"With clarity and passion John [Hutchison] persuades the reader into a new way of thinking, a new way of living, a new way of loving the God we so often question when things go wrong."

— CRAIG MCCONNELL
Writer and Teacher, Ransomed Heart Ministries

"One of Job's fickle friends, Eliphaz the Temanite, totally misunderstood the cause for Job's suffering. But he did get one thing right: 'Man is born to trouble as surely as sparks fly upward' (Job 5:7). Every journey through life includes time spent with uninvited traveling companions—sorrow, pain, heartache, and suffering. Dr. John Hutchison helps us understand why these guests, though uninvited, can be a valuable part of that journey."

— DR. CHARLES H. DYER
Provost and Dean of Education, Moody Bible Institute
Chicago, Ill.

"Beautiful in its concept and shape and scriptural fidelity, *Thinking Right When Things Go Wrong* tells us how 'joy and woe are woven fine' to strengthen our faith and glorify God. As such it is richly biblical, refreshingly countercultural, and immensely practical. This unique book provides the believing heart with a place to stand—and even sing—in the midst of trials and sufferings."

— R. KENT HUGHES
Pastor, College Church
Wheaton, Ill.

"John Hutchison provides personal hope, deep soul confidence, potential healing, and the courage to go on, through his biblical perspectives, life illustrations, and authentic examples of others who have experienced God's presence and strength when things go wrong. As a pastor and educator, I would highly recommend this book."

— DR. GORDON E. KIRK
Senior Pastor, Lake Avenue Church
Pasadena, Calif.

Thinking
RIGHT
When Things Go
WRONG

Thinking
RIGHT
When Things Go
WRONG

BIBLICAL WISDOM
FOR SURVIVING
TOUGH TIMES

John C. Hutchison

Kregel
Publications

Thinking Right When Things Go Wrong: Biblical Wisdom for Surviving Tough Times

© 2005 by John C. Hutchison

Published by Kregel Publications, a division of Kregel, Inc., P.O. Box 2607, Grand Rapids, MI 49501.

Library of Congress Cataloging-in-Publication Data
Hutchison, John C.
 Thinking right when things go wrong: biblical wisdom for surviving tough times / by John C. Hutchison.
  p. cm.
 Includes bibliographical references and index.
 1. Suffering—Religious aspects—Christianity. 2. Consolation. I. Title.
BV4909.H88 2005 248.8'6—dc22 2005022168

ISBN 978-0-8254-2810-4

Printed in the United States of America

07 08 09 10 11 / 6 5 4 3 2

To my family,
through whom God has richly blessed me—
Leah, Kristin, Kara, Casey, and Elliana.

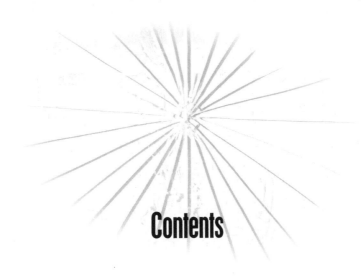

Contents

Foreword

In May 2003 I entered a seven-month period of darkness, during which I suffered deep depression and regular waves of anxiety. For thirty years I had not been significantly depressed, but during the twelve months leading up to May 2003, my family and I were hit with eight significant stressors. Given that I was already worn down due to several years of working too hard, it was all too much for me to handle. I began to awaken between two and three o'clock each morning and could not get back to sleep. It felt as if God had abandoned me, and my depression turned into despair. It was not a happy time.

When I read Professor Hutchison's manuscript, I saw in its pages the sort of help that would have rescued me in my own trials the year before. I jumped at the chance to write the foreword. I have known John Hutchison for fifteen years, and I have watched him handle his own ups and downs. He practices what he preaches. His life is congruent with the ideas you are about to ponder.

There are, indeed, several books in print on pain and suffering, but they usually fall into one of three categories. Some dwell heavily on the philosophical problem of why evil and suffering exist and do not attempt to minister to people who are in the midst of suffering. Other books refer to biblical passages but only in a superficial way, and they do not take readers deeply enough into the Word of God to gain the sort of help that people need in the midst of suffering. Some books are filled with personal, intimate stories of suffering with almost no biblical content.

All of these books have their place, but this volume does something different. It provides enough biblical "meat" to deeply nourish the soul, yet it is written in a warm and personal style that is accessible to us common folk. When you read this book, you will not only receive help for life's trials, you will also grow more deeply in your understanding of a biblical worldview on suffering. *Thinking Right When Things Go Wrong* breaks out of the mold and offers ancient wisdom about handling life's hardships that is refreshingly practical and life-related. Hutchison is a Biblicist, and this book is firmly—better, deeply—rooted in a careful and knowledgeable study of Holy Scripture. But Hutchison is also a pastor at heart, and he constantly addresses life's real dilemmas in authentic and practical ways.

The upshot of the book is that it provides biblical insights into the subject of trials and suffering, and thereby provides a rich context for Christians to process more effectively the difficult times of life—to see them as opportunities rather than obstacles. The voices of Jesus, Job, James, Paul, and Peter combine to tell us a great deal about God's purposes in these difficult times. For most of us, however, our emotional state or the sense of being abandoned by God prevents us from living out the precious truths of God's counsel. *Thinking Right When Things Go Wrong* is a tool that helps us understand the truth presented in the major biblical passages about trials and suffering, relate this truth to our own lives and ministry through illustrative stories and examples, and develop a thinking process that prepares our hearts for difficult times, thereby minimizing the shock and paralysis of such events.

Following an introductory chapter that shows the importance of this subject for Christians, the book divides into three main sections. Part 1 (chapters 1–4) identifies several specific benefits that the Bible reveals as positive results of experiencing suffering or persevering through trials. These chapters explain important principles found in passages such as Matthew 5:3–11; John 16:33; Romans 5:3–5; 2 Corinthians 1:3–5; 12:9–10; Philippians 1:13–18; Hebrews 12:7–11; James 1:2–4, 12; and 1 Peter 4:12–16. Each principle is illustrated with stories from Hutchison's own pastoral experience and life.

Part 2 (chapters 5–6) tackles perhaps the most difficult to understand teaching about suffering: how God's design in allowing suffering may be to bring greater glory to himself through the authenticity of our faith. Using the book of Job and the writings of Peter, these chapters explain that when suffering comes as a result of our faith in Christ, we actually become participants in the sufferings of Christ. Although this concept may be more difficult to relate to experientially, Hutchison shows that living out the truth of this principle will take us to deeper levels of spiritual maturity and commitment to Christ.

The final section of the book (chapters 7–9) returns to the major passages to look specifically at what we are commanded to do or think (chapter 7), and what God has promised to provide (chapter 9). Chapter 8 focuses on the unique role the Psalms can play during times of distress. In this important closing section, Hutchison motivates us to develop a thinking process about life that is distinctly countercultural—in some cases even against the grain of popular Christian culture. The goal is to prepare us to see trials as God sees them—as opportunities rather than obstacles.

This book is a must-read for anyone who wants to be good at life in the midst of suffering.

—J. P. MORELAND

Acknowledgments

My deepest thanks go to my daughter Kara and my pastor, Tim Morey, for their editing work and writing ideas. I am also grateful for the inspiration and encouragement given to me by my colleagues and deans at Talbot School of Theology—especially Dr. J. P. Moreland, Dr. Joe Hellerman, Dr. Dennis Dirks, and Dr. Michael Wilkins.

Introduction

"What do you think? Should we drive on or look for a motel?" I asked my wife as we slowed to a crawl on one of California's fastest freeways. We knew about tule fog in the San Joaquin Valley from earlier trips. At times during the winter, you can barely see the end of your own car hood, and you can only hope you will be able to see the car ahead of you if you need to stop. It was two days before Christmas, and we were driving north to Washington State.

I think if I can just follow a semi with fog lights, I'll be okay. But most of them are traveling way too fast for me! I had read stories of fifty-car pile-ups in the fog—the cars closely following one another at high speeds until the brake lights came on.

"Daddy, I can't see anything out there." The voice of my daughter Kristin brought my focus back to the most important things. We pulled off at the next exit, got the last room in a Motel 6, and waited until morning. The fog had changed our plans, but tomorrow would be another day.

If you have experienced the world famous tule fog of central California, or something like it, you know how disoriented you can feel when your normal senses are restricted. In fact, visual disorientation leads to fears that can paralyze us even more. In 1999, the tragic death of John Kennedy Jr., his wife, Carolyn, and her sister was likely a result of pilot disorientation. The National Transportation Safety Board concluded that Kennedy probably experienced "spatial disorientation," a form of vertigo, and when the navigation instruments contradicted his senses, he did not respond until it was too late. According to experienced pilots, when you fly "into the soup," one of the most important decisions you must make is not to trust your feelings as the final authority of what the airplane is doing. Your mind must be the boss, and the instruments your window to reality. Your life depends on understanding the information they provide.

Do you ever experience a sense of disorientation in life? I want to reassure you that you are not alone. For many of us, life's "tule fog" comes in the form of a personal trial or time of suffering when things are not what we expected. Interestingly, in Ecclesiastes 1:2, wise King Solomon uses a word to describe life that literally means "vapor" or "fog." It is sometimes translated "vanity" (NASB) or "meaningless" (NIV). Like pilot disorientation, stressful life experiences can send us into a tailspin if we trust the wrong information. Though our feelings about suffering are important to understand and express, they simply cannot be trusted as our final authority. Emotions may lead us astray. Like flying by instruments, we must trust in the most accurate description of reality we have—namely, the truth found in God's Word. Thankfully, God has revealed in the Bible a great deal about his purposes for trials and suffering. Our journey through life, as he designed it, will include bumps and potholes, and even deep valleys. Each of them has the potential to be an obstacle or an opportunity, a stumbling block or a stepping-stone, depending on how we respond.

The following worship song profoundly expresses this truth. The words were written for a friend whose husband had been killed just before their first wedding anniversary:

Masterpiece (Angie's Song)
I'm gonna hold on to what I believe
No matter what I feel or see
For You are faithful and able
To finish what You started in me

You have this way about You
Of taking what seems wrong

And making it a canvas
That You paint Your masterpiece on

I'm gonna hold on to what I believe
No matter what I feel or see
For You are faithful and able
To finish what You started in me

Let the strong winds blow
It won't change what I know
You are steadfast and true
And my eyes are on You
And I trust You, Lord

I'm gonna hold on to what I believe
No matter what I feel or see
For You are faithful and able
To finish what You started in me[1]

As Happy as Our Thinking Allows

Abraham Lincoln was one of the most successful leaders our nation has ever known, but he didn't live a charmed life by any stretch of the imagination. Consider some of the adversities he faced before he became president:

Age 7:   His family was forced out of their home on a legal technicality, and he had to work to help support them.
Age 9:   His mother died.
Age 22:   He lost his job as a store clerk. He wanted to go to law school, but his education wasn't good enough.
Age 23:   He went into debt to become a partner in a small store.
Age 26:   His business partner died, leaving him a huge debt that would take years to repay.
Age 28:   After courting a girl for four years, he asked her to marry him but she said no.

Age 37:   On his third try, he was elected to Congress, but two years later he was not reelected.

Age 41:   His four-year-old son died.

Age 45:   He ran for the Senate and lost.

Age 47:   He failed as the vice presidential candidate.

Age 49:   He ran for the Senate again and lost.

> Because times of suffering raise so many questions for us, they may lead to faulty reasoning about life, about God, and about his purposes.

For many of his adult years, Lincoln struggled with episodes of clinical depression, yet he overcame the debilitating effects of these setbacks to lead our nation in one of the most important chapters of its history. He once said, "Most folks are about as happy as they make up their minds to be."[2] In order to define a major point of this book, please allow me to adapt Lincoln's quote as follows: "Most folks are about as happy as their thinking allows them to be."

Happiness comes as a result of our choices, and the choices we make are a direct result of the way we think about life. Because times of suffering raise so many questions for us, they may lead to faulty reasoning about life, about God, and about his purposes. This is why we are given the wisdom of the Bible. Like putting on a pair of reading glasses, relying on Scripture enables us to see more clearly the things of life that are fuzzy and distorted. Our responses sometimes come from raw, hurting emotions, but they may also come from the errors of those who influenced us. When facing trials, we need all the help we can get, and the truth of God's Word working through the Holy Spirit's ministry in our lives brings us great hope.

Engaging in the Battle

Why is life so difficult? Certainly, knowing and using the resources God has provided for us will make a significant difference in the way we approach life. But even equipped with the best attitudes, life remains tough. Why is this? John Eldredge leads us to a critical presupposition embraced in this book:

> This is The Big Question, by the way, the one every philosophy and religion and denominational take on Christianity has been trying to nail down since the dawn of time. *What is really going on here?* Good grief—life is brutal. Day after day it hammers us, till we lose sight of what God intends toward us, and we haven't the foggiest idea why the things that are happening to us *are* happening to us. Then you watch lives going down with the Twin Towers, read about children starving in Ethiopia, and wham! If a good God is really in charge . . . all that.[3]

Eldredge responds to this question with a foundational scriptural truth, crucial in the life of a Christian:

> *We are* at *war!* I don't like that fact any more than you do, but the sooner we come to terms with it, the better hope we have of making it through the life we do want. This is not Eden. You probably figured that out. This is not Mayberry; this is not *Seinfeld's* world; this is not *Survivor.* The world in which we live is a combat zone, a violent clash of kingdoms, a bitter struggle unto the death. I'm sorry if I'm the one to break this news to you: you were born into a world at war, and you will live all your days in the midst of a great battle, involving all the forces of heaven and hell and played out here on earth.[4]

In order to fully understand the suffering and trials which befall us, we *must* understand this conflict. We must see our lives as part of a bigger story. Grasping that story better prepares us to face life as it really is. As we try to understand earthly trials, therefore, we will do so in the context of heaven and earth. This life is viewed in light of the life to come. It is the only way it makes sense.

To Those in the Midst of Suffering

We have all struggled with and learned from the difficult times of life. In the pages to follow, I will be sharing with you many stories from my life and the lives of people I have known, and how they mirror much of the wisdom taught in the Bible. You may be reading this book because you are going through a time of suffering right now, or perhaps look back to an unresolved trial in your past. As you will readily see, I am writing from a Christian perspective, and I appeal to the Bible, both the Old and New Testaments, as my authority for the claims I have made. However, I am *not* assuming you are a Christian or that you necessarily look to the Bible to guide your life. Regardless of your background, I invite you to read this book and consider the claims that are made in its pages.

Trials touch every life, yet I firmly believe that you will find the Christian, biblical explanation of trials to be a refreshingly authentic way to face each day. Life can be brutal, but a relationship with Jesus Christ offers peace and joy in the midst of trials. If that is what you seek, read on!

If you are a Christian and active in a Christian group, there are several approaches you can take in reading this book:

- *Personal encouragement during a trial.* A "quick reading" of the material in the book will provide encouragement and hope. Don't get bogged down with the details, but read the stories and look for insights and Scripture passages that will meet your immediate need and prepare you for the challenges ahead. Chapters 7, 8, and 9 will be especially helpful and encouraging.
- *Guide for personal Bible study.* One of my goals in writing this book is to motivate you to study Scripture. *Thinking Right When Things Go Wrong* often goes into depth explaining the background and interpretation of biblical passages. As you read, allow some time to study on your own the Scripture passages presented. Read them, meditate on them, and apply them to your life. Though much of the book is arranged topically, you will find special attention given to explaining the Old Testament books of Job, Psalms, and the wisdom of Proverbs. Use the discussion questions at the end of each chapter to stimulate your thoughts about applying these truths to your life.

- *Small group Bible study.* We all face trials, and one of the most important resources given to Christians is the encouragement of others in the church. I can't think of a better setting than a small discussion group to stimulate healthy dialogue and give support. The chapters are written and arranged topically to focus your group's discussion on one aspect of adversity at a time. Discussion questions are included at the end of each chapter, and the appendix provides suggestions for how to use these questions in small groups.

Henry David Thoreau in *Walden* spoke of people who "lead lives of quiet desperation."[5] God has far more for us than that. Though the burdens of life are not easy to bear, they can lead us forward to see our lives as part of a bigger, eternal story. Discovering that story helps us to experience the difficult times—trials and various kinds of suffering—with greater peace, assurance, and purpose. The trauma of suffering leads most people to ask two fundamental questions: What is the cause of this evil? and How should I respond to it? Though I believe the philosophical question of the origin of evil is an important issue, I have not addressed it in this book. Modern scholars have sometimes concluded that human suffering is incompatible with their view of a good God. As a result, they mistakenly redefine God's love or question his power to control evil. In contrast, earlier writers such as Thomas Aquinas, John Bunyan, Martin Luther, John Calvin, and Augustine, and even some modern writers such as C. S. Lewis, accepted pain and suffering as ultimately part of God's plan. I agree and have therefore chosen to focus upon the second question—how to respond to suffering. I believe this approach will be more useful for most readers.

At first glance, the arrangement of the major sections of the book may seem egocentric. By asking in the title of Part 1, "What's in It for *Me*, Lord?" it may seem as if our personal concerns are getting top billing over the next part, which is about glorifying God. As you read, however, you will see that this is *not* the intent. Chapters 4, 5, and 6 are the theological heart and soul of the book. Issues addressed there, including the element of mystery in our trials, the eternal significance of our responses, and the importance of glorifying God, are discussed in few other books on this subject. I have placed the tangible, experiential purposes

> Although the intrusion of a trial may imply that God has abandoned me, it may actually mean that my life is precisely on track.

for trials in the early chapters (1–3) simply because this is consistent with the way we experience life.

My first university studies were in electrical engineering, just before God led me to serve him in vocational Christian ministry as a teacher, pastor, and writer. Because engineers are by nature analytical problem-solvers, I admit that I have often approached life and theology in that way as well. The pursuit of this subject in Scripture has truly stretched me spiritually and deepened my walk with God. I have discovered that life's challenges are not just a series of problems to be solved but also an adventure to be lived with relationships to be nurtured.

For the journey, this adventure we call *life,* there is amazing wisdom and guidance found in the pages of the Bible. Not all our questions are answered, however, and suffering introduces unexplained mysteries that may puzzle us about God and life. Our raw emotions sometimes lead us to the wrong conclusions. Although the intrusion of a trial may imply that God has abandoned me, it may actually mean that my life is precisely on track. In our times of suffering, the Lord can do his greatest work, and we have the choice to blame God in bitterness or trust him implicitly. Margaret Clarkson has said it well, "It is not by miraculous deliverance that our faith grows, but by discovering God's faithfulness in the midst of our pain."[6]

Part 1

LIFE'S HARDSHIPS AND HEARTACHES

What's in It for Me, Lord?

Chapter 1

May I Have Your Attention, Please?

We had just begun eating a sumptuous Thanksgiving feast when the telephone rang. Calls from family were not unusual on holidays, especially because our new home in Dallas was fifteen hundred miles from our extended family. I tried to politely carry on the dinner conversation while my wife, Leah, answered the phone. However, the desperate tone of her voice in the adjacent room drew all of our attention away from the meal. "He did what? . . . He stole Dad's pickup and now you can't find him!" As Leah continued a brief conversation with her mother, I filled in some of the story of Leah's eldest brother for our guests.

Doug was ten years older than Leah, and he had grown up and moved out before she really knew him. He was a gifted businessman, a natural, who had made his first million dollars before he turned thirty. Then something began to deteriorate in his life that none of us really understood. Several businesses that he owned failed, and Doug simultaneously became very depressed. Over a period of several years, his manic-depressive condition (also called bipolar disorder) was accompanied by psychotic episodes during which he did bizarre things. On one occasion, he borrowed a brand-new Nissan sports car and drove it off a dock into San Diego Bay.

Such was the case on Thanksgiving Day 1983. My father-in-law had checked Doug out of a local hospital ward to join the family for dinner, but when his back was turned, Doug had driven off with the pickup truck. "Call us the minute you find him," Leah said to her mom. Though we continued eating, the dinner held little appeal now. Even polite conversation could not take away the sense of foreboding we felt.

The next call forever changed our lives as a family. Leah's dad and brother soon found the abandoned pickup truck—surrounded by police cars—on top of San Diego's highest bridge. Doug had committed suicide.

News like that, especially an unexpected tragedy, leaves you numb. I am generally a resourceful person, but I felt paralyzed. I am thankful that our good friends took charge and within minutes had arranged for our flight to California and child care for our two young daughters. They helped us pack and whisked us to the airport. Leah and I spoke few words on that trip, but one thing was certain: This tragedy had our undivided attention. In fact, the healing process after Doug's shocking death held our attention for many years to come.

> Trials are sometimes used by God as an "alert" system to refocus our priorities.

The trials of life, especially the unexpected ones, have a way of captivating our thoughts like nothing else. Trials are sometimes used by God as an "alert" system to refocus our priorities. In fact, few other experiences in life really capture our undivided attention. Right now, as you read this book, I have your attention to some degree, but not your undivided attention. Many people have the ability to think about more than one thing at a time, so they are rarely interested in focusing on only one thought or message. Though this ability to multitask may be useful in the workplace, a world of distractions may also numb us to God's "gentle whisper."[1]

"God whispers to us in our pleasures, speaks in our conscience, but shouts in our pains," writes C. S. Lewis in *The Problem of Pain*. "It is His megaphone to rouse a deaf world."[2] Lewis captures the relative effects of various forms of God's experiential "voice." Though the pleasant experiences of life may "whisper" to us something about a good God, they rarely move us significantly closer to him. God has more of a platform to speak through our conscience, but even at that deeper level, the moral voice of God can easily be interrupted or drowned out by other captivating philosophies. Suffering and tragedy, however, "shout" and even those with hardened hearts suddenly become teachable.

In my early years of ministry as a pastor, I saw this contrast played out at weddings and funerals. I was often called upon to officiate both, and I discovered that the opportunities to minister to people were considerably different between the two. For example, though I might prepare a wonderful wedding ceremony with a helpful message about marriage, few people at those weddings were really listening. Oh, they politely "listened," but not with undivided attention. The focus of their thoughts was on the happy bride and groom, as it should have been.

In contrast, witnessing death is a powerful teacher and object lesson that grabs the attention of all who will listen to the "shout" of God. For several years, I volunteered my services as a funeral pastor to families who preferred to have a Christian service but did not come from a Christian background or have a pastor to officiate. It was a wonderful opportunity to share Christ's love with people who did not have a church. As family and friends gathered to remember their loved one, I saw even the most hardened individuals wrestle seriously with their own mortality. Such is the case with the trials of life. They capture—even demand—our attention as nothing else can.

What exactly is the inaudible "voice of God" saying? Through trials we are challenged to examine our priorities and ask questions we rarely ask on a daily basis: Is my life focused on the trivial rather than on things that really matter? Have I become spiritually apathetic and lost my passion to serve God? Is there sin that needs to be confessed, and am I willing to turn from that sin and back to God? Have I become self-centered rather than caring about others around me? Do I love things more than people? Trials and suffering have an uncanny way of drawing our attention to life's needy areas and refocusing our priorities in several ways:

- from the trivial to that which is really important
- from self-centeredness to others-centeredness
- from spiritual apathy or sin to a stronger walk with God
- from materialism to valuing people and relationships

9/11

September 11, 2001, will forever stand as a day of infamy for most Americans. Though it is a day that many people would like to forget, it is one we should always remember. For hours, all communication was cut off and there was no way of knowing who was alive and who was dead. Life stood still and the only thing that mattered was the life of a husband or wife or dad or mom or beloved child. And then, for the fortunate, there was a phone call and a reunion. The embraces were never so sweet. For others, it was the sobering, sorrowing news that their loved one was indeed gone. On that day, our national psyche experienced something very tragic followed by something quite wonderful. New Yorkers cared for one another as the attack took the lives of so many. Police officers, firefighters, and run-of-the-mill citizens became heroes as they acted with courage and self-sacrifice. As the ripple effects reached across our nation, Americans for a time thought differently about life and about one another. Stories were told about families of people in the Twin Towers or of firemen and policemen who had tried to help.

For those of us who were not in New York City or Washington, D.C., there is no way we can even imagine what those people went through. Yet we also were moved to reevaluate our own lives. At the time, my wife was visiting her aunt in British Columbia. She tried everything she could to get to the airport, but all flights were grounded and the U.S.–Canadian border was closed. On September 12, she finally gave up hope of flying and instead drove a rented car fourteen hundred miles home. Even this ripple-effect experience of the otherwise distant tragedy made us value things we daily took for granted.

For many people, significant decisions followed 9/11, including the reconciliation of marriages and families that had been estranged for years. Some court cases based on petty charges were thrown out of court because judges and juries alike had a new sense of what was significant in life. This national tragedy illustrates what often happens through personal tragedy. Suffering not only focuses our attention, but it also moves us to reassess our priorities and shift our focus away from the trivial to the more important things in life.

The Lord Disciplines Those He Loves

One of these important things for Christians is our walk with God. Has a pattern of sin gained a foothold in your life? Has apathy caused your love for God to grow cold? The Scriptures make very clear statements about God's concern for this and his method of getting our attention about sin.

> "My son, do not make light of the Lord's discipline, and do not lose heart when he rebukes you, because the Lord disciplines those he loves, and he punishes everyone he accepts as a son." Endure hardship as discipline; God is treating you as sons. . . . We have all had human fathers who disciplined us and we respected them for it. How much more should we submit to the Father of our spirits and live! Our fathers disciplined us for a little while as they thought best; but God disciplines us for our good, that we may share in his holiness. No discipline seems pleasant at the time, but painful. Later on, however, it produces a harvest of righteousness and peace for those who have been trained by it. (Heb. 12:5–11)

This foundational biblical passage on the subject of trials and suffering in Christian experience is replete with ideas to shape our attitudes. Remember, our goal in this book is to learn what God is doing through life's difficult times. Times of hardship are undoubtedly the most challenging times in which to believe that God is at work, and thus they are the most important times to know what he is doing. We can understand God's purpose only by seeing trials and suffering as he sees them. The insight we gain allows us to "put on corrective lenses" that are not naturally a part of our thinking process but that enable us to *think right when things go wrong*. To take encouragement from Hebrews 12:5–11, we must see trials as discipline from a father who dearly loves us. We learn here that suffering and hardships, though unpleasant at the time, are worth enduring, because God's correction has the potential to produce great payoffs in life: harmony, peace, and a disciplined life.

I remember well the frustrated response of a young Christian named

Paula after I had preached a sermon on trials and related them to our relationship with God. She acknowledged that things like this were in the Bible but confessed she could not conceive of a God who would intentionally bring suffering into the lives of Christians. Some of our greatest questions in the midst of unpleasant experiences are, How could a good God have anything to do with this? and How could this possibly be for my good? Hebrews 12:5–11 claims that both are true. "My son, do not make light of the Lord's discipline . . . when he rebukes you, because the Lord disciplines those he loves, . . . he punishes everyone he accepts as a son. . . . God is treating you as sons. . . . God disciplines us for our good." These are straightforward statements about God's active participation in some of the unpleasant experiences of life and his design that they serve a good purpose. If God disciplines us because he loves us, then our trials must be understood in the context of the intimate relationship that a father has with his child.

> According to Hebrews 12:8, the experience of God's discipline assures us that we are *true* sons of God, not illegitimate ones. If God didn't discipline us, it would show he didn't care.

I knew instantly the reason Paula was struggling because I knew her family background. She had grown up with an overbearing, abusive father who disciplined out of anger (even revenge) rather than love. Her human model of fatherhood made the truth about God very difficult to accept or experience. Yet, there it was in Scripture, and it was clear. In spite of our experiences with imperfect human fathers, and contrary to many contemporary theories about parenting, God is a loving Father who sometimes uses trials and suffering to discipline his children. In fact, according to Hebrews 12:8, the experience of God's discipline assures us that we are *true* sons of God, not illegitimate ones. If God didn't discipline us, it would show he didn't care.

Initially, this phenomenon cannot be embraced emotionally because suffering perceived through human reason alone seems to be outside the plan of a loving God. If suffering is included in God's plan, we reason, then he must be a vengeful, angry God. But neither of these perceptions is true. When God allows trials into the lives of his children, it is always for our well-being and is motivated by love. C. S. Lewis wrestled with this dilemma in *The Problem of Pain* and concluded that our inability to understand God's relationship to human suffering is a result of our lack of understanding of two of God's attributes: his omnipotence and his divine goodness. First, God's omnipotence does not mean that he can do anything he wants. He cannot, for example, prevent us from making choices that result in suffering or trials or unhappiness, because he has given us the freedom of will to choose.[3] Second, according to Lewis, we do not fully understand the meaning of divine goodness and God's love. "The problem of reconciling human suffering with the existence of a God who loves is only insoluble as long as we attach a trivial meaning to the word 'love,' and look on things as if man were the centre of them."[4] Lewis's insights encourage us to seek an understanding of life's trials and suffering through a deeper understanding of God.

During the years when my daughters played with dolls, I once eavesdropped on a very serious conversation in one of their bedrooms. It seems one of their dolls had disobeyed in some way, and after placing her over the knee for a spanking, one of my daughters said, "Now we want you to know that we are not doing this because we are angry, we are doing this because we love you." For a parent, it was a priceless memory. Though spankings were rare in our household, the girls had learned those words from me. In their experience, the meaning of discipline and the message of love were closely related.

Hebrews 12:5–6 includes a quote from Proverbs 3:11–12, an Old Testament proverb encouraging a wise son to appreciate the discipline of his father as evidence of being a true son. In ancient times, a father would devote himself more fully to the upbringing of a true-born son in order to make him a worthy heir. That greater devotion would also probably mean greater discipline, so this advice encourages the disciplined child to accept this experience as evidence of the privilege of sonship.

The reference to Proverbs 3 in Hebrews 12 allows us to apply the latter passage more broadly than just to God's discipline for our sin. God does use trials and suffering to get our attention about disobedience. That is evident in expressions like "the sin that so easily entangles" (Heb. 12:1) and "in your struggle against sin" (Heb. 12:4). But the concept of discipline in Proverbs and in Hebrews includes both correction and instruction or training. Trials may be God's chastisement to get our attention, bring us to repentance, and restore our fellowship with him. They may also come as part of our training process when we are walking closely with God. God sometimes uses adversity to equip us and to pass along his wisdom to us. In a sense, hardship can function in much the same way as God's Word as described in 2 Timothy 3:16–17: "All Scripture is God-breathed and is useful for teaching, rebuking, correcting and training in righteousness, so that the man of God may be thoroughly equipped for every good work."

What is the bottom line of this process? Hebrews 12:11 ends with a description of Christians as "those who have been trained by [God's discipline]." Experiencing life's trials is likened to the process an athlete goes through in preparation for competition in a sport. The word used is a verb from which we get English words such as *gymnastics* and *gymnasium*. Even more significant, the meaning indicates a continual training experience rather than a single event. Anyone who has trained in athletics knows that getting in shape and developing excellence in a sport is a process requiring the development of muscles, coordination, and skills. Many of us have experienced the price that must be paid through participation in a favorite sport, but Olympic and professional athletes pay an even higher price to achieve the highest success. They will tell you that the goal cannot be reached quickly and the process is never easy. Their amazing athletic ability comes from years of commitment and endless hours of hard work to develop their talent and to be the best at their sport. As Christians, we are training for the most important contest of life and the stakes are even higher. Should we take it any less seriously?

Finally, the *goal* of this process in our lives is clearly seen in Hebrews 12:10–11: "God disciplines us for our good, that we may share in his holiness. . . . Later on, however, it produces a harvest of righteousness and peace." A similar passion is expressed in Psalm 119:67, 71: "Before I was afflicted I went astray, but now I obey your word. . . . It was good for me to be afflicted so that I might learn your decrees." This is Christlikeness!

Do all trials have the potential of producing Christlike qualities in me? Yes. Are all trials God's discipline for sin? No. God will reveal to you if sin is the issue. Don't make the same mistake as Job's friends, who were compelled by their theology to relate every trial and all suffering to sin. Not every hardship is the result of sin, but some are and that's why Hebrews 12:5–11, which focuses on the disciplinary na-

> Seeing God's goodness *during* the experience of a trial is difficult.

ture of suffering, is not a bad place to start in our prayers to God: "Lord, is there an area of persistent sin in my life that you are bringing to my attention and want me to confess?" The answer to this question is usually apparent very quickly. If that is not the case, the trial may not be intended for a corrective purpose.

The introductory words of verse 11, "No discipline seems pleasant at the time, but painful," reminds us that seeing God's goodness *during* the experience of a trial is difficult. The unpleasantness of the suffering sends us the message that something hurtful is taking place. But we must go beyond our own feelings and our human intuition to see this process through divine "lenses." A positive, teachable response to discipline produces the Christlike qualities of holiness, righteousness, and peace.

A Thorn in the Flesh

In 2 Corinthians 12:1–10, the apostle Paul gives an example of a trial in his own life that God allowed in order to keep Paul from a potential sin: "To keep me from becoming conceited because of these surpassingly great revelations, there was given me a thorn in my flesh, a messenger of Satan, to torment me" (v. 7). God's refusal to remove the "thorn" despite Paul's persistent prayers shows God's sovereign use of a trial as a preventative measure to shape the spiritual lives of his children.

This is a fascinating story in the apostle's life, and the implications for our own lives are far-reaching. Paul wrote 2 Corinthians in part as a candid defense of his apostolic authority against critics who had challenged his right to act in the role of an apostle. Like Galatians, 2 Corinthians is one of Paul's most autobiographical writings and reveals his great passion for Christian ministry. The apostle had a very close relationship with the Christians in Corinth. He had planted a church there (Acts 18) and was responsible for leading some of the people to the Lord before he went on to further ministry in Ephesus.

According to references in the Corinthian epistles to other letters, 2 Corinthians is probably the fourth letter Paul wrote to that particular church. Some false teachers had apparently infiltrated the church and led the Corinthian Christians astray through a false gospel; and they had also brought false charges against Paul (see 2 Cor. 10:7–11; 11:12–15). Because these teachers had deceived the Corinthians by boasting about their superior credentials, Paul is tempted to boast of his own qualifications (11:18, 21–23). He too is of the best Hebrew stock and has demonstrated unsurpassed dedication as a servant of Christ, even through trials and suffering. As Paul recounts his sacrificial service for Christ (vv. 23–29), he realizes that all the things he is "boasting" about would be seen by some as weaknesses and signs of failure. That is the reason he exclaims, "If I must boast, I will boast of the things that show my weakness" (v. 30). He later concludes, "For when I am weak, then I am strong" (12:10).

Continuing his boasting, Paul recounts a revelatory experience given to him by God fourteen years earlier. Though he refers to himself in the third person as "a man in Christ" (12:2), verse 7 reveals his identity. The vision he saw of the heavenlies was so overwhelming and beyond human experience that he could not describe it to other humans (v. 4). Perhaps these are the types of things that Peter, James, and John saw on the Mount of Transfiguration (see Matt. 17:1–13; Mark 9:2–10; Luke 9:28–36) or the apostle John saw in the throne room of heaven (see Rev. 4–5).

Presumably, Paul would have been prone to the sin of pride because of this experience, and God humbled him through trials that Paul refers to as "a thorn in the flesh" (2 Cor. 12:7 NASB). Bible scholars have put forth many theories about the identity of this nagging problem—everything from eyesight problems to epilepsy to recurring malaria to extreme headaches. The expression "in the flesh" seems to indicate a physical malady, but beyond that, we do not know enough to dogmatically draw conclusions. Theologian D. A. Carson, in agreeing that we do not have proof of the exact nature of Paul's "thorn," makes two observations: it afflicted Paul *after* his great revelation from God and was not a birth defect or a problem from earlier in life; and the difficulty was evidently something substantial and not a minor irritation. In 2 Corinthians 11,

Paul documents his experience with a variety of trials, but he seems to place this "thorn" in a separate category, pleading persistently that God would remove it (12:8).[5] Though the affliction was an extreme, nagging problem for Paul, God's will was to leave the trial and supply sufficient grace to sustain him through it (v. 9).

Paul's story serves as an illustration of our own experiences in at least three ways:

1. Paul's trial had a preventative purpose. Sometimes we may know the exact area of sin that God is addressing through discipline, but at other times he may be protecting us against a potential future sin, usually unknown to us. In this case, a positive response to suffering has the power to refocus our priorities and avert a spiritual disaster that we will never experience or even know about. Blind to the details, we can by faith rejoice and praise God for his infinite wisdom in providing the discipline and training we need.

2. By use of the "thorn," God was seeking to create a perspective in Paul's heart: "But he [God] said to me, 'My grace is sufficient for you, for my power is made perfect in weakness.' Therefore I will boast all the more gladly about my weaknesses, so that Christ's power may rest on me" (12:9). This positive view of such negative circumstances is profound and absolutely contrary to our natural inclinations.

3. Paul's suffering highlights the unknown or mysterious elements of our experience with God. Faith demands implicit trust that our heavenly Father knows best, even if he brings trials. In a situation like Paul's thorn in the flesh, we are encouraged to walk by faith, not by sight, even when it hurts. Our ability to do this draws heavily on our knowledge of God and our understanding of his attributes.

Sometimes, a trial is not something that happens to us but something that doesn't happen the way we hoped or prayed. When I completed my Ph.D. in Bible Exposition, my sights were aimed at a particular teaching job in a seminary I had loved dearly. Circumstantially, the prospects were good because my longtime mentor-teacher was retiring from his position about the time I would graduate. After I had built up great hopes, the news came back that I would not be getting the job. To add insult to injury, one of my best friends was the front-runner to receive the position.

Meanwhile, our family finances had been depleted through graduate school, and I had to take a nonteaching job to support my family. As weeks and then months passed, no further teaching opportunities came knocking at my door. Meanwhile two part-time jobs, as a janitor and a courier driver, simply fell into place to provide our needs. I was thankful to be able to support my family, but as I knelt to clean toilets and mop floors each week, I regularly prayed, "Lord, did I need a Ph.D. for this?"

Many years have now passed, and as a seminary professor, I have often reflected on that dry period in my life when God seemed to have forgotten about me. What would I have become if my life had been scripted exactly as I wanted it—the easy way? I can never know for sure, but I have good reason to believe I would not be the same teacher I am today. That "closed door" to the job I wanted soon led me to serve the Lord in a pastoral ministry, and it significantly shaped my sixteen years in church ministry and fourteen years as a professor. Even my part-time jobs along the way have reminded me what ministry is really all about. What do a teacher, a pastor, a janitor, and a courier driver have in common? They all exist to serve people. Get the picture? God's ways are not always our ways. His power is made perfect in our weakness.

The Grounded Airline Executive

Here's another example. Guy's professional career had never looked more promising. Twenty-five years ago, he had started as a part-time employee of one of America's successful airline companies. Now he was a vice president with more than five thousand employees under his charge. Over the years, his job had moved his family around every two to three years, but now he had found security at corporate headquarters. As Christians, he and his wife acknowledged the many blessings God had showered upon them. But soon things began to change dramatically.

The change began with Guy's perspective of success. Somehow, things looked different from the top. He began to take matters into his own capable hands and leave God out of the daily decision-making process. The demands of the job encouraged him to leave others out of his life as well. The required travel of the job meant that he and his wife saw each other very little. There were other things that captivated Guy's attention, more important things. He was nearly at the top of the ladder, and people frequently referred to him as the heir apparent to the company president. His colleagues treated him with great respect, regularly doing favors for him (like buying dinner) with the hopes that he would remember them after his ascendance to the top position. Guy was likable and dedicated, and his job and the people around him made him feel important. But sustaining life at such a high level is not easy. Things change, and they did for Guy. The first news came in the form of a hostile corporate takeover threat. After a long fight in the courts, the stock exchange, state legislatures, and even the U.S. Congress, Guy's company changed hands. The news was devastating—and too much for the company's president and CEO, Guy's good friend. On the night of the takeover, he committed suicide.

Guy's world was turned upside down, and there was nothing to hold on to. He had paid a big price to make it to this point—his personal walk with God was almost nonexistent, his marriage of twenty-three-plus years was failing, his best friend was dead. And now his corporate aspirations were quickly fading. It was like being on a sinking ship with no lifeboats, waiting to be rescued but not knowing whom to call upon. After trying to make things work during the first year after the takeover, Guy concluded that he needed to move on. The personal tragedy he had experienced seemed brutal, but he would later see—much later, unfortunately—that it had God's fingerprints all over it.

As he put out his résumé, he hoped that someone, perhaps one of his old friends or competitors, would recognize the credentials of this almost-CEO. Weeks passed, then months. After a year, he still had no job. For the first time in his life, he was not able to pay his bills. When Guy's checkbook showed its lowest balance, he began to rediscover the importance of relationships. As he and his wife worked together on the extended job search, they began to discover each other again. The trial of joblessness and financial insecurity continued for several years, including the loss of another good job through a corporate takeover. During this time, Guy's relationship with his wife and with other Christians became his greatest security.

More than twelve years have now passed since those years of unemployment and near poverty. Though his retirement plan was completely lost in the hostile takeover, God has restored all of it with perhaps an even better retirement package than his original plan. As for Guy's priorities, I will let his words speak for themselves as he reflects on that chapter of life some twenty years later:

> I haven't had a job like the one I had with all the prestige, but I would probably have had a life of marital strife for all my final years on this earth if God had not intervened. God has taught us a lot. Our greatest lesson was to learn that we could live very well on much less than we were accustomed. We never went hungry and always had a place to live. We drove cars that needed repair and were several years old. Life was different. When we had need, we would often get a call from our church telling us some money had been left anonymously. This was the most incredible part of our experience, and to this day, I still marvel at God's grace.[6]

Trials have a way of getting our attention like nothing else. In James 1:9–11, James describes the "messages" that come to Christians in two distinct economic situations—poverty and wealth.[7] Trials serve as an encouragement to the poor (people in "humble circumstances") that their true identity is found in the eternal riches they possess in Christ (v. 9). There is a warning to the rich, however:

> But the one who is rich should take pride in his low position, because he will pass away like a wild flower. For the sun rises with scorching heat and withers the plant; its blossom falls and its beauty is destroyed. In the same way, the rich man will fade away even while he goes about his business. (James 1:10–11)

Trials come as a warning for wealthy Christians to remain focused on their humble position before God, and not to trust in the power of wealth, which is only temporary anyway.

In Guy's case, adversity delivered him from a life of self-centeredness to one centered on deeply valued relationships; from a life of power and materialism to one of contentment; from spiritual poverty to a richer walk with God. You may not be a CEO, but chances are very good that the enticements of material wealth and success have succeeded in a "hostile takeover" of your life and priorities. Have you listened lately to the voice of God? Has he spoken to you through a trial of some sort to get you back on track?

Pain

In this chapter, we have examined one of the most important purposes of trials and suffering: capturing and holding our attention. If we are attentive to the voice of God, pain and adversity also redirect our thinking. They cause us to examine our relationship with God the Father and, if needed, to confess sin and spiritual apathy. Sometimes they can even protect us from potential sin. They also have the capability to redirect our priorities.

How is it that pain "shouts" its message to us, but the more pleasant experiences of life merely "whisper"? Why are the painful experiences of suffering such powerful teaching tools in our lives? Here the phenomenon of physical pain provides a helpful illustration. No one enjoys physical pain. The very fact that we avoid and fear physical pain is the beginning of understanding its purpose in the design of God. Yes, in the design of God.

Dr. Michael Ferrante, director of the UCLA Pain Management Center, works daily with patients who are experiencing extreme physical pain. He also teaches graduate students and medical interns about the subject of pain.[8] His working definition includes both acute and chronic types of pain: "Pain is defined as a sensory and emotional experience that is associated with actual or potential tissue damage or described in such terms."[9] The experience of pain is actually an amazing communication system that may be compared to other complex systems in our bodies, such as the respiratory system or digestive system. According to Dr. Ferrante, however, it is even more profound. When "actual or potential tissue damage" is detected by the nerve endings of receptor cells, the information is translated into a chemical and electrical code (through a process called *transduction*) and transmitted to the spinal cord. If no action is needed, the signal may stop at the level of the spinal cord, but in most cases it is sent electrochemically up the spinal cord to the brain, where the process of "perception" takes place. According to Dr. Ferrante, we understand almost nothing about the process of perception in the brain, despite sophisticated scientific analysis. What we do know is that these signals produce the necessary action to interpret and appropriately respond to the source of pain. They produce chemical substances that form a unique pain pathway down the dorsal horn of the spinal cord and back to the area of the painful input.

In my conversation with Dr. Ferrante about the mechanics of physical pain, I was most struck with his response to something he had studied in such detail all his life, reflected here in his own words:

> As I have studied the phenomenon of physical pain in the human body, I have often thought, "Where is the 'grand central station' of all this?" It is found in the dorsal horn of the spinal cord. The chemistry, the complexity, the beauty of that system is profound. I have often thought that the pain pathways in the dorsal horn of the spinal column must be one of the proofs for the existence of a God. Things of this complexity just don't happen by accident—they just don't occur! The beauty of it, the profoundness of it, the complexity of it, the fact that we have really only known about this for the last ten to twenty years—in my mind, things like this don't occur out of chance. There has to be a Creator, a Creator who was *extremely careful* in how he set this up, because the beauty of it, the interplay and balance of one group of chemicals against another, is profound.[10]

What are the attributes of physical pain that illustrate God's plan for other types of trials and suffering in our lives?

First, it gets our attention. The unpleasant experience of pain is captivating enough that we are forced to withdraw from other activities and investigate the reason for the pain. If we do not respond to the initial message, in most cases pain will shout louder through increased intensity. "Pain functions with such brutal efficiency that its message can preoccupy the brain and drown out all pleasurable signals," writes Dr. Paul Brand. "It travels along a hotline, insisting on priority. Moreover, its impact can spread out from the brain and ultimately involve the entire body."[11]

Second, the effectiveness of physical pain seems to be related to its repulsive, demanding nature. Neurological studies have been done with alternative kinds of sensors attached to the human body to compare their efficiency as warning systems. In one such study by Dr. Brand, professors of electrical engineering, bioengineering, and biochemistry were enlisted to develop an artificial mechanism to sense changes in pressure on areas like fingers or toes and to give a warning signal when that happened.[12] Various kinds of signals—audible and visible—were used to alert patients that their activity could potentially result in damage or injury. In many situations, the patients chose to ignore the warning signal and continue their activity. Ultimately, the only type of signal that would alter their behavior was something unpleasant like an electric shock that forced them to respond. The obvious conclusion was that the human body's pain system already does the same thing, and it is by far the most efficient way to do the job.

> Most physical pain has a temporary purpose.

Third, most physical pain has a temporary purpose. When a person in pain takes the appropriate action to resolve the problem, the pain leaves and is often not remembered.[13]

Fourth, pain is essential for the healthy functioning of the human body. When the body experiences a malfunction of the warning system of pain, serious damage can result. The most common example of this is the disease of leprosy, which results in the deadening of nerve endings and the inability to feel simple pain. Digits such as fingers or toes, and even limbs, can be worn off to stubs because they do not signal to the brain the presence of damage and the need for recuperation.

Medical doctors like Michael Ferrante and Paul Brand have concluded after years of study and observation that physical pain is one of God's greatest gifts to the human body. And so it is with the trials and sufferings of life. One of their God-given purposes is to get our attention and demand that it be focused on more important things. Whether the issue is sin or simply a need for a shift in priorities, trials often take on the positive role of moving us toward the resolution of a problem. Though unpleasant, pain is one of God's greatest gifts.

Trusting God with Pain

Aloha, a mother of two grown daughters, remembers the experience of taking her girls to the doctor during their childhood years: "Injections, stitches in the emergency room, and other childhood traumas— they knew I was the one who took them there, and they did *not* want to go. They did not understand why I was allowing something painful to be done to them. In the face of this, they clung to me, and only me. With my arms around them, my voice was what they needed above all else."[14] So it is with God. We may not fully understand the reason for the pain, but we can cling to him, listen to his voice, and trust that he has our best interests in mind.

> Can a mother forget the baby at her breast
>   and have no compassion on the child she has borne?
> Though she may forget,
>   I will not forget you!
>
> —Isa. 49:15

DISCUSSION QUESTIONS

1. Describe the effect that the events of September 11, 2001, had on you personally and on those you know. Why do you think cataclysmic events such as these cause us to refocus our lives so quickly? Has a personal trial ever had this effect on you? Describe what happened.
2. Read and think about the following quote from C. S. Lewis's *A Grief Observed*. What feelings expressed by Lewis have you also experienced while going through trials? What would you disagree with in his comments?

> Meanwhile, where is God? This is one of the most disquieting symptoms. When you are happy, so happy that you have no sense of needing Him, if you turn to Him then with praise, you will be welcomed with open arms. But go to Him when

your need is desperate, when all other help is vain and what do you find? A door slammed in your face, and a sound of bolting and double bolting on the inside. After that, silence. You may as well turn away.[15]

3. Read Hebrews 12:5–11. Why do most people (perhaps including you) have a difficult time equating God's love with his disciplinary action for sin in their lives? Explain the most important things about discipline for sin that are also consistent with God's love. If you are a parent, what principle(s) from Hebrews 12 do you try to use in the way you discipline your children?
4. Read 2 Corinthians 12:1–10. Why did God *not* answer Paul's prayer to remove this physical trial? Has God ever given you a "thorn" (an incessant, long-term problem) and refused to answer your prayers to remove it? What do you think he may have been teaching you through it?
5. Do you agree with German theologian Helmut Thielicke that the greatest deficiency among American Christians is that "they have an inadequate view of suffering"? How does American prosperity (in contrast to life in other parts of the world) diminish our spiritual growth? Has it affected yours?

Chapter 2

No Pain, No Gain

The sound of the crowds moving around me in Terminal 7 at Los Angeles International Airport seemed to fade into oblivion as I listened to Lois's words over the telephone. "Frank died peacefully in his sleep last night. I knew you would be back from Portland today, so I decided to wait to tell you. . . . I'd really appreciate it if you could stop by tonight." Lois's request was punctuated with an almost apologetic tone; she knew I had just returned from conducting the funeral service of my cousin, who had died of a brain tumor.

"I'll be happy to come over, Lois. Give me a few minutes to make one more phone call and pick up my bags, and I'm on my way." Although my emotional tank was on empty, I was glad to help in whatever way I could. As Lois and Frank's pastor, I had regularly visited the family during Frank's struggle with cancer; the news of his death did not come as a surprise.

I cannot say the same, however, for the next phone call I made from Terminal 7. Just two days earlier, a young man in our congregation had undergone medical tests after experiencing a severe headache. Ron had been our youth pastor several years ago, and being a local high school coach and dedicated marathon runner, he was a specimen of excellent health. "What did you find out from the doctor, Ron?" His extended pause told me something was wrong. "He's saying it may be a tumor on my brain. The doctors are running some more tests this week, but that is all I know now."

As I drove to Lois's house that night, I felt physically tired, emotionally drained, and completely bewildered by the things that were happening to good people all around me.[1] Serious trials had suddenly and unexpectedly touched my family and two of my friends in just a matter of weeks. Where was God to be found in all of this?

The Truth About Tribulations

In chapter 1, we saw that trials may be a "megaphone," a way in which God gets our attention about sin or misplaced priorities. Trials, however, are not merely attention-getting devices, nor are they only related to sin. In this chapter, we will look deeper into God's proactive purpose for us when we undergo trials or suffering. Romans 5:3–5 and James 1:2–12 make remarkably similar points about this subject and give us some understanding of the nature of trials themselves.

> The emotional impact of a trial is magnified because it is unpredictable and often comes suddenly.

Not only so, but we also rejoice in our sufferings, because we know that suffering produces perseverance; perseverance, character; and character, hope. And hope does not disappoint us, because God has poured out his love into our hearts by the Holy Spirit, whom he has given us. (Rom. 5:3–5)

Consider it pure joy, my brothers, whenever you face trials of many kinds, because you know that the testing of your faith develops perseverance. Perseverance must finish its work so that you may be mature and complete, not lacking anything. . . . Blessed is the man who perseveres under trial, because when he has stood the test, he will receive the crown of life that God has promised to those who love him. (James 1:2–4, 12)

What insights do these passages give to us for the difficult times of life? Here are just a few:

The emotional impact of a trial is magnified because it is unpredictable and often comes suddenly. Sometimes we are surprised by *what* befalls us, other times by *when* trouble comes upon us, and sometimes by both. James alludes to both of these elements in the expression, "whenever you face trials of many kinds." The phrase translated "whenever you face" has the sense of helplessly falling into the middle of something. In the parable of the Good Samaritan, Jesus uses the same expression to depict the traveler who "fell among thieves" (Luke 10:30 NKJV). In using this passive construction, James is saying that we "fall into various trials" (James 1:2 NKJV).

He also describes them as "trials of many kinds," literally, "of many colors." The stories of Scripture illustrate this variety. Job's trials were direct losses he experienced, followed by even more serious losses. He initially experienced the loss of property, good health, and the death of ten children. But his subsequent despair also included losing the respect of his wife, the support of good friends, respect as a leader in his community, and many more intangibles.

Many New Testament Scripture passages describe examples of persecution for following Christ. In 2 Corinthians 11:23–33, Paul recounts experiences of his own suffering as proof that he is a devoted servant of Christ. After naming specific men and women of faith, the "hall of fame" in Hebrews 11 recounts a nameless list of "others [who] were tortured and refused to be released. . . . Some faced jeers and flogging, while still others were chained and put in prison. They were stoned; they were sawed in two; they were put to death by the sword. They went about in sheepskins and goatskins, destitute, persecuted and mistreated. . . . They wandered in deserts and mountains, and in caves and holes in the ground. These were all commended for their faith" (vv. 35–39).

Life itself teaches us that circumstances that put our faith to the test come in a variety of forms and may come at any time. Like Job, who knew nothing about the heavenly conversation that led to his calamities (Job 1–2), it is often the surprise element of a trial that makes it much more difficult. Trials may involve actual tragedy, but sometimes our faith is tested by the fear of a potential loss. Abraham never had to actually kill his son Isaac as a sacrifice, but he was completely willing to do so in obedience to God. As a result, it is said that he "offered Isaac as a sacrifice" as if he had actually done it (Heb. 11:17; James 2:21). A trial may be defined as anything, actual or potential, that tests our faith in God.

> Trials are inevitable and are to be expected in life.

Recently, my wife underwent two medical tests that had the potential of very serious outcomes. One of them involved genetic testing to determine whether she carried a defective gene present in other members of her extended family. If she did, we were told, she would have a 90 percent chance of developing breast or ovarian cancer. Like many medical procedures, the results from both tests took about a month to come back. We were so thankful that both came back showing no defects! The danger was only potential rather than actual, yet the test of our faith was very real.

Trials are inevitable and are to be expected in life. Don't be surprised by trouble! Expect it! Anticipate it! Trials are the norm, even when we are walking with God. This very simple point may be a no-brainer to some people who have already learned to anticipate trials. They see their lives as part of a bigger story, a drama in which those who live for God are soldiers in a battle. "Our struggle is not against flesh and blood, but against the rulers, against the authorities, against the powers of this dark world and against the spiritual forces of evil in the heavenly realms" (Eph. 6:12).

My purpose in including this point is to challenge the popular notion that life for Christians is promised to be smoother or easier than it is for other people. Contemporary America enjoys prosperity like few cultures of the world, and we can be thankful for the blessings of God we enjoy every day. But our Christian witness has been inhibited by our ease of life. American Christians know little about real suffering, and we therefore consider trials out of place in our Christian experience. While touring churches in the United States, the seasoned German pastor and theologian Helmut Thielicke was asked what he observed most about American Christians. He responded, "They have an inadequate view of suffering."[2] This in turn leads to lack of preparation for the storms of life.

When James says "whenever you face trials," he assumes his readers are already undergoing them. We know that James's epistle is probably the earliest book of the twenty-seven New Testament writings, written about A.D. 45. Based on his salutation, "To the twelve tribes scattered among the nations," we know that his first readers were primarily Jewish Christians who had been scattered by persecution. Jewish Christians who truly followed Jesus' teaching found themselves in a hostile environment among other Jews of their time. Because Jesus had condemned the empty traditions of Pharisaical Judaism, Christian Jews were accused of antinomianism (holding views against the Mosaic law). As the conflict escalated, many Jewish Christians were excommunicated from the temple and synagogues, stripped of their possessions, stoned, beaten, and even killed. This is probably why James begins his writing with the subject of trials—it was the present experience of his readers.

The inevitability of trials was also expressed often in Jesus' words and ministry:

Do not suppose that I have come to bring peace to the earth. I did not come to bring peace, but a sword. (Matt. 10:34)

If the world hates you, keep in mind that it hated me first. . . . I have chosen you out of the world. That is why the world hates you. (John 15:18–19)

I have told you these things, so that in me you may have peace. In this world you will have trouble. But take heart! I have overcome the world. (John 16:33)

The expectation of suffering is reflected by the other New Testament writers as well:

They [Jewish temple leaders] called the apostles in and had them flogged. Then they ordered them not to speak in the name of Jesus, and let them go. The apostles left the Sanhedrin, rejoicing because they had been counted worthy of suffering disgrace for the Name. (Luke's words in Acts 5:40–41)

Dear friends, do not be surprised at the painful trial you are suffering, as though something strange were happening to you. (1 Peter 4:12)

In fact, everyone who wants to live a godly life in Christ Jesus will be persecuted. (Paul's words in 2 Tim. 3:12)

Jesus laid the foundation for this principle in the Sermon on the Mount, a message that defines his perspective of a truly godly person. Notice his emphasis upon the lowly, difficult experiences of life that most of us would not naturally choose:

> Blessed are the poor in spirit . . .
> Blessed are those who mourn . . .
> Blessed are the meek . . .
> Blessed are those who are persecuted
>   because of righteousness . . .
> Blessed are you when people insult you, persecute you
>   and falsely say all kinds of evil against you because of me.
>   —Matt. 5:3–5, 10–11

Our personal theology of trials and suffering is very important because it determines the way we think and react to suffering. Especially important is our ability to see God's relationship to the trials of life. One incorrect but common view says that a loving God would never decree (include in his will) suffering in the lives of Christians. There are several problems with this view, including the following:

- The Bible clearly says otherwise, as noted above.
- Scripture is replete with examples of God's will being accomplished through the experiences of trials and suffering of people— including the lives of Job, Jesus, Paul, and Peter. Jesus referred to the experiences of the man blind from birth (John 9:1–2) and the sickness of Lazarus (John 11:1–3) as happening "so that the work of God might be displayed in his life" (John 9:3) and "for God's glory" (John 11:4).

• If we begin with the premise that a loving God would not include in his will any suffering for someone he loves, then we must account for suffering with other unacceptable explanations. One such explanation is to blame all trials and suffering on Satan as a source of evil independent from God. There is some truth in this view. Satan, his demons, and his kingdom are the immediate source of much evil in the world. But to say that suffering and trials befall us independent of God's control leads to the heresy of dualism. In trying to "protect" God from the charge of being a source of evil (cf. James 1:13; 1 John 1:5), this view actually distorts other attributes of God, especially his sovereignty. If God is God, nothing happens without his permission.

Another explanation for the presence of suffering or trials is found in the ever popular "health and wealth" gospel, but it too leads to serious theological problems. Here the blame is placed on a lack of faith. The underlying philosophy of life says that God promises prosperity—good health and financial blessings—to all who have genuine faith in him. Likewise, if health or wealth are absent or taken away, the Christian's weak faith must be to blame rather than God. The following illustration of this view makes my point.

Doris was dying of cancer; the doctor's prognosis was that she had less than a year to live. But Doris was one of those people that everyone enjoyed visiting in the hospital. What a positive, upbeat view of life! I remember going to the hospital as a young pastor with the intent of encouraging her, but most times she was more of an encouragement to me. Everyone who knew Doris marveled at the faith of this middle-aged woman who had accepted the prognosis and was looking forward to eternity with the Lord.

About six months before her death, there was a marked change in the way some of her family members acted toward me. I felt estranged and unappreciated, and I did not understand the reason for this change until some time after Doris died. Several of the family members attended another church, and during Doris's extended bout with cancer their pastor began "ministering" to the family with a very different message: "If you had enough faith, Doris wouldn't be dying." I cannot even begin to describe the unnecessary anguish heaped upon this family during the years to follow, all because of a faulty theology of trials and suffering.

They not only grieved the death of their loved one but also felt tremendous guilt—and, later, anger toward God—because Doris was not healed. I can only assume the intention of the other pastor was a good one—to motivate them to greater faith—but his theology was seriously lacking something, which made it absolutely wrong. His incomplete view of God and the role of suffering in life resulted in immeasurable spiritual damage to many in that family.

> Trials have an important positive purpose in the Christian life.

Trials have an important positive purpose in the Christian life. One of the purposes of trials for the Christian is to demonstrate the reality of faith and nurture character development. This is where theology intersects life, where "the word of God is living and active. Sharper than any double-edged sword, it penetrates even to dividing soul and spirit, joints and marrow; it judges the thoughts and attitudes of the heart" (Heb. 4:12). James 1:3–4 depicts a process that is further described by Paul in Romans 5:3–5. The process is as follows:

suffering > perseverance > maturity or proven character > hope

A trial provides the opportunity for a Christian to enter into this spiritual growth process, which in turn has the potential to produce maturity, stability, security, and eternal hope. In order to fully understand how this works, let's work our way backward through the steps reflected above.

The results of the process (maturity or proven character > hope) are wonderful and presumably something that every serious Christian wants to achieve, to be "mature and complete, not lacking in anything" (James 1:4). Paul similarly describes this goal in Romans 5:4–5 as "character [produces] hope. And *hope does not disappoint us,* because God has poured out his love into our hearts by the Holy Spirit, whom he has given us" (italics added).

Are you disappointed with someone or something right now? It may be disappointment with God, or with other people, or simply with the circumstances that life has brought your way. Be encouraged that God can bring you something that will not disappoint, but which will bring assurance and great confidence about the future.

The concept of hope in Scripture is not just something we wish for with no guarantee of whether we will get it or not. Hope is God's assurance of the things he has already provided for us, including eternal life through God's Son Jesus Christ and the resources in this life to become more Christlike. The work of God's Holy Spirit within us, for example, provides us the ability to experience "love, joy, peace, patience, kindness, goodness, faithfulness, gentleness and self-control" through all kinds of life situations (Gal. 5:22–23). Scripture is replete with descriptions of God's work in the lives of Christians. In Ephesians 1:3–14, for example, Paul revels in the riches we have been given in Christ. All of this is included in the eternal *hope*. All Christians have already been blessed with the spiritual blessings we have in Christ, but not all Christians live as if those blessings were true. The difference is maturity. The word translated "character" in Romans 5:4 means, more precisely, "tested" or "proven character." Job said, "When he has tested me, I will come forth as gold" (Job 23:10). Pure gold or silver is not the raw ore but rather the product that comes forth after intense heat is applied. Similarly, proven character or maturity comes forth after we have gone through a growth process that includes testing.

The first part of the formula (suffering > perseverance > maturity) explains the growth process. It is here that many Christians "stall out" in their relationship with God and are unwilling to go further. If you have never wrestled with what I am about to say, you may even be tempted to stop reading here. Please read on! The truth is this simple: no pain, no gain. Without the first part of the process, the desirable qualities of Christian maturity, proven character, and hope simply will not happen. Let me put it more bluntly: When God allows suffering and trials into your life, he is providing a way to develop character qualities that can be produced in no other way. There are no shortcuts to maturity and proven character, only the narrow road of faith. Margaret Clarkson states it so honestly and clearly: "It is not by miraculous deliverance that our faith grows, but by discovering God's faithfulness in the midst of our pain."[3]

The term translated "sufferings" in Romans 5:3 refers to something that is pressed together or pressing in on us. It can also mean hostility from outward circumstances. We can relate to this, can't we? The concept of *stress* has become an accepted part of our vocabulary and lifestyle. As Christians, we live in a world that is hostile to the message of Christ, and there is continual pressure to conform. J. B. Phillips's paraphrase of Romans 12:2 says, "Don't let the world around you squeeze you into its mold, but let God remold your minds from within, so that you may prove in practice that the plan of God for you is good, meets all his demands and moves toward the goal of true maturity." We often use the word *stressful* to describe life in general. For Christians, however, even greater stress may come from the battle that is waging for the souls of people and the values of God's kingdom.

It is interesting to me that the usual way we pray amid this stress is to ask for deliverance: "Lord, I'm hurting; please take me out of this trial." Believe me, God understands the prayers of people in pain. Many of the Psalms are models of this type of prayer, or lament.[4] Likewise, Paul prayed fervently for deliverance from his thorn in the flesh (2 Cor. 12:8), as did Jesus when he anticipated the agony of the cross (Matt. 26:39). But are we also willing to pray with Jesus and Paul, "If removing the trial is not possible, may thy will be done"? As Clarkson so aptly observes, God's greatest purpose may not be accomplished through miraculous deliverance but by discovering God as we go through trials. This is why James, Paul, and Peter call upon us to rejoice—to consider joy absolutely compatible with suffering.[5]

Several years ago, one of my friends was going through a time of tremendous personal trial. As we talked and I promised to pray more specifically for him, he said, "I don't want you necessarily to pray that God will deliver me from this trial, but that he would give me the grace to bear up under it. I think I am learning that I don't want to waste any of the experiences God allows in my life." Humanly speaking, that is an odd way to look at suffering because our natural inclination is to want out of the fire. But as my friend had matured in his relationship with God, he learned to see trials and testing through different "lenses"—as an opportunity rather than an obstacle; a stepping-stone rather than a stumbling block. He didn't want to miss any opportunity to grow. His mature attitude embodies the word *perseverance* in our growth process:

suffering > perseverance > maturity or proven character > hope

Though some translations choose the word "patience" in Romans 5:3–4 and James 1:3–4, "perseverance" is more appropriate. Why? The Greek word used here is a very active and forceful term, rather than one of passive acceptance. The connotation of our word *patience* is too passive and implies noninvolvement. The word used by Paul and James does not mean patiently waiting for something to end. "It speaks of tenacity and stick-to-it-iveness."[6] It is an appropriate word to be used alongside the stress of sufferings. Perseverance describes resistance to pressure, and the ability to stand up under it. To persevere is to make conscious choices about how we respond to life's circumstances and to be persistent in following those choices. Please note that of the four stages of the growth process, perseverance is the only step that involves a significant choice and commitment on our part.

No Pain, No Gain

The expression "no pain, no gain" is often associated with the physical conditioning of an athlete. I have enjoyed sports all my life, but like many, I participated in the more rigorous, competitive sports only during my high school years. I have not forgotten, however, the agonizing process of getting in shape at the beginning of the season. Coaches seemed to know that a lazy, out-of-shape team would likely be a losing team. The hard work it took to get in shape often paid off later in wins.

I must admit that I have not continued the discipline of regular physical conditioning into my adult life, at least not on a regular basis. A few years ago, I became very convicted about this. I joined an athletic club and asked my neighbor Rick if he would teach me to play racquetball. Rick was not only an excellent player, but his job as a carpenter kept him in peak physical condition. He was a gracious racquetball teacher, and I began to pick up the basics of the sport rather quickly. After I learned the rules and techniques of the game, I figured I was ready to enter into serious competition. I can still remember the first game we played. I think the score was 3–21, and I was lucky to get those three points! Not only was the score humiliating, but when Rick invited me to play a second game, I had to admit I had no energy left. The spirit was willing, but the flesh was weak.

Losing that game to Rick was good for me because it renewed my desire to begin physical conditioning. I started a serious jogging program (though I did not tell Rick). Very soon I began to notice my improved stamina on the racquetball court. We increased from playing just one game to two, and then ultimately to playing three games each time out. During the next year, my scores became much more respectable, and I was even able to beat Rick a few times. I played better because I was in good physical condition.

Scripture uses an athlete as an illustration of Christian living for good reason. Paul wrote the following to the Corinthians, whose city was located just a few miles from the site of the Isthmian games, second only in popularity to the Olympics:

> Do you not know that in a race all the runners run, but only one gets the prize? Run in such a way as to get the prize. Everyone who competes in the games goes into strict training. They do it to get a crown that will not last; but we do it to get a crown that will last forever. Therefore I do not run like a man running aimlessly; I do not fight like a man beating the air. No, I beat my body and make it my slave so that after I have preached to others, I myself will not be disqualified for the prize. (1 Cor. 9:24–27)

Similarly, the writer to the Hebrews refers to the perseverance and discipline exhibited by a runner to exhort fellow Christians as they go through suffering: "Let us throw off everything that hinders and the sin that so easily entangles, and let us run with perseverance the race marked out for us" (Heb. 12:1).[7]

The pain of physical training is no fun when you are out of shape. With the hard work of persistent conditioning, however, things begin to change. Muscles develop and lung capacity increases, as does the psychological stamina it takes to "keep on keeping on." Through perseverance in the midst of life's struggles, much like my racquetball experience, we gain the benefits and encouragement of growth and maturity. But just as even the most gifted athletes will not succeed unless they "pay the price" and push themselves beyond the comfort zone of normalcy, so too with life's struggles. No pain, no gain.

What Does Perseverance Look Like?

In this chapter we have considered the process outlined by James and Paul in two important New Testament passages about trials:

suffering > perseverance > maturity or proven character > hope

We have no control over the trials of faith that will come our way on the journey of life, but we do have a choice about how to respond to them. Charles Swindoll says it well:

> The longer I live, the more I realize the impact of attitude on life. . . . The remarkable thing is we have a choice every day regarding the attitude we will embrace for that day. We cannot change our past . . . we cannot change the fact that people will act in a certain way. We cannot change the inevitable. The only thing we can do is play on the one string we have, and that is our attitude. . . . I am convinced that life is 10 percent what happens to me and 90 percent how I react to it.[8]

Remember, perseverance through a trial does not mean just passively waiting for something to change. It is a proactive quality whose longevity, persistence, and consistency are the products of right thinking. In this next section, we will explore the contexts of Romans 5 and James 1 to identify four key elements that define perseverance:

- Joy
- Submission
- Humility
- Prayer

Our desire is to see life's circumstances in the same way God sees them so that we might cooperate as much as we can with his training program.

Rejoice. One of the most misunderstood commands in the New Testament is the exhortation to rejoice amidst suffering (Rom. 5:3; James 1:2). For some Christians, this exhortation leads to discouragement because the emotion of joy or happiness seems entirely out of place during difficult times. Others experience the pressure from fellow Christians to keep up a super-spiritual façade for fear of being judged as an unspiritual Christian who lacks faith. Both of these extremes are unnecessary and reflect a misunderstanding of the command to rejoice. The biblical teaching of joy or rejoicing has more to do with a confidence in one's convictions than it does with emotion. Certainly the emotion of human happiness may accompany joy, but it does not begin there nor does it always end with a smile on our faces. When we rejoice in suffering, it is an expression of faith, a conviction that God is in control and that he is doing something constructive and good through this experience. Our en-joy-ment as Christians is in the belief that God is at work in our midst.

In his wonderful paraphrase of the New Testament, J. B. Phillips expresses James 1:2 in this way: "When all kinds of trials and temptations crowd into your lives, my brothers, don't resent them as intruders, but welcome them as friends!" Unrealistic? Humanly speaking, yes. But remember, our goal is to see life through the lens of God's Word. In suffering joyfully, there is potential to take our relationship with God to a new level. Our response of faith during trials not only brings glory to God but also builds character qualities in us that can be developed in no other way.

The joy presented in these verses is a deep contentment and peace that only God can produce. Sometimes, we rejoice through tears of grief—and that is okay, as well. As I have studied this quality in Scripture and observed it in the lives of godly people, I find the attitude of rejoicing quite similar to that of contentment. Paul illustrates this in his own life: "I have learned to be content whatever the circumstances. I know what it is to be in need, and I know what it is to have plenty. I have learned the secret of being content in any and every situation, whether well fed or hungry, whether living in plenty or in want. I can do everything through him who gives me strength" (Phil. 4:11–13). In the midst of a trial, both joy and contentment are qualities that do not happen naturally, but can come only from God. They proceed from a conviction that God is fully in control and has our best interests in mind. Rejoicing or being content goes well beyond simple, passive acceptance to include active participation in the plan that God has for us. We may not always know the details of that plan, but that is okay because we know God.

One of the most striking illustrations of peace amidst trials that I have ever witnessed came during the last few years of the life of a close friend. At the time she was diagnosed with leukemia, Sheila was one of my wife's dearest friends. She had become a Christian just a short time earlier, so she processed this devastating news in a new

> Submit to what God says is true rather than what you feel.

and fresh way. James 1:12 became her favorite verse in the Bible: "Blessed is the man who perseveres under trial, because when he has stood the test, he will receive the crown of life that God has promised to those who love him." Sheila personified what it means to "rejoice in the Lord." Her battle with cancer was a long, hard one, including a year of remission. But during that time she and her husband, L J, grew closer in their marriage than they had ever been in thirty-six years. Though Sheila was a very young Christian, her attitude of contentment had an effect on everyone who came in contact with her, especially some friends who did not know the Lord.

Submit to what God says is true rather than what you feel. The title of this book, *Thinking Right When Things Go Wrong,* is not merely contrived as a catchy play on words. Rather, "thinking right" expresses the key to a healthy response to trials (Rom. 5:3–4; James 1:3). Thinking right can only happen when we intentionally focus our thoughts on things that are true. If we trust the claims of God's Word and apply them to our lives, we begin to think as God thinks. The corrective lens of Scripture helps us to see life as God sees it. It is this knowledge that brings contentment in any situation. God's insight into what can be known gives us peace about the unknown. As someone has said, "Don't doubt in the darkness what God has shown you in the light."[9]

Take note of the similar emphasis on *knowing* in the writings of Paul and James. James says that we can find the joy in trials because we know that the testing of our faith develops perseverance (James 1:3). Similarly, Paul says in Romans 5:3–4, "We also rejoice in our sufferings, *because we know* that suffering produces perseverance" (emphasis added). "Knowing" in these passages is not merely grasping information about something intellectually, but is based on the Hebrew concept of knowing something through experience.

Where, then, is the place for emotion in difficult times? God created us to feel deeply and express emotion when we go through the agony of suffering. Perhaps the best illustrations of this in Scripture are the psalms of lament, such as Psalm 13:[10]

> How long, O LORD? Will you forget me forever?
>   How long will you hide your face from me?
> How long must I wrestle with my thoughts
>   and every day have sorrow in my heart?
> How long will my enemy triumph over me?
>   —vv. 1–2

Notice how the psalm begins with an honest expression of the heart: *Lord, I'm hurting, and it feels like you have forgotten me.* David is feeling abandoned, and he is not afraid to tell God about it. The inclusion of such psalms in Scripture provides examples of how we are to respond to the tough times of life. In the process of expressing his heart to God, David concludes the psalm with this conviction:

> But I trust in your unfailing love;
>   my heart rejoices in your salvation.
> I will sing to the LORD,
>   for he has been good to me.
>   —vv. 5–6

The psalm opens with an honest expression of what David is feeling while in the depths of suffering—honest words filled with deep emotion, even expressing doubts about God. But David always comes back to what he knows to be true. Anxiety and sorrow are not contradictory to joy, because David knows what he believes about God's faithfulness. So it is with our experiences of trial. We must focus our perspective on the truth about God and his revealed plan, rather than on our feelings about our circumstances.

Humble yourself before God. Author James Sire observes that when his life gets off track, he ultimately realizes he has forgotten one simple fact: "God is God, and I am not."[11] Though the quality of humility is not always explicitly mentioned in Scripture passages about enduring trials, it is everywhere assumed. Humility—and sometimes repentance—is needed in order for us to trust that God knows best, especially when the journey of life takes turns we would not have chosen. That is why experiences of suffering are usually the greatest tests of faith. God himself says, "My thoughts are not your thoughts, neither are your ways my ways" (Isa. 55:8). How about the calamities of Job? We will look at Job's relationship with God more closely in chapter 5, and we will see that God ultimately required Job to humble himself and repent of sin—the sin of pride (Job 42:1–6). Job's calamities did not come upon him because of this sin, but in the way that he responded before his friends, he failed to let God be God. How easy it is for any of us to take on the role of God, especially when the going gets tough.

After teaching for a few years at Biola University, I learned of an opportunity to serve as a part-time interim pastor in a church some distance from our home. Things were financially tight for our family at the time, and because I had about fifteen years of pastoral experience, I saw this job as a perfect opportunity. Initially, the prospects looked good and my hopes were high, but then someone else was offered the position. I remember being greatly disappointed because I had thoroughly analyzed all the information I knew, and the job seemed like a match made in heaven. It was not until several months later that I discovered God's wisdom in this great disappointment. Another interim pastorate opportunity arose in a Chinese congregation right in my neighborhood. The congregation and church leaders immediately embraced me, and I subsequently had several years of wonderful ministry there. Through the years, I have marveled often at the blessings that came out of that pastoral relationship. It only came, however, after God taught me something about "waiting on the Lord" rather than rushing to my own judgment. It reaffirmed a Scripture passage that has meant so much to my wife and me, "Trust in the LORD with all your heart and lean not on your own understanding; in all your ways acknowledge him, and he will make your paths straight" (Prov. 3:5–6).

James commands, "Submit yourselves, then, to God. Resist the devil, and he will flee from you. Come near to God and he will come near to you. Wash your hands, you sinners, and purify your hearts, you double-minded. Grieve, mourn and wail. Change your laughter to mourning and your joy to gloom. Humble yourselves before the Lord, and he will lift you up" (James 4:7–10). What does perseverance look like? James is echoing what Solomon says in Proverbs 3:34: God "gives grace to the humble."

Pray for wisdom amidst trials. Most Christians would openly admit that they do not pray enough. I'm convinced that a sincere, consistent prayer life is one of the most difficult spiritual disciplines because prayer itself is entering into a spiritual battle. God invites us to pray when we enter into times of trial, but especially to pray for insight as we go through difficult times:

> If any of you lacks wisdom, he should ask God, who gives generously to all without finding fault, and it will be given to him. But when he asks, he must believe and not doubt, because he who doubts is like a wave of the sea, blown and tossed by the wind. That man should not think he will receive anything from the Lord; he is a double-minded man, unstable in all he does. (James 1:5–8)

This gracious invitation into the mind of God has much encouragement to offer, but it has also been misunderstood at times. As we seek to understand what James is saying, it is important that we take note of the context in which he is writing. Because these verses are a continuation of the discussion that James begins in verses 2–4, we understand that he is giving a specific promise associated with a time of trial or suffering. It follows immediately on the heels of James's description of the process of perseverance and is therefore part of the answer to the question, What does perseverance look like? The prayer for wisdom is a God-given resource to help us persevere through trials. These verses are sometimes used to generally describe a prayer for guidance—for example, praying for wisdom in finding the right car to buy. Though other places in Scripture invite us to pray for practical daily guidance, that is not the point of James 1:5–8.

Prayer is our compass when we are lost in the wilderness and feel as if the universe has come crumbling down around us. Perhaps you've heard the story of the army that was battling in a deep valley, led by a general who was perched on the hills above. The soldiers, who were in touch with the general by radio, at times felt disoriented and even defeated, but they remained confident because the general was able to see the big picture and give them strategic directions to win the battle. Similarly, the valley of trials severely limits our perspective, but through prayer we have direct contact with God, who has an infinitely bigger vantage point and can give us wisdom to carry on in the battle. Can you trust him to do that?

James reassures us that God understands our feelings of inadequacy during trials. The conditional "if any of you lacks wisdom" is stated in such a way that it assumes it is true for everyone. The encouragement that "he should ask God" is an invitation to regularly, repeatedly come to God with our requests for wisdom in the midst of trials. Thus we might read the invitation literally: "Because each of you lacks wisdom (to meet the trials of life victoriously), you should—continually, repeatedly—ask God, who gives generously to all without finding fault, and it will be given to you." The literal rendering may not read very smoothly, but it depicts the extravagant nature of God's offer. Though trials are often a mysterious part of life, God does not intend to leave us without help.

A second part of the passage that is sometimes misinterpreted begins with verse 6. The conditional statement "but when he asks, he must believe and not doubt" has led some Christians to a faulty understanding of the nature of faith during trials. It is sometimes suggested that this verse means that the only effectual faith is one that shuts out all negative thoughts and dwells solely upon God's answering our prayer as we have asked it. This naturally leads to the conclusion that if we doubt or waver in our confidence, God might not answer our prayer because of our lack of faith.

"If you had enough faith, Doris wouldn't be dying." The story of Doris and her bout with cancer told earlier in this chapter may be an extreme example, but it illustrates how devastating this type of theology can be. Defining *faith* in this way is more psychological than biblical. It is a Christian version of the power of positive thinking in which the effectiveness of prayer is linked more to my positive thinking than to the power of God.

Who, then, is the one who doubts, the "double-minded man" in this passage? Donald Burdick describes him as follows:

> [He is one who is] double-souled. It is as though one should declare, "I believe," and the other in turn shouts, "I don't!" This sort of instability is not only apparent when the man prays; it marks all he does. In his personal life, his business life, his social life, as well as in his spiritual life, indecisiveness negates his effectiveness.[12]

The doubter described here is not one who has the legitimate fears we all face in uncertain times but rather one who professes to follow God but regularly does not. It might be someone who professes to believe in God, but when one closely observes his lifestyle there is little evidence of such faith. This condition, then, to "believe and not doubt" in our prayers for wisdom amidst trials, simply calls us to live authentically as true disciples of Christ. If our lifestyle shows a serious wavering between creed and practice, we cannot expect that God will answer our prayers for further wisdom.

This Is Not *Instant* Gratification!

In a world of instant communication, fast computers, and fast food, where we expect immediate gratification to our every wish, perseverance is a rare virtue. James says, "Blessed is the man who perseveres under trial, because when he has stood the test, he will receive the crown of life that God has promised to those who love him" (James 1:12). Much like Jesus'

words in the Beatitudes[13] or the introductory word of several psalms,[14] the
word "blessed" here should be translated
with a shout of exuberance: "O the happiness of the one who perseveres under
trial!" In other words, God (through
James) promises a deep, transcendent
sense of happiness *if* we do not give up
when the going gets tough.

> James refers to two common images to describe the reason for and the results of perseverance.

James is a master of the use of illustration (as was his half brother,
Jesus), and he refers to two common images in his world to describe the
reason for and the results of perseverance. First, "when he has stood the
test" was a term used in the first century for the testing of coins and
precious metals to see whether they were genuine. Perseverance through
trials is much more than just passively waiting for the storm to pass. The
very process is proof that we are "the real thing"—that is, true children
of God who are living exactly as God intended us to live. "In this you
greatly rejoice, though now for a little while you may have had to suffer
grief in all kinds of trials. These have come so that your faith—of greater
worth than gold, which perishes even though refined by fire—may be
proved genuine and may result in praise, glory and honor when Jesus
Christ is revealed" (1 Peter 1:6–7).

A second result of perseverance is pictured in the phrase "he will receive the crown of life that God has promised to those who love him."
This illustration takes us back to the world of athletics in that day when
the victor was rewarded with a crown of oak, laurel, or other leaves fash-
ioned into a wreath. This is the same crown that Paul refers to in 1 Corinthians 9:25: "Everyone who competes in the games goes into strict
training. They do it to get a crown that will not last; but we do it to get a
crown that will last forever." If you are looking for quick payoffs or escape hatches here, you don't understand the process of perseverance.
"No pain, no gain" sometimes includes *waiting* in the midst of trials.
Psalm 40:1–2 describes it well:

> I waited patiently for the LORD;
>   he turned to me and heard my cry.

> He lifted me out of the slimy pit,
>   out of the mud and mire;
> he set my feet on a rock
>   and gave me a firm place to stand.

"It is not by miraculous deliverance that our faith grows," says hymn writer Margaret Clarkson, "but by discovering God's faithfulness in the midst of our pain."[15] Are you in the slimy pit, the mud, and the mire right now? It's hard to find a firm place to stand, isn't it? Make a conscious decision to persevere. Don't give up on God because the ground is shaky. He will again set your feet on a rock. And when he does, you will be able to look back to this time as one of the greatest times of growth you have ever experienced.

Temptation or Trial? Obstacle or Opportunity?

In this chapter, we have explored the spiritual growth process that can take place during times of trial or suffering. In Romans 5:3–5 and James 1:1–12 we have seen that the heart of this process is perseverance. By trusting God rather than our emotions or natural instincts, we can see how something very negative can be transformed into something positive. The context of James 1:1–12 is interesting, because the subject of the ensuing discussion in verses 13–18 seems to switch from "trials" to "temptations," yet the same root term is used for both words: "trials" (vv. 1–12) and "tempted" (vv. 13–18). Almost all English translations have correctly recognized the contextual shift in emphasis and distinction between these subjects. Trials are described as experiences allowed by God to produce growth and maturity in our lives. Temptations are depicted as coming not from God, but rather as enticements to sin from our own evil desires. Though the ultimate source and purpose of trials and temptations are quite different, they are really opposite sides of the same coin. The same experience in life may be either a trial or a temptation, depending upon our response to it. A particular set of circumstances can either result in sin, or become a wonderful spiritual growth process through faith and perseverance. Viewed through different lenses, obstacles may in fact be opportunities. What we perceive to be a stumbling block might actually be a stepping-stone to a deeper experience with God. Something with the potential to be destructive can become one of the most constructive experiences of our lives.

Consider the medical practice of vaccination, a procedure that produces immunity against some viruses and bacteria by introducing live or altered antigens into a person's body. The presence of these "enemy cells," in turn, stimulates the human immune system to produce antibodies that remain to fight against more dangerous forms of the disease at a later time. A similar process happens when we catch various strains of the flu or colds; the acquired immunity protects us from catching that particular strain of virus again. However, the only way this process works is through exposure to actual viruses and bacteria that subsequently triggers a battle in the immune system.

> Maturity and proven character can only come through the difficult experiences that develop them.

Similarly, God allows trials and experiences of suffering into our lives to "toughen" us and prepare us for life on earth and life in eternity. Our response to present trials determines whether we will face the future with greater strength and maturity. As expressed in Hebrews, "No discipline seems pleasant at the time, but painful. Later on, however, it produces a harvest of righteousness and peace for those who have been trained by it" (Heb. 12:11). Maturity and proven character can only come through the difficult experiences that develop them. Our sovereign heavenly Father is a master at shaping a unique spiritual formation program for each one of us. He knows our limits and our weaknesses. He reassures us that "no temptation [trial] has seized you except what is common to man. And God is faithful; he will not let you be tempted beyond what you can bear. But when you are tempted, he will also provide a way out so that you can stand up under it" (1 Cor. 10:13).

DISCUSSION QUESTIONS

1. Reflect on your maturity level at this stage in your life (either personal or spiritual maturity). What significant events or influences have helped you to mature and become stronger? If any of them were trials and difficult times, explain how these were a benefit to you.

2. Explain in your own words the process described in James 1:3–4 and Romans 5:3–5. Share an example of this process from your own life or one that you have observed in the life of another.

3. How would you respond to a young Christian friend who asked the following question: "I was just reading about facing trials in Romans 5 and James 1, but I do not understand the command to rejoice in the midst of them. This seems like denial of the problem and is certainly not very authentic. Why would I ever do that?"

4. What are some of the cultural factors in Western or American society that make perseverance a quality that is not admired, pursued, or encouraged by many? Why does the Bible say it is an important quality?

5. Using information revealed in James 1:2–18, explain the difference between trials and temptations. Are trials and temptations ever the same thing?

Chapter 3

Stretching the Soul

Defeat, even more than victory, may lead to significant times of spiritual transformation. Sorrows sometimes stretch out places for joy in our hearts. In the first two chapters, we have seen that God may be doing his greatest work in situations when he seems entirely absent. In this chapter, we will look at three additional examples of how God works through difficult circumstances in our lives. First, the circumstances surrounding a trial sometimes lead to the salvation of souls, either of the one who is suffering or of others who observe a response of faith. Second, a courageous response to suffering provides an example to other Christians and inspires them to boldly live for Christ in the same way. Finally, trials sometimes provide unique preparation for ministry to others who are going through the same kind of suffering.

Stretching the Soul for Salvation

Trials and tragedy are never welcome visitors in our lives. They come as intruders, grabbing our attention like nothing else. They pierce to the very depths of our souls and ask questions we try to avoid. Listen to Mike's story, shared in his own words:

> I came to Jesus late in life through trauma. I was not a particularly bad person, just neutral. I was "culturally" Christian and educated with twelve years of Roman Catholic schooling. I did believe in

God and that Jesus was God, but it all seemed so otherworldly. I guess I was an existentialist and a relativist like most of my generation. The meaning of life was whatever you ascribed it to be. God was not personal but rather an abstraction.

I was well known in my field of medicine and took great pride in the fame I received while teaching at prestigious Ivy League universities. My marriage at one time had been happy but had become colder over the years. My wife and I were growing apart, and she seemed to prefer it that way, though I did still love her.

Then my wife suddenly died. I had been away as a visiting professor, and when I arrived home the next day, the TV was strangely on and the house was not very tidy. I immediately called her name and went looking for her. I found her blue and unresponsive lying on the bed: obviously dead for quite some time.

Do you know what hell is? Hell is being a physician, administering CPR to your dead spouse, and you know she's dead. Hell is not what painters or artists describe. It is not red-dressed creatures with horns and pitchforks. I was shown hell for a fleeting few minutes. Hell is absence. It is an emptiness that is unfathomable. No recourse. No goodness. It is the absence of a solution. Hell is the absence of God, for without God there is no goodness.

I considered suicide for about forty-eight hours. I felt "dirty." I felt that I had to "get clean." I didn't know why I had these feelings. Within this time period I had to arrange for the funeral. My wife was "culturally" a Baptist. I went looking for a minister.

It was late in the day, and the pastor was tired. I called the church, and he agreed to meet with me. I later found out that he had recently performed a number of funerals. He was exhausted and wanted no part of any further funerals. For some reason, still unknown to him to this day, he took this last one on and didn't pass it to a colleague. I visited him for the first time that afternoon. I poured out my soul to him. I wanted to "get clean." Time passed after the funeral. The pastor and I kept in touch.

As time passed, I began to consider the options for my life. For some reason, I somehow felt that I had been given a second chance at life, whatever that meant. I began to ask questions: What makes a good life? How do you know what is right and wrong? How do you know what is good and evil? What is the meaning of life? You can ask these questions in the framework of an introductory philosophy class. You won't find the answers to them until the search becomes desperate, the reason to get up in the morning.

During this intense time of searching, I was extremely depressed. I really didn't like the person I saw on the inside when enough of those layers had been peeled away. I was being broken. I was reaching my limits as an individual. I was reaching the end of myself. Who or what would I find?

Mike's tragedy and subsequent search for answers represents the story of so many. We are preoccupied with ourselves and other things, and we fail to pursue that which is most important—our relationships with others and, most importantly, with God. The death of Mike's wife led him to pursue truth, and ultimately the pastor who officiated at the funeral became a source of light to Mike. Mike started praying and reading the Bible, though he didn't absorb it all at first. Ultimately, that pastor led Mike into a relationship with Christ.

That seemed very strange to me at first. A personal relationship with God? I was desperate. Could this be true? Then the pastor showed me John 3:16, which I think I understood for the first time in my life: "For God so loved the world that he gave His one and only Son." This was no longer an abstraction.

So what is the meaning of life? Jesus Christ is the meaning of life, for without Him, there is no meaning. He is the Alpha and the Omega. It took me forty-four years to figure that out. I had to have all the defense mechanisms torn away. I had to be broken and desperate. I had to fall into a long, deep, dark pit. And when I had finally hit bottom, do you know who I found there? I found Christ.[1]

The death of Mike's wife was truly a tragedy, but good can come out of tragedy. Romans 8:28, perhaps more than any other passage in the New Testament, has brought reassurance to Christians who are going through difficult times: "And we know that in all things God works for the good of those who love him, who have been called according to his purpose." In some cases that "good" is the salvation of others. Paul writes a few verses later, "What, then, shall we say in response to this? If God is for us, who can be against us? . . . Who shall separate us from the love of Christ? Shall trouble or hardship or persecution or famine or nakedness or danger or sword? . . . No, in all these things we are more than conquerors through him who loved us" (Rom. 8:31, 35, 37).

Joseph, one of the sons of Jacob in the Old Testament, had much to be bitter about. As a teenager he enjoyed prosperity and the devotion of his father, who saw Joseph's birth as a special gift of God in his later years (Gen. 37:1–10). Joseph's brothers were jealous, however, and plotted to kill him. His life was spared when one of his brothers stood up for him, but Joseph was sold into slavery and ultimately lived his early adult years as a slave in Egypt (vv. 11–36). How easy it would have been for him to hate his brothers and become bitter toward God. Without any fault on his part, everything he enjoyed in his early prosperous life had been taken away from him, and now he was doomed to live the hopeless life of a slave.

But "the LORD was with Joseph" (Gen. 39:2), and his status as a slave was upgraded to that of a servant in the house of Pharaoh. Eventually, he became one of Egypt's most powerful leaders during that time in history (Gen. 41). Rather than responding in bitterness to God, Joseph continued to serve God in whatever circumstance he found himself. Though Romans 8:28 would not be written for another two thousand years, Joseph believed this truth and practiced it in his life. Ultimately, his brothers traveled to Egypt because of famine, and when they learned that Joseph was not only alive but a ruler in Egypt, they feared he would take revenge on them.

Joseph's amazing response in Genesis 50:19–20 is the Romans 8:28 of the Old Testament, "Don't be afraid. Am I in the place of God? You intended to harm me, but God intended it for good to accomplish what is now being done, the saving of many lives." Though at the time Joseph's sale into slavery was a tragedy for him and his parents, it resulted in the physical salvation of all the descendants of Jacob. During extreme years of famine, the twelve tribes of Israel were blessed in the prosperity of Egypt because of the faith of this one young man. Faith in the midst of trial. Joseph's brothers feared, and we might expect that Joseph would be bitter, angry, and even revengeful as a result of his trial. But he wasn't. Likewise, when we face adverse circumstances, we too must ask ourselves, "Am I in the place of God?" How do I know what good God may be able to bring out of even the greatest tragedy? Times of trial are the *most* difficult times to live by faith because it seems as if God has abandoned us. Yet, God is able to take the circumstances of every trial or tragedy and produce hope. Our response becomes the key.

Paul's Prison Ministry

A significant trial in the life of the apostle Paul was his confinement in a Roman prison—not once but twice! He writes of the first Roman prison experience in Philippians 1:12–18, but with quite an unexpected tone of *joy*. Paul was the quintessential positive thinker, and he had good reason to be. Unlike our psychologically induced power of positive thinking today, where the power is found in believing something hard enough, Paul's power was found in God and in the confidence of knowing that God is at work amidst every trial. Paul rejoiced over the salvation of many others through the trials he experienced. Since this is one of Scripture's classic passages on trials, let's explore it in more depth.

There is little debate that the most effective evangelist and church planter in the early church was the apostle Paul. Acts 13–20 documents ten years of his life during which he took three missionary journeys preaching Christ, planting new churches, and establishing training centers in Antioch, Ephesus, and Corinth. Though Paul regularly faced persecution for this ministry, his mission was successful by anyone's standards.

When he was arrested in Jerusalem, his life was in great danger (Acts 21–23) and everyone assumed his ministry was over—everyone, that is, except Paul! He was born a Roman citizen, and citizenship had its privileges, including the right to appeal a capital offense all the way to Caesar.

Protection by the Roman guards who transported Paul from Jerusalem to Rome for trial actually saved his life from a Jewish mob (Acts 24–28). On this trip, Paul was able to share the message of Christ with some of the most powerful rulers of his time: Felix (Acts 24), Festus (Acts 25), and Agrippa (Acts 26). Upon his arrival in Rome (Acts 28), Paul was placed under house arrest, which meant confinement to rented quarters with a Roman guard chained to him and some visitors allowed. Luke the historian describes this in verses 30–31, "For two whole years Paul stayed there in his own rented house and welcomed all who came to see him. Boldly and without hindrance he preached the kingdom of God and taught about the Lord Jesus Christ." During this time, Paul also wrote to several churches in a group of writings called the Prison Epistles, which include the letters to the Ephesians, Philippians, and Colossians (and a personal letter to Philemon, who lived in Colossae). Understanding the context in which Paul wrote to the Philippians helps us to appreciate his remarkable attitude of joy. In Philippians 1, he cites three positive results that came from his negative circumstances: the gospel advanced inside the prison; the gospel advanced outside of the prison; and the gospel advanced through the work of inspired friends.

1. The gospel advanced inside the prison. "Now I want you to know, brothers, that what has happened to me has really served to advance the gospel. As a result, it has become clear throughout the whole palace guard and to everyone else that I am in chains for Christ" (Phil. 1:12–13). We can assume from Paul's words that his friends in Philippi saw his confinement as an end to his ministry. How typical when you love someone! Because of love and compassion, we often jump to the conclusion that a trial prevents God from carrying out his work. Paul, seeking to encourage them, says, "No!" This trial has actually enabled the message of Christ to reach the highest echelon of Roman society. The palace guard—or Praetorian Guard—was Caesar's elite corps, responsible for guarding his household. In the United States, they would be equivalent to the Secret Service.

Paul's references to chains indicate that his house arrest included being chained to one or two soldiers at all times, a typical arrangement for a prisoner awaiting trial. There is great humor in the irony of this situation. Paul's friends saw him as chained to Roman guards, but Paul saw the guards as chained to *him*—a captive audience! Over a period of two years, a succession of imperial soldiers were privy to Paul's conversations with his visitors, overheard him as he dictated letters to various churches, and no doubt had many personal discussions with Paul themselves. To encourage his Philippian supporters, Paul rejoiced that the gospel was being preached to a segment of Roman society that likely would have never heard it apart from his arrest.

How do you respond to the trials of life? Do you see the glass as half empty or half full? Suffering is never enjoyable emotionally, but one of the things we learn from Paul's example is the importance of viewing trials from a greater perspective, as part of a bigger story than our own. His optimism is not just a gimmick or a technique of positive thinking. He is genuinely confident that he has good reason to see hope even in humanly hopeless circumstances, because God is at work there doing something that could be done in no other way.

Paul's words about this trial are filled with expressions of joy and rejoicing (Phil. 1:3, 18, 26). His attitude changes obstacles into opportunities, stumbling blocks into stepping-stones. Biblical joy, however, is not primarily a superficial feeling but rather a deep conviction. This kind of joy is closer in meaning to a sense of contentment than the emotion of happiness. We may hurt and even grieve in the circumstances of a trial, but remain joyful (content and confident) because we know that God is at work in our midst. Are you facing or have you faced tough circumstances? Is it possible that through them God is bringing about the salvation of those who do not know Christ? Sometimes, the full story of God's work amidst trials can only be seen through the passing of time—sometimes only in eternity.

Craig and Carolyn Kelford were active in our church for many years, and were regular participants in our adult fellowship group. Craig worked as an administrator in a world missions organization and Carolyn was a teacher at the local high school. Then tragedy struck. Their son Craig, who was on the high school track and field team, was struck and killed by an errant discus during a meet. The news reverberated throughout our community. Expressions of love came from our church and youth group, from local high school students and teachers, and from the surrounding community. Young Craig's memorial service was packed with hundreds of teenagers and staff from the high school. And because the Kelfords represented such a typical family and their loss was so tragic, the Los Angeles news media carried the story in the newspapers and on television.

But the Kelfords were *not* a typical family in their response to this tragedy. Yes, they grieved deeply at the loss of their son and never hesitated to express that grief publicly when they talked about Craig. In the midst of their deepest sorrow, however, they talked about their faith in Christ. When other parents might have pursued lawsuits or reacted in anger toward the coaches who had supervised the track meet, the Kelfords responded publicly with grace. When they met with the young man who had thrown the discus, they reached out to comfort and reassure him. Craig's memorial service remembered his life but focused on Jesus and the hope he can give to everyone who trusts in him. Carolyn and Craig found that the message of their son's life attracted the attention of hundreds of high school students who rarely thought about their need for Christ. Many were saved and today are walking with the Lord because the Kelfords believed that God was at work even in their darkest hour. They responded as they did because they saw all of life, even the most difficult trials, as part of a bigger story.

2. The gospel advanced outside of the prison. "It is true that some preach Christ out of envy and rivalry, but others out of goodwill. The latter do so in love, knowing that I am put here for the defense of the gospel. The former preach Christ out of selfish ambition, not sincerely, supposing that they can stir up trouble for me while I am in chains" (Phil. 1:15–17).

Here the apostle acknowledges that there were competitive, rival preachers who were using his imprisonment as a means to discredit him and become more "successful" themselves. Who were these rivals? Certainly, Paul's successful ministry stirred up controversy from different groups. Some simply opposed the message of Christ among the Gentiles (Acts 17:32) and others among the Jews (Acts 13:50; 14:19). They claimed to be presenting the gospel of Christ, but were actually presenting a distortion of it that Paul calls "really no gospel at all" (Gal. 1:6–7). In Philippians 1, however, Paul is talking about another type of rival, whose message was evidently the pure gospel of Christ, but the motives for preaching came from envy, rivalry, and selfish ambition (Phil. 1:15, 17).

Perhaps they were envious of Paul's fame and success as an evangelist and church planter. We can surmise that they were privately gloating about Paul's confinement and publicly maligning him, "supposing that they can stir up trouble for me while I am in chains" (v. 17). Unlike the false teachers, however, their message was still the true gospel.

Life isn't always fair. How do you respond to injustice and unfairness? Maybe a better question is, How do you respond to injustice and unfairness when you are doing exactly what God wants you to do? Paul's ministry had been stopped short by circumstances (arrest and imprisonment), but the pain was exacerbated by narcissistic preachers who maligned his good name, seeking to promote their own ministries.

I can envision Paul reflecting on Joseph's story: "Am I in the place of God? You intended to harm me, but God intended it for good to accomplish what is now being done, the saving of many lives" (Gen. 50:19–20). This kind of attitude is the only explanation for the apostle's response: "But what does it matter? The important thing is that in every way, whether from false motives or true, Christ is preached. And because of this I rejoice" (Phil. 1:18). Paul saw his life as part of God's bigger story, and by thinking right when things went wrong he was able to rise above his circumstances—and his critics—to experience joy. The joy Paul describes is not primarily a warm, emotional feeling, but instead is a deep, personal contentment that God is at work. This is "Christian positive thinking" at its best. Rather than denying the truth about his situation, Paul honestly faced the obstacles before him and saw them as opportunities to advance the cause of Christ. We can do the same, because the ultimate experience of joy comes in knowing that we are part of God's bigger story.

3. *The gospel advanced through the work of inspired friends.* "Because of my chains, most of the brothers in the Lord have been encouraged to speak the word of God more courageously and fearlessly" (Phil. 1:14). Paul's courageous response to negative circumstances not only produced more opportunities for him to present the gospel, but it also served as an example to other Christians, inspiring them to boldly follow Christ in the same way. Paul's positive response as a victor rather than a victim renewed courage in other Christians to become more bold in their witness as well. Courage inspires courage.

When Pearl Hamilton, a gifted Bible teacher and director of women's ministries at our church, succumbed to leukemia in 1993, it was devastating to all who had benefited from her ministry. Nevertheless, the memorial service was a grand celebration of the courage and faith that Christ had given to Pearl in her last days. As the service ended, my wife's friend Sheila leaned over to her and said, "I could never be like that." Little did she know that just two weeks later she would hear the early news of her own cancer. During the next five years (including two years of remission), Sheila's life became like Pearl's. Though she felt completely inadequate in her weakness, the example of courage and faith she had seen in Pearl became her own story as well. Sheila's remaining years made a significant spiritual impact on the people around her, a circle of friends probably no one else could have reached. At her memorial service, as I looked out over the crowd that had filled the auditorium, I remembered the words Sheila had uttered there just five years earlier, "I could never be like that." Inspired by Pearl's faith in the face of death, Sheila had become "like that," and her faith in turn became a testimony to others who followed.

Not all of us are called upon to face the traumatic circumstances of terminal illness (I'm thankful for that!), but we ought not to underestimate the impact our faith might have in the more mundane events of everyday life. When we face trials of any kind, one of the most important steps we can take is to draw on the support of others in the body of Christ. Galatians 6:1–2 says that when we struggle with temptation and sin we should not try to face it alone, but instead "carry each others burdens, and in this way you will fulfill the law of Christ." First Corinthians 12 describes Christians as members of a body, and "if one part suffers, every part suffers with it" (v. 26).

The dynamic influence of shared "body life" provides a number of advantages when we face trials. First, we receive the support and encouragement of friends at a time when we most need it. Second, we share an accountability for our faith, encouraging us to persevere even when the going gets tough. Third, our response of faith, even in very small trials, serves as an encouragement to others to do the same. Through prayers and mutual support, friends become "partners" in the faith, and seeing us respond courageously spurs them on to do the same. Paul's attitude about his circumstances was the key. Rather than wallowing in self-pity, he saw (through the eyes of faith) the strategic opportunity God had placed before him.

Getting Your B.D. Degree

Thus far in this chapter we have seen how trials can stretch out places for joy in our hearts. Dire circumstances can lead to the salvation of others in a variety of ways. Suffering may be God's way of preparing the heart of an unbeliever for Christ, of opening up doors for the gospel where none existed, or of motivating Christians to present Christ more courageously. These are all depicted in Paul's attitude about imprisonment in Philippians 1:12–18. But the "stretching of the soul" has another purpose in serving God. Suffering has the potential to provide a unique preparation for future ministry, especially to others who may go through the same kind of suffering. In 2 Corinthians 1:3–4, Paul worships God with this insight: "Praise be to the God and Father of our Lord Jesus Christ, the Father of compassion and the God of all comfort, who comforts us in all our troubles, so that we can comfort those in any trouble with the comfort we ourselves have received from God."

You are a minister. Sure, you may not have seminary training or be listed on your church's pastoral staff, but in God's program you are a minister. Not only that, but the Bible says that you may be called to a specialized ministry with others. First Peter 4:10 says, "Each one should use whatever gift he has received to serve others, faithfully administering God's grace in its various forms." Second Corinthians 1:4–6 teaches us that preparation for a ministry with others may come through the experiences of life:

> [God] comforts us in all our troubles, so that we can comfort those in any trouble with the comfort we ourselves have received from God. For just as the sufferings of Christ flow over into our lives, so also through Christ our comfort overflows. If we are distressed, it is for your comfort and salvation; if we are comforted, it is for your comfort, which produces in you patient endurance of the same sufferings we suffer.

The life of Moses serves as a wonderful illustration. During the first forty years of Moses' life he was raised in the privileged position of an adopted son in Pharaoh's household (Exod. 2:1–10). In Acts 7:22, we learn that "Moses was educated in all the wisdom of the Egyptians and was powerful in speech and action." Because the Egyptian empire was the most powerful and prosperous nation of its time, with universities second to none, Moses truly had an impressive résumé. His Egyptian training in leadership skills, warfare, languages, and literature would later become essential to him in his service for God. Effective leadership skills and training in warfare were to help him lead the wandering Israelites to the Promised Land. Training in various languages, literature, and law enabled him to write the Torah, in which we find evidence of an educated, creative writer who recorded the five scrolls of Genesis through Deuteronomy.

But God's training program for Moses also required something beyond a degree from an Egyptian university. It was his B.D.—his "Backside of the Desert" degree. After killing an Egyptian official, Moses was forced to flee, at the age of forty, into the primitive life of the wilderness (Exod. 2:11–15) where he spent another forty years of his life (until he was eighty!). As he reflected back on the privileged years of his early adulthood, I'm sure there were many times when Moses saw his service for God as finished because his life as a fugitive was an unexpected turn in the road. He had remained faithful to God (Heb. 11:25–26); why had God not continued to bring him success? With all the training he had received in Egypt, why was he now tending sheep?

The answer to these questions is simple, but Moses could not see it at the time: He was working on his B.D. degree. Through his experiences in the Midian wilderness, he learned essential skills and developed character traits that would be needed later in his ministry. Just as he learned patience leading sheep, he would later need it regularly leading the "flock" of Israel in similar desert conditions. Moses learned important skills of wilderness survival, but more importantly he developed the humble heart of a servant-leader. At the burning bush (Exod. 3), God called Moses to do the work he had been prepared for, and at first Moses refused. Perhaps he had learned the lesson of humility too well, but perhaps he simply thought his life of service was over.

Has God taken you through a series of courses toward your B.D. degree? Maybe he has, and you didn't recognize it for what it was. B.D. degrees are earned only in the classroom of life's experiences, experiences that rarely seem important at the time and that are often accompanied by the silence of God rather than his clear revelation. Sometimes it seems as if God is absent altogether, and only later do we see his faithful presence through the trial. It has always been encouraging to me that Abraham, Moses, and other great leaders did not fully understand what God was doing when he called them. All of them earned B.D. degrees through the experiences of life.

At the beginning of chapter 1, I shared with you the story of the tragic death of my brother-in-law on Thanksgiving Day. During the year prior to his death, Doug had moved to Dallas to receive treatment in a Christian counseling center. During that time, he sometimes lived in our home, an arrangement that was a real challenge for us with two small children. It was Leah's and my first exposure to someone going through severe depression. I can remember a number of times when we had no clue how to help him, when Leah would try to console him in one part of the house while I was getting our children out the back door to stay with neighbors. The experience of trying to help Doug in his state of depression was truly frustrating for us. We would have avoided it if we had not felt the obligation of our family relationship. Yet during that trying time we became much more familiar with the nature of depression, and in so doing became more understanding of and empathetic to others who face that disease. We read books, talked to doctors, and learned from firsthand experience. God gave us many opportunities to use that experience in the years that followed. Though I do not consider myself a trained counselor, I understand some of the realities of depression much more clearly because of the family encounters we have had with it.

God's Grace Is Sufficient

God is good, and his grace and comfort are completely adequate for every experience of our lives. Second Corinthians 1:3–7 centers on the theme of comfort in the midst of trials. The key word "comfort" (or "encouragement") appears ten times in these verses, as either a verb or a noun. The verb form conveys the sense of God's consistent, constant, and unfailing ministry in our lives. His ministry to us is not "hit-and-miss"; nor does it ever fail.

Paul, a man in the midst of trials (2 Cor. 1:8–11), begins his letter not by focusing on his circumstances but by focusing on God, who is in control of Paul's circumstances. His doxology is thus, "Praise be to the God and Father of our Lord Jesus Christ, the Father of compassion and the God of all comfort" (2 Cor. 1:3). The expression "Father of compassion," which means the source or originator of compassion, echoes the sentiments of many of the Old Testament writers in their statements about God.

> Because of the LORD's great love we are not consumed,
>   for his compassions never fail.
> They are new every morning;
>   great is your faithfulness. . . .
> Though he brings grief, he will show compassion,
>   so great is his unfailing love.
>
> —Lam. 3:22–23, 32

> You will again have compassion on us;
>   you will tread our sins underfoot
>   and hurl all our iniquities into the depths of the sea.
>
> —Mic. 7:19

> The LORD will surely comfort Zion
>   and will look with compassion on all her ruins.
>
> —Isa. 51:3

> I, even I, am he who comforts you.
>
> —Isa. 51:12

> As a mother comforts her child,
>   so will I comfort you;
>   and you will be comforted over Jerusalem.
>
> —Isa. 66:13

As a father has compassion on his children,
so the LORD has compassion on those who fear him.
—Ps. 103:13

The LORD is good to all;
he has compassion on all he has made.
—Ps. 145:9

Paul's worship in the midst of suffering shows his growing knowledge of and love for God.[2] Through trials he was able to see more clearly God's limitless reservoir of compassion, leading him to rely even more heavily on God (2 Cor. 1:9). The root of the Greek word for *comfort* means "to come alongside and help." It is the same word used in John 14–16 to describe the Holy Spirit as "the comforter." The literal meaning of the English word *comfort*—"with strength"—reminds us that the comfort God supplies comes to us from an infinite source of strength.

> The literal meaning of *comfort*—"with strength"—reminds us that the comfort God supplies comes to us from an infinite source of strength.

Herein lies the dynamic relationship between trials and comfort described in this passage: Our experiences in trials equip us to minister to others more effectively. Because we have a shared experience with those who later go through the same thing, it enables us to empathize with them. Not only that, but we also gain a certain level of credibility through our common experience. But the most important factor is not our shared relationship with other people; rather, it is the deepening of our relationship with God. Experiencing God's comfort brings us into a more intimate relationship with him, which in turn provides us with a deeper reservoir of compassion for others. My capacity to show mercy is directly related to the depth of my experience with God.

It isn't necessary, in order to minister, that we experience *exactly* what someone else has experienced, but it does help, as my wife and I learned when a young couple in our church suffered a miscarriage. The husband, Ken, was devastated, and his young wife, Nancy, even more so.

They had waited so long for Nancy to get pregnant, and now just a few weeks later, the good news had been stolen from them. Pregnancies that end in miscarriage are statistically more common than most people know, but when it happens to you the statistics bring no comfort. Leah and I came alongside and tried to be a source of comfort, but there were certain words we carefully avoided in our conversations. It was not ours to say, "I know how you must feel," because we really didn't know. We had two healthy children and had never experienced a miscarriage. But did that mean our concern was not appreciated? Of course not. Ken and Nancy knew we cared, but the empathy we felt and the words we shared always had their limits.

As it happened, a new friendship with another couple in our church became the key to Ken and Nancy's emotional recovery. I arranged for the couples to meet because I had seen this dynamic work before. Ken and Nancy needed to be encouraged by others who had gone through the same circumstances, who had personally experienced the comfort of God in this particular kind of trial. Their shared experience immediately brought them to a deeper level of understanding and compassion. Hearing the other couple's story of renewed trust in God was exactly what Ken and Nancy needed in the days ahead.

Although everybody goes through trials in general, experiences such as miscarriage, the death of a child, suicide of a family member, depression, alcoholism and other addictions, and cancer represent unique circumstances that will not happen to everyone. In these situations, the deepest capacity for ministry often comes from those who have gone through the same trial *and* have experienced God's grace and comfort through it. In 2 Corinthians 1:4–6, we see that our Christian experiences are intended by God for ministry. Though our culture encourages intense individualism, the church does not. We are members of a living organism (1 Cor. 12), and within that organism our shared experiences benefit one another.

God can use the power of shared experiences to significantly touch others. Have you seen trials in this way? Have you considered the spiritual gifts and unique spiritual journey that God has given to you? Though most of us would rather point to our strengths and victories as tools for serving God, his unique ministry for us will more likely draw upon our weaknesses, trials, and times of suffering. Reflecting on his own "thorn in the flesh," Paul writes,

> Three times I pleaded with the Lord to take it away from me. But he said to me, "My grace is sufficient for you, for my power is made perfect in weakness." Therefore I will boast all the more gladly about my weaknesses, so that Christ's power may rest on me. That is why, for Christ's sake, I delight in weaknesses, in insults, in hardships, in persecutions, in difficulties. For when I am weak, then I am strong. (2 Cor. 12:8–10)

As we have seen through the example of Paul's life, God can work through trials in our circumstances as well. Whether equipping us for more effective ministry, inspiring others through our responses of faith, or leading others to personal salvation, God may be doing his greatest work when we least suspect it. God's ways are not always our ways (Isa. 55:8–9).

DISCUSSION QUESTIONS

1. Give an illustration from your own life (or of someone you have known) that illustrates the truth of Romans 8:28.
2. After reading Paul's imprisonment story in this chapter, respond to the following questions: Typically as you face challenges in life, do you approach them with the attitude that the glass is half empty (pessimistically) or half full (optimistically)? What past role models or influences in your life shaped you to look at life that way? What influences in your present Christian life affect your attitudes in this area?
3. Have you ever been unjustly criticized when doing good, as Paul experienced from rival preachers (Phil. 1:15–17)? How did it make you feel? Were you able to "keep on keeping on" despite the criticism?
4. Have you ever experienced a trial in your own life that later prepared you to minister to someone else who was going through a very similar situation? How does the truth of 2 Corinthians 1:4–6

encourage you when facing such trials? In what specific ways did that experience better prepare you to help others?

5. After reading about Moses' desert experience in this chapter, reflect on some of the difficult, humbling experience you have gone through. Were any of them God's training for a "B.D. degree"? What specific qualities did you learn through them that later made you a better servant?

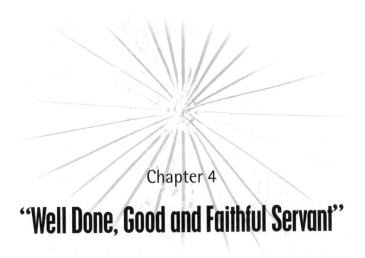

Chapter 4

"Well Done, Good and Faithful Servant"

It was like a moment frozen in time. The trauma ward was quiet as I sat by the bedside of my father-in-law, Tad. I had just watched his vital signs fade away to nothing. The preceding days had been difficult ones for everyone in the family. Several days earlier Tad, a retired welder, had blacked out and fallen on his patio. The blow to his head had placed him in a comatose condition with a serious brain hemorrhage. The specialists in the trauma unit at Mercy Hospital had done everything they could, but they were keeping him alive only through life-support machines. After several days, the prognosis moved from bad to worse, and we knew we had to let Tad go. This is exactly what he would have wanted, but it didn't make the decision any easier. Tad loved life so much that it didn't seem like even eighty-four years were enough.

After everyone had said their good-byes and cried together, Tad's youngest son, Bruce, and I stayed with him while life support was removed. Very quickly he was gone. Bruce went to tell the family, and I was left there with Tad. Curtains drawn, it was one of the most private and personal experiences I have ever known. I cried and I prayed, because I had loved this man so much. Ever since Leah and I were married, twenty-seven years earlier, he had treated me like one of his sons. As I sat there beside the bed, time stood still.

Then I did something spontaneously that came as a surprise even to me. I began to talk to Tad. Not to the body, for there was an overwhelming sense that he was no longer in that body. But I spoke nevertheless:

"Tad, I don't know if you can hear me right now. But if you can, I know that God is saying to you, 'Well done, good and faithful servant . . . enter into the joy of your Lord.'" I kept repeating those words from Matthew 25:21 as I thought about the reality of what had just happened. Death is truly the intersection between two worlds. When the nurses came, I had no problem leaving the bedside, because I knew that Tad was no longer resident in that body.

> If we fail to see how our lives now are part of a bigger story, we will never understand God's purposes in suffering and trials.

I have been in the room several times after someone has just died, and I always have the same sensation that the person is no longer there but is nonetheless present, if you know what I mean. So it was with Tad. I don't know whether his soul could hear me or not, and it doesn't really matter to me. What does matter is that Tad was immediately welcomed into the presence of God (2 Cor. 5:8). At his memorial service, I told the story of my relationship with this quiet man whose life had reflected Jesus. That more than three hundred people attended the funeral said it all: Tad was a man who had faithfully followed Jesus and who had touched the lives of everyone around him. Now in heaven, he is enjoying the rewards of faithful service from his life here on earth.

Quo Vadis?

In order to understand God's purposes for trials or suffering in our lives, we must look beyond the intersection of two worlds—beyond death to the afterlife. You may be saying right now, "How can death and what happens afterward have any relationship to my present trials?" It reminds me of the words of Henry David Thoreau, the nineteenth-century philosopher and author, who on his deathbed was asked by a preacher, "Quo vadis?" (which, translated, means, "Where are you going?"). Thoreau answered, "One world at a time!" Though the subject of death may not seem relevant, I think you will see that by looking beyond death we can find some of the most important insights about suffering in this life. In fact, if we fail to see how our lives now are part of a bigger story (including death and beyond), we will never understand God's purposes in suffering and trials.

Let's review where we have been thus far in order to understand where we are going in the next few chapters. In chapters 1–3, we utilized the lenses of God's Word to help us identify tangible, positive results that can come through the experience of trials. Suffering has the potential to make us more mature in character, more caring about others, and often brings our drifting minds back to the most important issues of life. These positive outcomes are all visibly seen in the lives of those who "think right when things go wrong." By looking through the lenses, we can more clearly see God's work in progress.

In this chapter, we will move to another dimension of thinking right that goes beyond our human experience and is not visibly seen. We are embarking on one of the most important subjects of all: how our response to suffering is related to our eternal relationship with God. If you can grasp this and make it part of your thinking, you will join the writers of Scripture and thousands of other believers in seeing life's trials the way God sees them. This chapter focuses on the rewards in heaven that are directly related to the sufferings of this life. Our contemporary culture thinks very little about life after death, which may be why trials and suffering are such difficult subjects to grasp.

The Crown of Life

The most clearly stated verse in Scripture about the relationship between our present trials and future heavenly rewards is in James 1:12, "Blessed is the man who perseveres under trial, because when he has stood the test, he will receive the crown of life that God has promised to those who love him." How we respond during difficult times does matter. In some mysterious way, the faith we exhibit through perseverance under trial is directly related to the rewards God will give us for faithfulness. If James were the only writer in the Bible to say this, it would not be nearly as convincing. But as we'll see, Paul, Peter, John, and Jesus himself describe the same thing.

James's statement and the verses that follow it raise three interpretive questions. First, is the promised crown of life a result of perseverance through trials (James 1:2–11), or is it specifically a result of obedience to God's warning to resist temptation and sin (vv. 13–18)? Secondly, what exactly is promised in the word "blessed" and the phrase "the crown of life"? And finally, when is this "crown" received?

Let's take a closer look at each of these questions.

1. Does the promised crown of life relate to trials or to temptations? One of the questions regarding the context of James 1:12 is whether it is a conclusion to the paragraph that precedes it or an introduction to the subject of temptation, which follows it in verses 13–18. The best understanding, in my view, is to see verse 12 as a capstone to the discussion of trials (vv. 2–12). In verse 9, the "brother in humble circumstances" refers to a Christian who is financially poor. This would not have been unusual for first-century Jewish believers, who were often persecuted and scattered because of their faith (v. 1). This "brother" is encouraged to rejoice and take pride in his new position (as a Christian). Similarly, as the poor man is told to put the trials of his earthly poverty into perspective, so the rich man is told to forget the prestige of his earthly riches. Theologian R. C. H. Lenski summarizes verses 10–11 as follows:

> Faith in Christ lifts the lowly brother beyond his trials to the great height of a position in the kingdom of Christ, where as God's child he is rich and may rejoice and boast. Faith in Christ does an equally blessed thing for the rich brother; it fills him with the Spirit of Christ, the spirit of lowliness and true Christian humility. . . . As the poor brother forgets all his earthly poverty, so the rich brother forgets all his earthly riches. The two are equals by faith in Christ.[1]

This equality exists because human distinctions (rich vs. poor) are temporary in God's plan. Our temporal life experiences are part of a bigger story. From this perspective, verse 12 serves as a capstone to the preceding section on trials. Building upon the experiential benefits of persevering through trials—the building of character and maturity—James adds an eternal incentive for perseverance: the crown of life.

2. How are we blessed if we persevere? What is the crown of life? The repeated phrase in the Beatitudes ("Blessed is the one who . . ."), which are part of what is commonly called the Sermon on the Mount (Matt. 5:1–12), reminds us of exclamations in the Psalms (1:1; 32:2; 34:8; 84:12) and Proverbs (8:34). All of these expressions have the same thrust, an enthusiastic statement of the profound joy found by one who perseveres. Matthew 5:12 could be translated, "O the happiness of the one who perseveres under trial!" Our joy is not because all is going well (in trying circumstances, we may not feel like being joyful), but the promised blessedness or happiness is found in what we know to be true about the future. A similar idea is found in James 1:2–3: "Consider it pure joy . . . whenever you face trials of many kinds, *because you know that. . . .*" (emphasis added). Experiencing joy is contingent upon believing what God says is true. That's what faith is. In James 1:3, God promises reward in this life, but verse 12 promises reward in the life to come.

Perhaps the simplest way to understand the crown of life is to read it as "the crown, that is eternal life." The Grecian cultural imagery of a *stephanos,* or victor's crown, is found not only here in James but also in several other New Testament passages. In the Greek and Roman athletic games, a victorious athlete was honored with a wreath of laurel, oak, or even celery, placed upon his head as a crown. Our modern Olympic awards ceremonies are patterned after this ancient tradition, though today we recognize three winners instead of just one, and the wreaths have been replaced by gold, silver, and bronze medals. Several New Testament writers, and especially Paul, use this vivid Greco-Roman illustration to picture the crown of eternal life that will be received by each Christian. In order to better understand James 1:12, we can compare it to some other New Testament passages:

> Blessed are you when people insult you, persecute you and falsely say all kinds of evil against you because of me. Rejoice and be glad, because great is your reward in heaven. (Matt. 5:11–12)

> Everyone who competes in the games goes into strict training. They do it to get a crown that will not last; but we do it to get a crown that will last forever. Therefore . . . I beat my body and

make it my slave so that after I have preached to others, I myself will not be disqualified for the prize. (1 Cor. 9:25–27)

For what is our hope, our joy, or the crown in which we will glory in the presence of our Lord Jesus when he comes? (1 Thess. 2:19)

For I am already being poured out like a drink offering, and the time has come for my departure. I have fought the good fight, I have finished the race, I have kept the faith. Now there is in store for me the crown of righteousness, which the Lord, the righteous Judge, will award to me on that day—and not only to me, but also to all who have longed for his appearing. (2 Tim. 4:6–8)

When the Chief Shepherd appears, you will receive the crown of glory that will never fade away. (1 Peter 5:4)

Do not be afraid of what you are about to suffer. I tell you, the devil will put some of you in prison to test you, and you will suffer persecution for ten days. Be faithful, even to the point of death, and I will give you the crown of life. (Rev. 2:10, written by the apostle John to the church of Smyrna)

The twenty-four elders . . . lay their crowns before the throne. (Rev. 4:10)

The crown of righteousness is spoken of by Jesus, Paul, Peter, and John. By and large, it pictures the day when we will fully experience eternal life. As we look closely at these passages, however, we see that there is more than just a general reference to eternal life; there is also some type of reward for faithfulness. Paul describes it as faithfulness to his ministry, even when he was facing death: "For I am already being poured out like a drink offering, and the time has come for my departure. I have fought the good fight, I have finished the race, I have kept the faith. Now there is in store for me the crown of righteousness, which the Lord, the righteous Judge, will award to me on that day" (2 Tim. 4:6–8). James

1:12 is extremely significant, for it indicates that in heaven God rewards our perseverance through trials on this earth.

The parable of the talents told by Jesus in Matthew 25:14–30 illustrates beautifully that we are called to be faithful servants while our master is gone, and we are to use wisely the gifts and resources God has given to us. This accountability applies to everything we possess, as well as to the opportunities God places before us. We choose either to live by faith or do it on our own. One day we will each give an account before God, much like the servants do in the parable. The judgment seat of Christ is where this will happen (2 Cor. 5:10). Living by faith accomplishes our greatest purpose in this life for it brings glory to our Creator and Lord. In turn, God rewards this faithfulness. Because times of suffering and trials represent the most difficult times to live a life of faith, it makes sense that God will reward us in a special way for persevering through them. I do not know exactly what eternal rewards are, but I do know that if we could somehow look beyond death, hearing God's words, "Well done, good and faithful servant," would be all the motivation we'd need.

What does this mean in practical terms as we face life's most difficult times? Do you ever feel as if God has abandoned you; that your trial is too great to bear; that you are ready to give up? We all do. In those moments, it is vitally important that we see life from another perspective. We must view circumstances through the "corrective lens" of Scripture in order to refocus on the truth about our situation. Those dark moments actually have eternal significance! Regardless of the circumstances, regardless of how we feel, we have the choice at that moment to live by faith or give up. When we persevere in faith, we're given a promise of blessedness or joy, and by God's grace we will one day be commended by God for our faithfulness. Our lives are part of a bigger story, a drama that is unfolding in the heavenlies. When we understand this, it allows us to see every situation in life, especially the difficult ones, as faith opportunities that carry eternal significance.

A friend told me that when Billy Graham was asked whether he would receive rewards in heaven, his response surprised everyone. Dr. Graham said that if we were able to know how others in heaven were rewarded, we'd find that those rewarded the most would not be the international evangelists but the little old ladies who prayed faithfully for souls to be saved. I think he is right. The only criterion given for rewards is faithfulness to God with the treasures, talents, time, and opportunities he has given us. My father-in-law referred to himself as "just an old welder." Yet after becoming a Christian in his adult years, he consistently lived out what it means to be Christlike. Though Tad never preached a sermon in his life, most of those who attended his funeral could tell you stories of "sermons" they had seen in the life of an honest, hardworking businessman with authentic faith. His kind, considerate approach to people gave him instant rapport with almost anyone he met. Though I couldn't hear heaven from the trauma unit that day, I believe God welcomed him with those words, "Well done, good and faithful servant."

3. *When is the crown of life received?* The crown promised to us in James 1:12 and a number of other passages is probably received when a Christian enters into the presence of God. In 1 Corinthians 9:25 (NASB) it is called an imperishable crown because eternal life will not fade away, unlike an athlete's wreath of laurel or oak. In my opinion, an event mentioned in 2 Corinthians 5:10; Romans 14:10–12; and 1 Corinthians 3:10–15 describes this. In 2 Corinthians 5:1–10, Paul contrasts the earthly experiences of Christians who now know of their "eternal house in heaven" (v. 1), yet must go on living away from the Lord. How do we do this? "We live by faith, not by sight," says Paul (v. 7). On earth, as in heaven, we are to "make it our goal to please him" (v. 9). What is our motivation? "We must all appear before the judgment seat of Christ, that each one may receive what is due him for the things done while in the body, whether good or bad" (v. 10). This event is sometimes called the bema seat of Christ because of the Greek word Paul uses in this verse. The bema was the seat of a Roman official, who would act in judicial cases and in some cities give awards to competing athletes. Bema seats have been found in essentially every major Roman city, as well as in Roman colonial cities such as Corinth, Philippi, and Ephesus. Paul uses the metaphor of a judge to picture the judgment that awaits all of us as Christians. This judgment is not a determination of who goes to heaven and who goes to hell; it is rather Christ's evaluation of "the things done while in the body, whether good or bad." All who stand before this judgment are believers headed for heaven.

Paul's other recorded letter to the Corinthians describes the results of this evaluation. In 1 Corinthians 3:11–12, he uses the illustration of a building to show how human workers might use different kinds of building materials to build upon the foundation of Jesus Christ (v. 11). Paul says that each of us should be careful how we build, for "the Day" will reveal that some building materials are lasting (gold, silver, costly stones) and others worthless (wood, hay, straw). The test will be by fire, which is probably referring to the holy presence of the Lord Jesus at the bema seat (vv. 10, 12–13). Based upon other passages, we can conclude that these eternally valuable works are the ones done in faith. For these we receive rewards.

The other works are burned up and worthless in God's sight. In this sobering passage about accountability, I am encouraged that God's grace is always present alongside his holy judgment. Describing some of our works before the bema seat, Paul says, "If it is burned up [in the presence of Christ's holiness, the Christian] will suffer loss; he himself will be saved, but only as one escaping through the flames" (1 Cor. 3:15). This all serves as a reminder that while our salvation in Christ is secure, the choices in life that we make as Christians do matter to God, for we are to live by faith, and not by sight. Some of our deeds are of eternal value and some are not.

I do not know exactly when the bema seat of Christ will take place, because Scripture does not clearly say. In Revelation 4–5, the "twenty-four elders" are depicted as worshipers around the thrones of the Father and the Son, and the elders are described as "dressed in white" with "crowns of gold on their heads" (4:4). In my opinion, this symbolizes believers who have already been rewarded at the bema seat. Thus, one may conclude that the judgment seat of Christ takes place after our physical death, in preparation for us as believers to enter the presence of the Lord in heaven. The ultimate purpose of the crowns received is described in verses 9–11:

> Whenever the living creatures give glory, honor and thanks to him who sits on the throne and who lives for ever and ever, the twenty-four elders fall down before him who sits on the throne, and worship him who lives for ever and ever. They lay their crowns before the throne and say:

> "You are worthy, our Lord and God,
>   to receive glory and honor and power,
> for you created all things,
>   and by your will they were created
>   and have their being."

As a popular contemporary praise chorus expresses, "It's all about you, Lord!" The ultimate purpose of rewards (crowns), according to Revelation's vision into heaven, is worshiping God. Think of it. When we live by faith, including persevering through trials and suffering, we will receive a reward in heaven. That reward, the crown of life, gives us a greater capacity to worship and enjoy God forever.

Fast Food, Webcams, and Instant Gratification

I consider myself a Christian who sincerely loves God and values the process of spiritual growth in my life. I can accept (though I don't enjoy) the experiences of trials and suffering as a part of God's plan for me, and I want to learn how to face them more effectively. But like many Christians, I'm not "grabbed" by the truth about heavenly rewards like I think I should be. How about you? Apathy is perhaps one of the greatest barriers to our gaining a deeper understanding of trials. In this section, I propose several cultural factors that have shaped us more than we are probably aware. The first is our demand and expectation of instant gratification.

My wife and I recently entered a new chapter of life called grandparenthood. Our first grandchild, Elliana, has already brought immeasurable joy into our lives, and she is just seven months old. She lives a thousand miles away, so I am very thankful for modern air travel and technology, which makes it possible to see our daughter, son-in-law, and Elliana much more often. We have installed a webcam on our computer, which enables us to carry on conversations "face-to-face" and see Elli's antics live on the computer screen. Isn't modern technology wonderful!

Progress in this age of information technology has also changed our expectations about our day-to-day lives. After using a cable hookup or

DSL to retrieve computer images, for example, I find it frustrating when I have to wait on a dial-up connection. I become impatient and frustrated if I have to wait long in line at a "fast-food" restaurant. The list goes on. This age of technology has also become an age of speed and instant gratification. In changing our expectations, it has also changed the things we value most, and what we are willing to wait for.

Alongside this compressed time framework, an aggressive individualism dominates our Western culture. As a result, we process life looking for the immediate rather than the eternal. We value experiences that deliver tangible, experiential, and immediate payoffs, but we don't want to bother with those that transcend us. Waiting on the Lord, a wonderful, biblical growth experience, seems like waiting on a dial-up connection. Even persevering through a trial, though I know intellectually that it is important, seriously disrupts my preferred pace of life. To God's promise of the crown of life and rewards in heaven, we say with Thoreau, "One world at a time!"

The Good Life

A second influence of modern culture that distracts our affection for the things of heaven is materialism—valuing that which is temporal and material over the eternal. This goes hand in hand with the demand for instant gratification because it exalts a happiness derived from the things of this world rather than from God. I am struck by the worldview of the New Testament writers, but especially apostles Paul and Peter. Their lives were filled with many trials, but they viewed hardship as temporary and paling in significance to the glory yet to be revealed. By focusing on heaven, they were able to persevere through trials on earth. Here are a few excerpts from their writing that reflect this attitude. All of them were written during times of great suffering:

> I consider that our present sufferings are not worth comparing with the glory that will be revealed in us. (Rom. 8:18)

> Therefore we do not lose heart. Though outwardly we are wasting away, yet inwardly we are being renewed day by day. For our

light and momentary troubles are achieving for us an eternal glory that far outweighs them all. So we fix our eyes not on what is seen, but on what is unseen. For what is seen is temporary, but what is unseen is eternal. Now we know that if the earthly tent we live in is destroyed, we have a building from God, an eternal house in heaven, not built by human hands. Meanwhile we groan, longing to be clothed with our heavenly dwelling. . . . Now it is God who has made us for this very purpose and has given us the Spirit as a deposit, guaranteeing what is to come. . . . We live by faith, not by sight. We are confident, I say, and would prefer to be away from the body and at home with the Lord. (2 Cor. 4:16–5:2, 5, 7–8)

Yes, and I will continue to rejoice, for I know that through your prayers and the help given by the Spirit of Jesus Christ, what has happened to me will turn out for my deliverance. I eagerly expect and hope that I will in no way be ashamed, but will have sufficient courage so that now as always Christ will be exalted in my body, whether by life or by death. For to me, to live is Christ and to die is gain. (Phil. 1:18–21)

Similarly, Peter writes the following words during a time of intensive persecution of Christians in the Roman empire under Nero:

In this you greatly rejoice, though now for a little while you may have had to suffer grief in all kinds of trials. These have come so that your faith—of greater worth than gold, which perishes even though refined by fire—may be proven genuine and may result in praise, glory and honor when Jesus Christ is revealed. Though you have not seen him, you love him; and even though you do not see him now, you believe in him and are filled with an inexpressible and glorious joy, for you are receiving the goal of your faith, the salvation of your souls. (1 Peter 1:6–9)

Paul and Peter both lived lives of intense persecution for their faith and died a martyr's death at the hands of Nero. Yet both men express the same attitude of loose attachment to life in this world, and both looked forward to what they would experience in the presence of the Lord. They considered the circumstances of the present world (including trials) as incomparable to the glory of being with the Lord in eternity, and this bolstered their spirits amidst trials.

The influence of affluence is a subtle yet powerful force in our Western worldview; few of us consider the influence it has over our Christian attitudes. I know almost no one who thinks like Paul or Peter, and this explains in part why we are so ill-equipped to go through trials. I have been privileged to serve the Lord in vocational Christian ministry for almost thirty years, including eighteen years as a pastor in a church. I have cared for the lives of the very rich, and in some cases people who had nothing. Most, including my family, are in the category of middle-class Americans, who on a world scale are among the rich. How have these factors influenced our Christian outlook on life?

For some, the influence of wealth is far more powerful than the influence of Christ. Shortly after I began serving as pastor in one of my ministries, a businessman visiting our church explained that he and his wife were looking for a new church home and asked me if I would have lunch with him the next week. I had just begun a sermon series on the topic, "What Jesus believed about money," so I anticipated that some of our conversation might be about that subject. It was, in fact, the only topic we talked about. This businessman was the area director of a well-known Christian organization, whose recruits worked on the basis of "pyramid sales." He asked me what I thought of that organization, whether I planned to preach about money often, and what I believed the Bible taught about materialism. After that lunch, I never saw the man again, so I can assume my answers were not what he wanted to hear.

How attached are you to the things of this world? Remember, materialism is not measured by how many things you possess but to what degree those things possess you. For most of us, the influence of materialism is subtle. We enjoy the material blessings of life as gifts from God, and so they are! But our willingness to obey Christ goes only as far as it is convenient in our lifestyles. We recklessly view ourselves as owners of life's goods, rather than simply managers as the Bible teaches. Though heaven is a place we may want to go some day, we have become attached much more to planet Earth. This way of thinking makes a difference when a crisis comes.

The Evidence of Things Not Seen

Hebrews 11 is sometimes referred to as the "hall of fame of faith" for its very practical presentation of Old Testament believers who acted by faith and were rewarded by God. The chapter is especially helpful in our study of trials. These Old Testament men and women had at least two things in common: (1) they demonstrated what practical faith looks like while facing trials; and (2) their faith illustrates a foundational principle, which is introduced in Hebrews 11:1: "Now faith is being sure of what we hope for and certain of what we do not see."

Noah, for example, was warned about a judgment to come by a great flood though he could not imagine where God would get such amounts of water. Nevertheless, he preached the message by faith (v. 7). Abraham, by faith left the comforts of his prosperous home to pursue a land and a culture he had never seen (vv. 8–10). He and Sarah conceived Isaac when Sarah was barren and both were far too old (vv. 11–12). By faith, Abraham obeyed God and raised a knife to kill Isaac as a sacrifice, believing that God would somehow still produce a great nation from Isaac's line (vv. 17–19). By faith, Moses refused to enjoy the comforts of life among the Egyptians and left Egypt to lead his people (vv. 24–26). All of these people believed in something they could not see except through the eyes of faith.

After presenting an impressive cavalcade of men and women who lived by faith, the writer of Hebrews encourages his readers, who are themselves going through serious trials as Christians, to follow their examples:

> Therefore, since we are surrounded by such a great cloud of witnesses, let us throw off everything that hinders and the sin that so easily entangles, and let us run with perseverance the race marked out for us. Let us fix our eyes on Jesus, the author and perfecter of our faith, who for the joy set before him endured the cross, scorning its shame. . . . Consider him who endured such opposition from sinful men, so that you will not grow weary and lose heart. (Heb. 12:1–3)

In this example, the "lenses" of faith enable us to see things we cannot naturally see. True faith has always required belief in things not yet seen. But how does the kind of faith described in Hebrews 11 fit into the values of our Western culture?

Why the Modern Mind Cannot Understand Suffering

Peter Kreeft, in his excellent book *Making Sense Out of Suffering,* has a very helpful chapter called "Why Modernity Can't Understand Suffering," in which he argues that components of our post-Enlightenment thinking present an "intellectual obstacle" to a full understanding of this human experience. [2] Kreeft focuses on the thinking and beliefs of modernism,[3] though I believe his insights are applicable to some aspects of postmodernism as well.[4] The following contrasts help to explain the shift in societal thinking that led to a gradual rejection of the truth expressed in Scripture:

1. *To the premodern mind, "objective reality" meant God, or the gods, or some reality beyond this world. To a modernist, the concept of objective reality now means the physical universe.* After the birth of modern science, the quest for knowledge shifted from a knowledge of virtue or moral ideals to a more practical kind of knowledge proving man's conquest of nature. This transition is quite evident when one looks at the shift in thinking that took place from the birth of modern science through the Darwinian period. The earliest pioneers (e.g., Francis Bacon, Robert Boyle) stated explicitly that they were doing science to discover more about the perfections of the Creator in order to bring glory to him. Within three hundred years, Darwinian evolutionary theory was denying the existence of a creator.[5]

2. *Prior to the modern era, people generally believed in an objective moral law, but the intelligentsia of the modern age would no longer be controlled by supernatural ideals and instead relied on the natural forces of their own heredity and environment.* Value systems moved away from objective standards to subjective experience. Romans 1–2, though written long before the rise of modernism, is an apt description of the shift that took place in humanity as a result of sin. In

Romans 1:21–32, Paul describes a natural progression from rejection of God as Creator to idol worship to distorted morals:

> Although they knew God
>> They neither glorified him as God
>>> Nor gave thanks to him
>>>> But their thinking became futile
>>>>> And their foolish hearts were darkened
>>>>>> Although they claimed to be wise they
>>>>>> became fools.

This shift is also reflected in three references to "exchanges" in the passage.

- "They exchanged the glory of the immortal God for images"; that is, idolatry (Rom. 1:23).
- "They exchanged the truth of God for a lie" (Rom. 1:25).
- "Their women exchanged natural relations for unnatural ones"; that is, immorality (Rom. 1:26); and men were "inflamed with lust for one another" (v. 27).

3. *To the premodern mind, suffering was accepted as a moral challenge to be lived, and sometimes a mystery to be accepted.* Because of humanity's claim of power over nature, modernists saw suffering as scandalous and the greatest problem to be conquered.
4. *To the premodern mind, sin was seen as individual and in some way related to most suffering.* Modern thinking either denies the concept of sin completely (because, they say, there is no absolute moral truth) or redefines sin to be societal (cruelty to others, intolerance, etc.). Therefore, the modern mind sees the Christian message of the Cross as seriously lacking and inadequate. "If Christ conquered sin," the reasoning goes, "then why did he not abolish suffering and dying?" Biblical Christians, in contrast, see modernism as incomplete because it ignores the primary problem—individual sin.
5. *Every traditional society in the premodern era gave its people an otherworldly perspective on this world.* Belief in the existence of some sort

of heaven and some sort of hell was held by almost all societies. Modern belief removes any serious belief in hell, and sometimes heaven as well. If heaven is accepted, it is for everyone and has no relationship to this life. Thoreau's "one world at a time!" is the classic response of a modernist who sees no connection between this life and the next.

What Does This Mean and Where Is It Going?

There is much more that could be said about the cultural shifts from premodern to modern thinking, but my primary intent here is not a philosophical discussion about culture. More important is the recognition that cultural norms determine the way that people process life, and modernist presuppositions have, in fact, clouded the issue regarding suffering. Without belief in God, sin, objective morality, or an afterlife, we in Western culture have been seriously handicapped in our ability to understand the place of trials or suffering in our lives. Suffering becomes a problem to be solved, and so far we haven't solved it.

In this chapter, I have sought to shed some light on one aspect of suffering by discussing Scripture and culture. Retracing our steps, we looked at James 1:12 as an important statement that God rewards perseverance through suffering. Faith in God, especially in times of trial, will ultimately result in a heavenly crown of life. This consists of more than just making it to heaven; it refers to eternal rewards for faithfulness that we will enjoy in eternity. This knowledge, or anticipation, can bring us blessedness or joy on earth while we are going through trials. The New Testament writers, and especially Paul, saw their earthly lives as part of a bigger story, and they encouraged us to do the same.

Why do promises such as the one found in James 1:12 have so little impact upon our personal experience? For the most part, we have been conditioned by our culture to think differently. For example, the age of technology and information has taught us to value things that come quickly and bring instant gratification, quite different from the experiences of perseverance through a trial and rewards received in heaven. Additionally, materialism has taught us to value the things we possess in this life and give little thought to their relationship to the life to come;

yet trials have meaning only if they are seen in light of a bigger story beyond this world. And finally, modernism has produced a culture in which faith in things not seen is out of place and even ridiculed. The philosophical underpinnings of modernism see suffering as merely one more problem to be solved.

As a child of the modernist culture in America, I have found the Bible to be a much more reliable guide than the science-based norms I was taught through my formal education and my culture. Postmodernism has introduced some interesting shifts of emphasis, especially in Western thinking. Here are several examples, contrasted and compared with the five earlier points about modernism:[6]

1. The postmodern mind represents a swing back toward a supernatural understanding of the universe and a recognition of the existence of a real spiritual world. Scientific naturalism is still influential, but it is no longer revered as a worldview beyond challenge. This swing, however, is not necessarily a move back toward an embrace of the God of Christianity but to one of many gods.
2. Postmodern thinking has continued and strengthened the trend *away from* an absolute moral standard. More than ever, morality is seen as relative to each particular culture, and any notion of a universal moral standard is generally seen as an oppressive attempt to impose one culture's set of norms on another.
3. Though the postmodern mind rejects the assertion of humanity's dominance over nature, suffering is still a scandal and a mystery. Rather than being seen as a challenge to be lived through, however, suffering casts doubt on whether God and/or the universe is just. For the postmodernist, the existence of suffering is a major obstacle to reliance on God, and sometimes to any belief in God.
4. Like modernism, the postmodern generation either denies the biblical concept of sin, or redefines it as societal and not individual.
5. The postmodern shift is restoring a belief in an afterlife, though not always in traditional Western categories. Eastern beliefs in reincarnation, Nirvana, Buddhist conceptions of nothingness are also supported in a pluralistic culture.

I am encouraged by some (though not all) of the shifts introduced by postmodernism in my children's generation. Acceptance of a reality beyond the physical world, for example, is a step back in the right direction. An openness to accepting mysteries in our world that will never be fully understood is important when wrestling with the subject of suffering. However, postmodern thinkers, like those of us who were raised in a modernist environment, still struggle with the mystery of suffering in our human experience. The reason, in part, is that they have not come to grips with the question of authority—where to find truth. Only through the lens of Scripture will we be able to grapple with the essential issues of trials and suffering of this life. Even then, we must not be so arrogant as to believe we will find all the answers. But if we humbly submit ourselves to the eternal God and pursue a relationship with him, even the mysteries become more acceptable, because we can know that they ultimately are purposeful in the mind of our Sovereign God. Most of all, our cultural milieu of modernism and postmodernism provides great opportunities to live authentic Christian lives that are anchored firmly in the truth.

DISCUSSION QUESTIONS

1. In James 1:12, what do you think "the crown of life" is? How does perseverance through a trial in our present lives affect our receiving a crown in the life to come? (In other words, how does perseverance logically relate to our ultimate reward?)

2. Why does the promise of eternal reward (see James 1:12) *not* motivate most people today? Why is it important for Christians especially to think about this idea often?

3. Why is the illustration of an athletic contest used so often in Scripture to picture rewards in the life to come? From this chapter, name some examples of illustrations from athletics that help to explain your experiences in the Christian life.

4. After reading the section of the chapter called Why the Modern Mind Cannot Understand Suffering, give an illustration of some reasons why modern thinkers struggle with this subject. What stumbling

blocks have you observed in contemporary viewpoints that make a
biblical view of trials inconceivable for most people?

5. Would you consider yourself a "modern" or "postmodern" thinker
   in the way you view some of the mysteries of suffering in our world?
   Do you believe there are mysteries that God never intended for us to
   understand about life on earth? If so, why would that be so?

Part 2

LIFE'S HARDSHIPS AND HEARTACHES

What's in It for You, Lord?

Chapter 5

It's All About You, Lord

A bloodcurdling scream came from the upstairs room of my daughter Kara. This had happened before, but my instincts told me to run quickly to her aid. The smile on her face as I entered her room told me that Kara was enjoying the newly discovered "power of the scream" to get immediate attention. This time I had an idea. "Have you ever heard the story of the boy who cried wolf?" I asked.

"No, Daddy, tell it to me." Kara loved stories, and as she settled into my lap I recounted that age-old tale of how misusing a cry for help may one day backfire when you really need it. After finishing I said, "Now, Kara, do you understand what that story is all about? Do you see how dangerous it is to scream when nothing is wrong?"

"Yeah, Dad, I understand."

The rest of the day progressed without incident, but the very next morning another scream from her room resulted in a slightly slower response from me. "Dad, don't worry. Nothing is wrong. But I just love that story about the boy who cried wolf. Will you tell it to me again?"

The power of a story. While our children are growing up, we realize how much they love to have stories read to them. That love goes with us throughout our lives. The Bible, authored by many human writers who spanned fifteen hundred years across several cultures, relies significantly on stories to make its points. Because God, the Divine Author, orchestrated the writing process of Scripture, we can assume that he too understands the power of story to teach moral and spiritual lessons. Jesus

111

Christ demonstrated this through the use of many parables, and the stories in the Old Testament narrative represent a majority of that portion of the Bible.

One such story from the Old Testament book of Job has much to say about the trials in our lives.

> In the land of Uz, there lived a man whose name was Job. This man was blameless and upright; he feared God and shunned evil. He had seven sons and three daughters, and he owned seven thousand sheep, three thousand camels, five hundred yoke of oxen and five hundred donkeys, and had a large number of servants. He was the greatest man among all the people of the East.
>
> His sons used to take turns holding feasts in their homes, and they would invite their three sisters to eat and drink with them. When a period of feasting had run its course, Job would send and have them purified. Early in the morning he would sacrifice a burnt offering for each of them, thinking, "Perhaps my children have sinned and cursed God in their hearts." This was Job's regular custom. . . .
>
> One day when Job's sons and daughters were feasting and drinking wine at the oldest brother's house, a messenger came to Job and said, "The oxen were plowing and the donkeys were grazing nearby, and the Sabeans attacked and carried them off. They put the servants to the sword, and I am the only one who has escaped to tell you!"
>
> While he was still speaking, another messenger came and said, "The fire of God fell from the sky and burned up the sheep and the servants, and I am the only one who has escaped to tell you!"
>
> While he was still speaking, another messenger came and said, "The Chaldeans formed three raiding parties and swept down on your camels and carried them off. They put the servants to the sword, and I am the only one who has escaped to tell you!"
>
> While he was still speaking, yet another messenger came and said, "Your sons and daughters were feasting and drinking wine

at the oldest brother's house, when suddenly a mighty wind swept in from the desert and struck the four corners of the house. It collapsed on them and they are dead, and I am the only one who has escaped to tell you!"

At this, Job got up and tore his robe and shaved his head. Then he fell to the ground in worship and said:

> "Naked I came from my mother's womb,
>   and naked I will depart.
> The LORD gave and the LORD has taken away;
>   may the name of the LORD be praised."

In all this, Job did not sin by charging God with wrongdoing. . . .

[A short time later, Job was afflicted] with painful sores from the soles of his feet to the top of his head. Then Job took a piece of broken pottery and scraped himself with it as he sat among the ashes.

His wife said to him, "Are you still holding on to your integrity? Curse God and die!"

He replied, "You are talking like a foolish woman. Shall we accept good from God, and not trouble?"

In all this, Job did not sin in what he said. (Job 1:1–5, 13–22; 2:7–10)

God Behind the Seen

This captivating story of one man's experience with tragedy comes directly from the Bible and is the basis for the Old Testament book of Job.[1] Yet if you are familiar with the details, you have probably noticed something missing. What about the part of the story where God and Satan are talking about Job, and God gives Satan permission to bring these trials into his life? You are absolutely correct; there is more to the story. Embedded within Job 1–2 is a parallel drama that takes place in heaven, two conversations between God and Satan that result in cataclysmic events on earth. Please understand why I left these out of the original story. What you read above is exactly the way Job experienced life! He didn't know about these conversations in heaven when life collapsed on him! In fact, though much detail is given about the events that follow these tragedies, nowhere do we find that God ever revealed this information to Job. Trials and suffering came upon him without any warning or reason given.

And so it is with us as we live behind the veil of our human experience. Life happens, and some of it is not what we would have chosen. No script, no clues, just the brutal realities of suffering. But God does not want us to assume that this suffering is purposeless, and that is why the background details are added to Job's story in the Bible. We are being let in on more information than Job knew, in order to enable us to understand more clearly how trials can be directly related to a test of faith. We are taken behind the scenes to understand that Job's response to these tragic events became the proof of the authenticity of his faith, and when Job persevered in his faith commitment, God in heaven received honor and glory. By reading Job's account, we can see more clearly that our life experiences are part of a bigger story with eternal significance.

As we add to our understanding of trials by investigating this Old Testament story, I will explain what I believe to be the meaning of the book of Job. The two most important truths (I call them Big Ideas) that come from this book are very simple, yet foreign to our human experience. The mystery element of trials makes the teaching of Job a crucial component in our understanding of suffering in the Christian life.

It's All About You, Lord

The first Big Idea from the story of Job is found embedded in the account of his calamities (Job 1–2). The story teaches us that trials or suffering may sometimes come upon us to demonstrate the authenticity of our faith in God, which in turn brings glory to God. The background for Job's tragedy on earth is revealed through two conversations in heaven between God and "the satan." The term *satan* is a word that simply means "the accuser," and this aptly describes what he is about to do. Satan is a fallen angel (Isa. 14:12–15; Ezek. 28:1–9; 2 Cor. 11:14), and in Job he is with other angels in the presence of God. We have no way of knowing whether this was normal or out of the ordinary, but the next event to happen is extremely important in the message of this book.

Because Satan is in the role of the accuser, most people jump to the conclusion that he initiated a challenge to God about Job. But it is actually the other way around! On both occasions, God speaks first and issues a challenge to Satan, "Have you considered my servant Job? There is no one on earth like him; he is blameless and upright, a man who fears God and shuns evil" (Job 1:8; 2:3). God's impressive description of Job's faith and life is exactly the way we are introduced to him in 1:1. These descriptions portray him as a godly man of integrity whose ethical, honest, and exemplary life came as a result of his sincere, obedient walk with God. What is the implication of God's challenge to Satan? Simply that Job walks with integrity not for selfish reasons but because he loves and worships God.

Job was a man who had everything—and then tragedy struck. Through God's revelation in Job 1–2, we are able to understand what happened to precipitate this. After God challenged Satan to consider the authenticity of Job's faith, Satan ("the accuser") retorted that Job's faith in God existed merely because of the material blessings he had received (Job 1:2–3, 10), and the protection ("hedge") God provided for Job and his family (v. 9). "Strike everything he has," Satan charged, "and he will surely curse you to your face" (v. 11). When Job's faith does not collapse after the first tragic losses, God again initiates a conversation with Satan. His second commendation is even greater, noting that trials had been brought on Job without any cause (Job 2:3). This statement by God is very important to our understanding of Job's later discussion with his friends, because we know that none of Job's calamities were brought on by his sin. Satan's second attack was to remove Job's good health, which resulted in a series of other losses as well.

A common story on planet Earth is about a good man who has tragic losses. The philosophical question, Why do bad things happen to good people? has been around since Adam and Eve. We have pursued here a closely related variation of that question: Why do bad things happen to godly people? In previous chapters, we have seen some specific reasons for suffering that may be experientially observed and explained. In chapter 4, we looked (by faith) at the heavenly promise of rewards for faithfulness given to those who persevere through trials. Now, in this chapter, we will address the most complex truth we have yet encountered. We must turn "Godward" in our thinking.

> Suffering in life
> is not about us but
> about God.

The Lord allows some suffering in our lives to demonstrate the authenticity of true faith and to bring glory to himself. This is more difficult to comprehend because it is a mystery that we will not fully understand until we're in heaven—and perhaps not even then. Because it is something that is not experiential, we must accept it by faith. In short, this story about suffering in life is not about us but about God, with the ultimate purpose of bringing glory to him. Paul says in 1 Corinthians 10:31, "So whether you eat or drink or whatever you do, do it all for the glory of God." Now, I suspect that most of us would say "Amen" to this in theory, because theologically we know that the God who created us and all the universe should always be receiving worship and glory for who he is. But accepting this on an emotional level and practically living it out is another thing. To know that trials or tragedies befall us and that God's purpose in it is to somehow glorify himself through our response does not immediately satisfy most of us. Yet, God says through the prophet Isaiah,

> "My thoughts are not your thoughts,
>   neither are your ways my ways,"
>   declares the LORD.
> As the heavens are higher than the earth,
>   so are my ways higher than your ways
>   and my thoughts than your thoughts.
>   —Isa. 55:8–9

Here we must trust God's plan and purposes, whether or not we understand them. We sometimes live with mystery, and when we respond with faith in God, we achieve his greatest purpose and bring glory to him. The longer I live, the more I realize that this is ultimately what life is all about for a Christian; knowing that my life is part of a bigger story beyond this world does bring encouragement and hope in tough times. As my "muscles" of faith are exercised, tested, and developed, this particular aspect of suffering means more and more. But we must be willing to live with some mystery, because God does not always provide all the answers.

The Veil of Faith

Try to summarize the entire book of Job in one word. What word would you choose? Most would probably choose the word *suffering*. It is a book about suffering, to be sure, but in reality many of our questions about suffering are not answered. I think a better summary word is *faith*. The book of Job is a book about a faith that is tested in the most difficult setting of life—suffering. I do not believe that the story of Job is the scenario for every trial that comes into the life of a Christian. My sense from other Scripture passages is that some trials simply come as a result of living in a fallen world and are not necessarily orchestrated by God to prove something about faith. Other trials come through our own personal sin and are simply there to draw us back to God. But the story of Job describes the circumstances surrounding many of our trials, especially those that come upon us for no known reason.

A number of years ago, our oldest daughter, Kristin, began to have periodic fainting spells. We were advised to take her to a neurologist, who ran tests on her, including an EEG (electroencephalogram, designed to measure brain waves). The doctor who interpreted the results described her brain waves as "borderline abnormal." Now what does that mean? Is that the same as borderline normal? The prognosis was even more frustrating, because our primary doctor was on vacation and could not authorize another set of tests for two weeks. Thankfully, Kristin was young enough to be blissfully ignorant of the concerns. But Leah and I, as her parents, were beside ourselves. Brain tumor? Epilepsy? Where did this come from? She seemed to be otherwise very healthy, so why this? The two-week wait, which as you might imagine was filled with a lot of prayer, actually became an amazing time of learning to trust God. The "peace of God, which transcends all understanding" did guard our hearts and minds

(Phil. 4:7). When our doctor returned, we requested a second EEG, and both tests were then reviewed by a pediatric neurologist. His interpretation: nothing abnormal on either test! The perceived "abnormalities" reported by the other doctor proved to be normal in a preadolescent. The fainting never recurred. I have reflected many times on that experience with the thought, "What was that all about, Lord?" In the final analysis, nothing was actually wrong with our daughter's health. But the perception that something was wrong served just as well to test our faith.

A New Testament passage such as Ephesians 6:10–20 makes it quite clear that we are engaged in a spiritual battle, in which we fight against spiritual forces of evil. Thus, the heavenly drama regarding Job's faith looks much like the opposition described in the New Testament. In chapter 8, more will be said about the effective spiritual resources we possess for these situations, but here my purpose is to point out the spiritual battle that is raging at a deeper level than we can see or experience. In recent years, some excellent material has been written on the subject of spiritual warfare. Authors such as Clint Arnold and Neil Anderson have provided excellent exposition of key Scripture passages and a solid theological discussion of this topic.[2] Frank Peretti built upon this concept in his novels, though we must remember that they are written to be novels and not theology texts.[3] Resources like these have provided a needed reminder that events in our lives and the world around us are directly related to the drama of a spiritual battle in heavenly places.

Meanwhile . . . Back on Planet Earth

All of this discussion about spiritual warfare in the heavenlies is possible because in Job's story the veil has been pulled back to allow us to see God's discussion with the accuser. But remember, Job did not know about this, and in the course of daily life, neither do we. The robbers who took Job's possessions, the lightning that struck his flocks, the windstorm that killed his children, and even the terrible disease that attacked his body were tragic events like you would see on the evening news. There was no obvious indication that these things were caused by Satan and allowed by God. The only clue is the unusual "coincidence" that so many tragic events occurred simultaneously.

I don't make it a practice to try relating all events in life to a deeper spiritual conflict. Part of the dynamic of faith is a willingness to live with some mystery in our spiritual lives. But when believers encounter an unusual intensity of trial, or frequency of trials—or both, in my opinion the explanation may be that it is a test of faith. Even though Job was beset by "natural" events, the story intentionally makes the point that these tragedies came in rapid succession. This is the purpose of the often-repeated expression, "While he was still speaking" (Job 1:16–18). We get the message that Job received an inordinate amount of bad news all at one time.

Life sometimes happens this way for us, as well. The summer of 2004 was a crazy time for Leah and me—an unusual coincidence of some very difficult circumstances. Our trials during that period of time were not as extreme as Job's, for we did not lose a loved one or suffer with agonizing diseases. But many trials came at once. Within one particular week, my wife underwent some medical tests that required us to wait a month for the results. Hanging on one test was the possibility of some sort of heart or blood pressure abnormality, and the other test, as mentioned in an earlier chapter, was given to determine whether she had a genetic defect like several members of her family.

The second test was of greater concern because if she possessed this defective gene, it meant a 90 percent chance of ovarian or breast cancer, likely requiring a decision about preemptive surgery. This worry was multiplied times four because if my wife possessed the defective gene, our two daughters and one granddaughter would also potentially be at risk. My prayers were focused on four of the most important women in my life, and I couldn't get all the terrible possibilities out of my mind.

During this same period, we were helping my eighty-year-old mother through knee-replacement surgery and the intense physical therapy that follows. This situation was greatly complicated by the fact that my dad has Alzheimer's and my mother is the primary caregiver. They live one thousand miles from us, so a plan to take care of my mom included provisions to take care of my dad, as well. During this time of disruption in his life, my father entered into a new, more difficult stage of Alzheimer's. Immediately after this, Leah and I traveled to San Diego to help her eighty-four-year-old mother face spinal surgery and the recuperation process afterward.

These were some of the major challenges faced during this short time period, in addition to normal responsibilities in our jobs and the challenges of everyday life. I hesitate to add this to the list, but because we are pet lovers it was significant: during this same summer our dog went completely blind. I learned something about myself during those months: I can generally cope with one or two trials and maintain reasonably strong faith, but so many at one time left me disoriented. Still, when life has been tough, God has been good and he has always supplied grace when we needed it.

What are we to conclude about this unusual sequence of trials? Is it just a coincidence that they occurred during the same month I was planning to devote myself to writing a book about going through trials? I don't think so. I do not remember ever facing so many challenges at one time, and though I can't prove it, I believe these were intended to test the quality of my faith, whether I can live out the things I am writing about, all for God's glory.

Job's Initial Response: An Example We Can Grow From

The book of Job provides great lessons of faith. The first is recorded in Job's response to the initial set of tragic losses (Job 1:20–22). We can observe in Job some of the following attitudes and practices:

1. He freely expressed mourning and grief in response to his suffering and losses. Tearing his robe and shaving his head (Job 1:20) were common cultural practices to express grief. Tearing one's clothing was a physical expression of being inwardly "torn up" by the ordeal. Similarly, shaving one's head was symbolic of the loss of personal glory. In Job's dialogue with his friends, recorded in Job 2–3, we can also find some cultural practices that allowed people who were emotionally hurting to express themselves. All of these were normal ways in which one would express grief emotionally and physically. Job models for us a very healthy place to start when we go through suffering. Some cultures have historically expressed mourning through loud wailing; most cultures do so with tears. Psychologists tell us that a grieving process is absolutely essential for those who experience the death of a loved one.[4] Grief is expressed in various ways, but it must be expressed in order to maintain a healthy emotional state.

When my father-in-law died, we all experienced a great void in our lives after his passing. It was so sudden—literally a matter of days that he was in the trauma unit. Processing that loss and expressing our grief has been different for each family member. Though Tad will always be missed, all of us have gone through our own process of letting him go and adjusting to life afterward. If you have experienced the death of someone close to you, or other devastating losses, do you feel the freedom to cry or otherwise express your deep despair? If this strikes you as a meaningless question, it may be because you naturally express your emotions in crisis situations. But some, for various reasons, do not. Perhaps you come from a family that just does not express emotion outwardly. In other families, and even some cultural groups, men are expected to be more stoic, and crying is unacceptable. Some Christians reason that if we know a loved one has gone to heaven, we should not feel sorrowful about their passing. As a result, they actually discourage the expression of grief. But remember, expressing appropriate grief is not for the person who is gone but for the survivors, who are experiencing a real loss. When I minister to families who have lost a loved one, I am much more concerned about those who are stoic and expressionless than about those who are expressing their grief. Job's response begins with appropriate mourning and grief.

2. He worshiped God and expressed implicit trust in God's plan.

> Then he fell to the ground in worship and said:
>
> "Naked I came from my mother's womb
>   and naked I will depart,
> The Lord gave and the Lord has taken away;
>   may the name of the Lord be praised."
> —Job 1:20–21

I find this response an amazing example and challenge to my faith. Here we see Job move from expressing his feelings to making a statement of faith. Not everyone is able to do this as immediately as Job apparently did, but it is important that we begin to think in terms of God's sovereignty and faithfulness as soon as possible. Job is a shining example of someone who is "thinking right when things go wrong." We already know he is hurting, but even in this time of darkness he continues to trust what he learned to be true in the light. He is focusing on God instead of on the immediacy of his problems. Most translations of the Bible arrange these words in poetic form because they seem to represent a memorized saying. With a posture of worship, Job reflects on what he knows about God—in this case, God's benevolence, love, and sovereignty. He reasons that because we come into life with nothing and leave with nothing, it is God who gives us all we have on this earth. Being God, he can also take it away. This relates very closely to a third principle.

3. *He recognized the proper place of his worldly possessions and family— as gifts from God.* By seeing himself as a manager or steward of all he has on earth, rather than as an owner, Job reminds himself to keep his possessions in proper perspective. Because everything he has came from God, he must be willing to submit to God's will if God takes everything away. In principle, this is easier to apply to material possessions, but what about the death of Job's children—and all of them at once? In the story's introduction, we learned that Job was very close to his sons and daughters and regularly prayed for their spiritual lives (Job 1:4–5). Now, after their deaths, he is *by faith* affirming the truth that God is God, and he—Job—is not. Because God gives children as gifts to parents (Ps. 127:3), we do not own them, but rather must entrust their lives to God, including premature death. I am thankful that most of us who are parents are not called upon by God to face this. I have come alongside a number of young parents who have grieved the death of a child. I observed my wife's parents when they lost their eldest son at age forty-one. There is something unnatural when a child dies before a parent. Yet it happens to many people, and it happened to Job. His response was not denial, for he had already expressed profound grief. Instead, his response was one of implicit trust in God during one of the greatest losses he could experience.

4. *He did not blame God for his suffering.* A natural human response to tragic loss, especially the death of a child, is to blame God. Psychologists tell us that anger—expressed toward others and toward God—is one of

the stages of grief. But Job 1:22 says, "In all this, Job did not sin by charging God with wrongdoing." After Job's second major experience of suffering, the terrible skin disease that inflicted sores over his entire body (Job 2:7–8), Job's wife had had enough: "Are you still holding on to your integrity? Curse God and die!" she counseled her husband (v. 9). Again Job demonstrates by his answer that he did not blame God: "Shall we accept good from God, and not trouble?" (v. 10).

Have you observed the typical response of the "man on the street" to tragedy? When terrible events occur on a personal or global scale, we often hear, "Why does God let such things happen?" Yet we rarely hear the name of God invoked when wonderful things take place. Those who do not have a relationship with God are even hesitant to refer to something as a miracle, lest they give any credit to God; but when tragedy strikes, they see God as responsible. We all have the propensity not only to expect good things as normal, and even to take credit for them, but also to blame God for everything bad. In this sense we are more like Job's wife. Job's response is extraordinary. This is why he is given to us as an example of faith.

5. He did not sway from his personal convictions, even when those closest to him disagreed. Job's great faith was also shown by his resolve to obey God even when others criticized him. I believe that Job's wife has received far too much criticism from those who explain this story. Let's not forget the trauma that had also befallen her. She had experienced all the same tragedies as Job (with the exception of sickness); she was a mother who had recently lost all ten of her children in one day. In addition to these trials, her husband had now contracted a grotesque disease. When Job's friends saw him for the first time, they could hardly recognize him because of the sores (Job 2:12). We can safely say that Job's wife believed her husband was dying, or at least that life as they knew it was over. I have often asked myself and others who read this story, "Would your response in such circumstances be more like Job's or like his wife's?" Job's wife was simply responding to the hopeless feeling of life unraveling before her eyes, just as we would. It is Job's response that is extraordinary. Though his words to her seem harsh—"You are talking like a foolish woman"—we must remember that the term *foolish* as defined in Scripture is one who lives as if God doesn't exist.[5] Job was saying that his wife's response was like that of someone who doesn't have a relationship of trust with God. But I know how I feel when my wife is deeply discouraged. I trust her judgment about things and face difficult times looking to her for strength. How difficult it must have been for Job to maintain his faith all alone!

The central and largest section of the book of Job (chapters 3–41) reveals the drama of others who abandon him—his four friends. In the next section, we will look more closely at their reasons—which are different from Job's wife's reasons. Though they came with the intent to encourage their friend, their lengthy dialogue with Job was a great disappointment. The intensity of the argument steadily increased as Job and his children were accused of sins that brought on God's wrath. In the wake of this further abandonment by his closest friends, Job must decide whether it is worth it to still trust in God.

Have you ever faced difficulties all alone? Have you ever felt as if those you trust the most have let you down and don't understand what you are going through? Job had the courage to face his trials alone and maintain his trust in God.

Is It a Sin for a Christian to Be Depressed?

After the glowing example of faith recorded in Job chapters 1 and 2, his story takes a rather surprising turn in chapter 3 as he speaks in tones of human depression:

> After this, Job opened his mouth and cursed the day of his birth. He said:
>
> > "May the day of my birth perish,
> >   and the night it was said, 'A boy is born!'" . . .
> > Why did I not perish at birth,
> >   and die as I came from the womb? . . .
> > Or why was I not hidden in the ground like a stillborn child,
> >   like an infant who never saw the light of day? . . .
> > Why is light given to those in misery,
> >   and life to the bitter of soul,

> to those who long for death that does not come,
>> who search for it more than for hidden treasure,
> who are filled with gladness
>> and rejoice when they reach the grave? . . .
> For sighing comes to me instead of food;
>> my groans pour out like water.
> What I feared has come upon me;
>> what I dreaded has happened to me.
> I have no peace, no quietness;
>> I have no rest, but only turmoil."
>>   —Job 3:1–3, 11, 16, 20–22, 24–26

Put simply, Job wishes he had never been born—or he wishes he had died at birth. Because neither of those things happened, he wishes he could die now. In deepest despair, he wants to give up living. Why the sudden and radical shift in mood from his words of faith in Job 1:20–22? And as a corollary to this question, I want to bring up an issue that has produced some debate among Christians. Is it a sin for a Christian to be depressed?

Most people, if they have experienced life at all, have encountered human depression. Some have experienced it personally; others have seen it in loved ones and friends, both Christian and non-Christian. I believe we see examples of depression in several biblical characters, including Job (Job 3) and Elijah (1 Kings 19:1–5). Obviously, all human maladies—physical, emotional, psychological, and spiritual—result indirectly from the effects of sin on the human race. But this is a different issue than attributing a particular sickness, in this case extreme emotional despair, to sinful attitudes. Sin obviously can and often does have negative psychological effects. David's words in Psalm 32:3–4 and Psalm 51 speak of both physical and emotional effects when he was unrepentant of sin. Therefore, depression *may* come from a sinful lifestyle. I believe that both Job and Elijah, however, experienced depression following traumatic events in their lives, but *not* as a result of personal sin. In the Lord's follow-up ministry to both of them, he does not call their depressive feelings sinful. We will see that Job does repent for sin later in the story, but the sin is not his feeling of great despair in chapter 3.

Several years ago, one of our daughters traveled three thousand miles to attend a Christian university in an exchange program. Although she is very sociable and has an outgoing personality, she found it extremely difficult to adjust to this new situation and subculture. Despite her typically upbeat and positive personality, she became depressed and ultimately dropped out of school for the rest of the semester. When we met her at the plane on her return, it was obvious she needed an extended time of healing. As it happened, she struggled with mild bouts of depressive feelings for several months. A friend who is a psychiatrist assured us that some depression is short-term and nonrecurrent, and this was the case in our daughter's situation. The depressive feelings ultimately left and have not returned. In the years since, I have reflected on this experience because it was so out of character for our daughter, whose personality is naturally cheerful and positive. Yet, the experience of depression for her was very real, and even with great encouragement from all of us, she could not simply talk herself out of it.

As a pastor and a professor, I have observed the effects of depression on Christians and have tried to provide help and encouragement when possible. Sometimes, depressive feelings can be caused by physical factors such as loss of sleep or poor diet. Experts tell us that some depression, often called clinical depression, comes from a chemical imbalance in the body and brain, which is often treated with medication to restore the balance. Effective counseling and the emotional support of friends and family are other important elements that can help someone going through depression.

When I teach on Job 3 in a college classroom, I often conclude by inviting anyone who might be struggling with depression to talk with me afterward. On one occasion, a young woman with tears in her eyes reluctantly came forward after class and said she had struggled with depression for several years. Though she had received some counseling, it had been short-term and she had eventually given up. The depressive feelings, however, haunted her throughout college. I recommended a Christian counseling center at our university but discovered she could not afford it. Seeing an opportunity for fellow Christians to help, I approached a businessman friend who I knew had the gift of giving and asked if he would be willing to provide the finances for the needed counseling. At the end of that semester, I was again approached by the young woman, again with tears in her eyes, but this time they were tears of gratitude. The effective Christian counseling she had received had significantly helped her deal with her depression.

For those of us who have not personally experienced depression, there is a tendency to gloss over its seriousness with advice such as, "Snap out of it!" Don Baker, a respected pastor of a large church, had visited people in the psychiatric ward of the local hospital. Little did he know that one day he would go through severe clinical depression and others would visit him there. He later described some of his feelings:

> It is impossible for those who have never been depressed to fully understand the deep, perplexing pain that depression causes. Four interminable years I appeared healthy, without bandages and without crutches. There were no visible scars, no bleeding, and yet there was the endless, indefinable pain that no doctor's probing fingers could locate—no drug could totally relieve. There was always the pain and along with it the desire for oblivion—an oblivion that would only come in minute snatches of restless sleep. I seemed to be out of touch with reality. Life was a blur, often out of focus. My life seemed to be nothing but pretense and fantasy. No one really cared, I felt—not even God. The only solution—at times—seemed to be suicide. To be told that Christians never get depressed only pushed me deeper into my black hole of depression.[6]

The subject of depression is too complex to fully discuss here, but I do not want to gloss over the extreme mood swing that we see in Job chapter 3, and I want to come back to the question of why Job's mood shifts so dramatically after his declaration of faith in 1:20–22? To find the answer, we must observe some important factors in the story.

First, time had passed since Job's initial losses, and perhaps the reality of his tragic day had set in. We do not know how much time elapsed between the tragedies of chapter 1 and his sickness in chapter 2. But even if it was just a few weeks, by the time Job was inflicted with the terrible sores, he was immersed in grief over the death of his ten children. This does not negate Job's initial statement of faith; it simply acknowledges that time enabled Job to see the gravity of the situation.

Second, when Job initially responded in Job 1:20–21, he was not yet suffering with the physical disease that afflicted him later. One might expect that physical suffering under these conditions would lead anyone to despair.

Certainly, the passage of time and his own illness affected Job's perspective, but a third factor strikes me every time I read the story. By the time Job's friends visit him (Job 3), the extent of his losses has become much clearer to him. Not only has he lost his possessions, servants, children, and good health, he has suffered the following losses, as well:

- Loss of ministry as a counselor and spiritual leader to others (Job 4:3–6)
- Loss of physical strength, power, hope, patience, success (Job 6:11–13)
- Loss of support, devotion, and comfort from his friends (Job 6:14–17; 16:1–5)
- Loss of sleep, hope, sense of meaning in life (Job 7:4, 16–20)
- Loss of sight and weight because of his disease (Job 17:7)
- Loss of intimacy with his wife, and the respect of his friends, servants, and the younger generation (Job 19:9–20; 30:1)
- Loss of the prime of life, intimate fellowship with God, respect as a leader in his community, appreciation of his ministry by others (Job 29:4, 7–11, 21–25)

Psychologists tell us that changes in life, especially losses, lead to the highest levels of human stress. "Stress tests" available in magazines or on the Internet can help us identify potential stressors in our lives and estimate the cumulative level of stress. On a typical 100-point scale, the most stressful event is the death of a spouse (100 points).[7] Other major stressors include divorce (73 points), marital separation (65 points), death of a close family member (63 points), personal illness (53 points), and so on. When we add up the points for all the stressful events we have experienced in a year, we can see whether we have been subjected to unusually high levels of stress and estimate the risk of physical or emotional consequences. In Job's case, I believe that the cumulative effect of so many losses in such a short time disrupted his entire life. Job is not suicidal, but he despairs that life no longer has meaning for him.

Again, I find no indication that God considered Job's response sinful. Although despair or depression may be related to sin, it is not always the case. Certainly, when God later called Job to repentance for another sin—pride (Job 40:1–5; 42:6)—he could have also referred to Job's lack of faith, but he does not. Like the laments of the psalmists, Job 3 is the honest cry of a man who has lost almost everything.

With Friends Like These, Who Needs Enemies?

The central and largest portion of the book of Job (2:11–42:6) is often called "dialogue." In ancient wisdom literature, this term is actually a genre, or type, of wisdom writing. The drama of the book of Job is building up to Job's dialogue with God in chapters 38–42. In his misery, this is what Job wanted most, for he believed God may have some answers to the mystery of his suffering. First, however, he had to endure the criticism and attacks of several friends, who ironically came to comfort him. The dialogue between Eliphaz, Bildad, Zophar, and Job takes place in three exchanges, or rounds of discussion (4–14; 15–21; 22–31), followed by the speech of a fourth, younger, friend named Elihu (32–37). All of these men came with good intentions, to "sympathize with [Job] and comfort him" (2:11). Instead, they did neither. At first, they followed the ancient Middle Eastern custom of respect, by allowing the grieving man to speak first. When Job did not speak for seven days and nights, neither did they. Their respectful economy of words did not last, however, and once they started talking, their dialogue seemed endless, as reflected in Job's words:

> I have heard many things like these;
>   miserable comforters are you all!
> Will your long-winded speeches never end?
>   What ails you that you keep on arguing?
>   —Job 16:2–3

When will you end these speeches?
Be sensible, and then we can talk.
—Job 18:2

Their messages were actually very simple theological points that they
wanted to make to Job. And their points are precisely the reason we are
examining this portion of Job's story—because I have a theological point
to make as well! Their perspective of Job's situation may be summarized
as follows:

- *Presupposition:* God blesses good people and brings suffering to sinners
- *Observation:* Job, you are suffering
- *Conclusion:* Job, you are a sinner and must repent

> The theology of
> Job's friends was wrong
> because it was
> incomplete.

Throughout this series of dialogues,
Job keeps insisting that he is innocent
and has committed no sin to bring
God's discipline upon him. We, the
readers of Job's story, know that Job is
right, for we have heard this from the
very mouth of God (Job 2:3). But Job's
blameless and upright reputation is no match for the rigid, loveless theology of his friends. The more Job insists on his innocence, the more
intense and passionate the discussion becomes. At one point, Bildad even
insinuates that Job's children brought death upon themselves by sinning
(8:2–6), which is a far cry from the original words of comfort he intended to convey.

These men were driven by a wrong theology of suffering and trials.
Their theology was not entirely in error, because God does promise to
reward the righteous and discipline those who sin. This is the basic principle of law that Moses wrote in Deuteronomy 28 and that is reflected in
the simple wisdom of Proverbs. The theology of Job's friends was wrong
because it was incomplete. They treated life in neatly defined theological categories, and even placed God in a box! But sometimes God works
in mysterious ways, and allows a righteous person like Job to suffer. This
is also part of his plan. If this possibility is not a part of our theology,

then our theology is wrong and may be as destructive as Job's friends' theology was to Job.

A supposed biblical teaching that is very popular is "prosperity theology," sometimes referred to as the "health and wealth gospel." On the surface, it seems innocent enough because it claims to encourage faith. Followers are motivated by inspirational teachers and preachers to look to God "in faith," and they are promised material blessings and good health if they do.

There are many things about prosperity theology that disturb me, for I have seen it consume lives and divert the affection of Christians away from God and onto themselves. It is an incomplete theology and filled with half-truths. Yes, God may and often does give good health and material blessings to those who follow him. But these are *not* absolute promises, even in the Old Testament Law or the principles of Proverbs. God is God, and the story of Job has been recorded to help us see the complexity of God's ways. Modern prosperity theology teaches that if we have not yet reached a position of financial prosperity, it is because we do not have enough faith. Prosperity theology teaches that sickness comes as a result of sin, and that God guarantees healing to those with enough faith. I've already told you about my involvement with a wonderful Christian family that was losing a loved one to cancer. Oh, the unnecessary guilt heaped upon them when they were told, "If you had enough faith, Doris wouldn't be dying!" This is the theology of Job's friends, and it places God in a box. His ways are not our ways (Isa. 55:8). Our trust of him, even when we do not understand his ways, is what faith is all about.

The Impatience of Job

The climax of Job's story is reached when God finally speaks to Job (Job 38–42). This section reveals the second Big Idea about trials in the book of Job. Remember, the first Big Idea was that trials or suffering may come upon us to demonstrate the authenticity of our faith in God, which in turn brings glory to God. Therefore, trials may be related to sin but in some cases are not. But what keeps me going through times of suffering, especially trials that come upon me for no known reason? A quote from Margaret Clarkson perfectly expresses the second Big Idea: "It is not by miraculous deliverance that our faith grows, but by discovering God's faithfulness in the midst of our pain."[8]

Job waited desperately for God to provide some answers for his suffering and to defend his claims against the false accusations of his friends. But God remained silent while Job was falsely accused. Like us, Job desperately wanted answers to the questions about his suffering:

> I loathe my very life;
>   therefore I will give free rein to my complaint
>   and speak out in the bitterness of my soul.
> I will say to God: Do not condemn me,
>   but tell me what charges you have against me.
>   —Job 10:1–2

> But I desire to speak to the Almighty
>   and to argue my case with God. . . .
> Now that I have prepared my case,
>   I know I will be vindicated. . . .
> Only grant me these two things, O God,
>   and then I will not hide from you:
> Withdraw your hand far from me,
>   and stop frightening me with your terrors.
> Then summon me and I will answer,
>   or let me speak, and you reply.
> How many wrongs and sins have I committed?
>   Show me my offense and my sin.
>   —Job 13:3, 18, 20–23

> Oh, that I had someone to hear me!
>   I sign now my defense—let the Almighty answer me;
>   let my accuser put his indictment in writing.
>   —Job 31:35

One of the more challenging aspects of faith is waiting on God's timing. We wait upon the Lord to provide answers to our questions about the future, but sometimes he moves very slowly. For example, a good friend of mine is going through a transition time in his life right now as God seems to be leading him to an entirely different ministry. He has confidence that he is experiencing God's leading, but nothing about the future is clear. So many practical factors about life for him and his family hang in the balance, but God is silent right now. So it was with Job. His friends had disappointed him, and now God himself was not responding as Job had hoped. This precarious place in life, one of confusion and waiting on God, is exactly where God wants us. When the apostle Paul prayed for the removal of his thorn in the flesh and God did not answer, Paul learned a simple truth through the waiting process: "When I am weak, then I am strong" (2 Cor. 12:10).

Job Flunks the Science Exam

When God finally speaks in Job 38–42, his words represent one of the most amazing passages in the Bible. At last! This is exactly what Job had been waiting for! Or was it? Job expected God to speak to his friends and to defend Job against their criticism. But God speaks to Job alone.[9] Job expected God to give answers to his moral dilemma about life, but God's speech is filled with questions—seventy of them—and they seem to have nothing to do with Job or his problems. God's initial speech (Job 38–40) consists of questions about how the physical universe runs. Some examples:

> Where were you when I laid the earth's foundation?
>> Tell me, if you understand.
> Who marked off its dimensions? Surely you know!
>> Who stretched a measuring line across it? . . .
> Have you ever given orders to the morning,
>> or shown the dawn its place? . . .
> Have you comprehended the vast expanses of the earth?
>> Tell me, if you know all this.
> What is the way to the abode of light?
>> And where does darkness reside? . . .
> Do you know the laws of the heavens?
>> Can you set up God's dominion over the earth? . . .

> Do you send the lightning bolts on their way?
>   Do they report to you, "Here we are"?
> Who endowed the heart with wisdom
>   or gave understanding to the mind? . . .
> Do you know when the mountain goats give birth?
>   Do you watch when the doe bears her fawn?
> Do you count the months till they bear?
>   Do you know the time they give birth?
>   —Job 38:4–5, 12, 18–19, 33, 35–36; 39:1–2

These are just a few examples of the questions that God asks Job about the origin of the physical universe, the oceans, sunrise and sunlight, the dimensions of the earth, light and darkness, snow and hail, storms, lightning and thunder, water and ice, the constellations of stars, and the birthing process of animals.

I grew up on a farm in rural Washington State, and throughout those years we raised many types of farm animals. Through those experiences, I personally witnessed the birth of almost every animal on the farm, and I can testify that they rarely needed our help. The wisdom found in the animal kingdom—we sometimes call it instinct—is evidence of the amazing wisdom of the Creator.

Though I have not formally studied astronomy, I have sometimes done my own study of the constellations of stars. Recently, we went on a vacation to the Sierra Nevada Mountains, and our hosts had a powerful telescope set up that allowed us to look at the endless stars of the Milky Way. One dark night, we were overwhelmed as we gazed at these sights, in their vastness a powerful reminder of the infinite wisdom it takes to create and sustain our physical world. As Psalm 19:1 says, "The heavens declare the glory of God; the skies proclaim the work of his hands."

But what about Job's distress? God not only failed to answer his questions, but he also changed the subject! Job was speechless before God—and he obviously failed the science exam! Only God could know the answers to such questions, and that is precisely the point. God, through his majestic statement about his wisdom in the physical universe (Job 38–41), was reminding Job what was also true about God's wisdom in the moral and spiritual universe. In a sense God was saying, "Job, you have no idea how the physical world came into being or how it functions, yet daily you experience it and you trust me to govern it. Though you don't understand all that takes place in your life, can you trust me?" God was calling Job to greater faith, even if Job did not have all the answers to the questions of life.

Like Job, when we encounter trials or suffering it seems to us that being delivered from the problem, or at least knowing the answers to the "why" questions, would satisfy us most. But our greatest need is not to know answers but to know God more intimately. In times of crisis, trial, and suffering, what we need most is a deeper experience of God. As Clarkson reminds us, "It is not by miraculous deliverance that our faith grows, but by discovering God's faithfulness in the midst of our pain."[10] This is what Job means in his response to God, "My ears had heard of you but now my eyes have seen you" (Job 42:5). His "eyes" were the eyes of faith. He had now experienced a more intimate relationship with God than he'd had before. In verses 2–3, he praises God by affirming his attributes:

- omnipotence: "I know that you can do all things."
- sovereignty: "No plan of yours can be thwarted."
- omniscience and wisdom: "Surely I spoke of things I did not understand, things too wonderful for me to know."

All of this appropriately leads to repentance by Job: "I am unworthy—how can I reply to you?" (Job 40:4) "Therefore I despise myself and repent in dust and ashes" (42:6). As previously noted, this is not repentance for some hidden sin that Job's friends believed brought his trials. This is repentance for the sin of pride, when in his frustration Job had demanded God to defend him before his friends and answer his questions.

Seeing Life in Perspective

It's not about you. The purpose of your life is far greater than your own personal fulfillment, your peace of mind, or even your happiness. It's far greater than your family, your career, or even your wildest dreams and ambitions. If you want to know why you were placed on this planet, you must begin with God. You were born *by* his purpose and *for* his purpose.[11]

So begins the first chapter of Rick Warren's best seller, *The Purpose Driven Life,* a book that challenges people to think beyond themselves as they try to discover life's meaning. This also applies to the difficult, trying times of life. In this chapter we have explored an ancient story from Hebrew wisdom literature that is one of the Bible's most important books about faith, trials, and suffering. It is a story about a man who suffers but does not know the reason. When this story was preserved in writing, through the inspiration of God, it included some information about a spiritual conflict in the heavenlies that precipitated Job's trials. Job's faith on earth became a demonstration that his love for God was authentic, and through this process greater glory was brought to the Lord in heaven. As far as we know, when Job lived out these circumstances on earth he never knew of the heavenly background that we read about in Job 1–2.

And such is life for us. Some suffering comes without explanation or obvious reason. How do you respond to that kind of experience? Can you live with some mystery in your spiritual life? Are you willing to let God be God? In some cases, the only reason we experience suffering is that greater glory might be brought to God in heaven. Through the "lenses" of faith, we can learn with Job that what we need most is not answers but to know God more intimately.

DISCUSSION QUESTIONS

1. Have you ever had a Job-like experience by being faced with a series of trials all at once? How did you respond? What did you learn?
2. What troubles you about the story of Job? What has been encouraging for you? What is the main point (big idea) the story of Job is trying to teach?
3. In Job 1:20–22 and 2:9–10, what do we observe in Job's attitude, actions, and perspective that serves as an example to us? Give an example of how you could apply one of Job's comments to a trial you are going through (or have recently gone through).

4. In Job 3, do you think Job was depressed when he says he wishes he could die or had never been born? How could his thinking be so different than just a short time earlier (Job 1:20–22; 2:9–10)? Have you ever experienced a trial when your attitude was much like Job's in chapter 3? Explain how you handled it.

5. Why was God's "science lesson" in Job 40–42 so difficult for Job to understand? What do you think God was trying to teach Job through it? How does it relate to some of the trials you are experiencing right now?

Chapter 6

What a Privilege!

A muscular offensive lineman from the Florida State University football team was distributing Christian literature at an event sponsored by Campus Crusade for Christ. He had just become a Christian, and this activity was both new and scary for him. A younger, slightly built student perused one of the Christian brochures, looked squarely into the football player's face, and spit at him. "That's what I think of your Jesus!" he said.

The natural response for the lineman would have been a massive cross-body block. But this young Christian had been told that he might receive persecution when standing up for Christ. Pulling out his handkerchief, he said, "I want you to know that Jesus can wipe away your sins just as easily as I wipe this spit from my face." He politely walked away. Even more than the brochure, the love of Christ embodied in the football player's humility and gentleness delivered the most convincing message. One year later, both men were serving in Christian ministry together.

"For the word of God is living and active. Sharper than any double-edged sword, it penetrates even to dividing soul and spirit, joints and marrow; it judges the thoughts and attitudes of the heart" (Heb. 4:12). There is no question that God's Word all by itself can transform a person's life. Whether it's a Gideon Bible in a hotel room drawer, or a gospel tract handed to a friend, the Word of God conveyed in the pages of Scripture has effectively reached people with the good news about Jesus Christ.

> There is no question that God's *preferred* method of evangelism is to *embody* Christ's message in people like you and me.

But there is also no question that God's *preferred* method of evangelism is to *embody* Christ's message in people like you and me. That is why Christ came to earth. Through the Incarnation, God revealed himself in a new and visible way. This is also why Christ left, so that he might send the Holy Spirit to dwell with us so our lives would reflect Christ to the world.

If you're at all like me, you are not a masochist, and you would probably avoid the experience of pain whenever possible. Similarly, you try to get along with most people and do not enjoy rejection or being hated by others. Is that true? Well, I have important news for you. If you are a Christian and live accordingly, you will be persecuted, hated, and rejected by other people. Guaranteed. It has nothing to do with you, and everything to do with the one you represent—namely, Jesus Christ. But when the persecution comes, it will often *feel* as if it is directed at you, and you will *feel* like giving up. However, by knowing the truth through a clear, biblical thinking process, you will be able to see these unique trials for what they are. Here is the truth in the words of the apostle Peter:

> Dear friends, do not be surprised at the painful trial you are suffering, as though something strange were happening to you. But rejoice that you participate in the sufferings of Christ, so that you may be overjoyed when his glory is revealed. If you are insulted because of the name of Christ, you are blessed, for the Spirit of glory and of God rests on you. . . . If you suffer as a Christian, do not be ashamed, but praise God that you bear that name. (1 Peter 4:12–14, 16)

When a Problem Becomes a Privilege

In previous chapters, we have examined many purposes for trials, but there is a particular kind of suffering that is in a category by itself: persecution. My daughter Kristin recently returned from a trip to Germany and Switzerland. On the last day of the trip, she lost her wallet, which contained a credit card, ATM card, and all her cash. Along with all the hassles of canceling the charge cards, she had to borrow $50 from a Good Samaritan stranger (a Christian) in order to get to the airport so she could return home. Now, that experience was a trial, but it is not the kind of trial we are considering in this chapter.

In 1 Peter 4, the apostle refers to persecution or suffering that comes as a direct result of living for Christ. It is persecution received when we are faithful to God by bearing the name of Christ and standing up for what is right. In this category of trial, the wrath of others is directed toward us but is fueled by a hatred for Christ and all that he stands for. When this happens, it often comes as a surprise, the last thing we would expect in response to Christlikeness. Peter says, "Do not be surprised" (v. 12) or "do not be ashamed" (v. 16), but rather "rejoice" (v. 12) and "praise God" (v. 16) because "you are blessed" (v. 14) through this experience.

Now let's return to the story of the football player told at the beginning of this chapter. What an embarrassing confrontation for this new Christian! Do you think his natural response to spit on his face would have been to rejoice and praise God? I can imagine every muscle tightening as he considered what to do. But though he was a young Christian, someone had taught him how to think right when things go wrong. Someone had taught him that persecution of this kind is likely, and when it happens we're to remember the words of Peter, "Do not be surprised at the painful trial you are suffering, as though something strange were happening to you. But rejoice that you participate in the sufferings of Christ, so that you may be overjoyed when his glory is revealed. If you are insulted because of the name of Christ, you are blessed, for the Spirit of glory and of God rests on you. . . . If you suffer as a Christian, do not be ashamed, but praise God that you bear that name" (1 Peter 4:12–14, 16). Thinking right when things went wrong transformed the young man's anger and enabled him to respond in love (produced by the Holy Spirit), rather than take revenge according to his own emotions. As a result, he not only avoided an ugly confrontation but also attracted another unlikely individual into the kingdom of God. Obstacles become opportunities when we are able to see that the problem of persecution is really a unique privilege.

Why Are We Surprised?

Peter's words in 1 Peter 4:12–19 are perhaps the clearest statement in Scripture about this particular kind of trial. As we explore the topic in more depth, we will see that Jesus, Paul, Luke, John, and the author of Hebrews had much to say about the subject as well.

Peter's epistles were written at a very difficult time for early Christians. During the years of Nero's reign, and especially after A.D. 64, any religious sect that was not willing to participate in emperor worship was seen as a threat to Caesar. Christians were blamed for the great fire that burned much of Rome in A.D. 64, and persecution was especially intense until A.D. 68 when Nero died. Some Christians were burned at the stake or sent to their deaths through gladiators or wild animals; some were covered with pitch, tied to poles, and used as human torches in Nero's gardens. The persecution of Jewish Christians also continued by their own countrymen, prompting many of them to flee into other parts of the Roman Empire. This explains why Peter's message is directed to so many regions of the Roman Empire: "To God's elect, strangers in the world, scattered throughout Pontus, Galatia, Cappadocia, Asia and Bithynia" (1 Peter 1:1).

His advice in 1 Peter 4:12, "Do not be surprised at the painful trial you are suffering, as though something strange were happening to you," is a reminder that persecution for the cause of Christ is to be expected. Peter had been present in the Upper Room and had heard Jesus say:

> If the world hates you, keep in mind that it hated me first. If you belonged to the world, it would love you as its own. As it is, you do not belong to the world, but I have chosen you out of the world. That is why the world hates you. Remember the words I spoke to you: "No servant is greater than his master." If they persecuted me, they will persecute you also. If they obeyed my teaching, they will obey yours also. They will treat you this way because of my name, for they do not know the One who sent me. . . . He who hates me hates my Father as well. (John 15:18–23)[1]

I have given them your word and the world has hated them, for they are not of the world any more than I am of the world. (John 17:14)

On that important evening, the Lord was preparing his disciples for his departure from the earth, and reminding them of something he had regularly taught: Persecution is inevitable, and it will come from people who do not know God and therefore have a hatred for Christ.

Later, when the Lord called Ananias to minister to Saul (who became the apostle Paul) immediately after his conversion to Christianity, his instructions included a direct reference to suffering for the cause of Christ: "I will show him [Paul] how much he must suffer for my name" (Acts 9:16). Paul's life and teaching confirm this reality as well:

When we are persecuted, we endure it; when we are slandered, we answer kindly. Up to this moment we have become the scum of the earth, the refuse of the world. I am not writing this to shame you, but to warn you, as my dear children. (1 Cor. 4:12–14)

For it has been granted to you on behalf of Christ not only to believe on him, but also to suffer for him. (Phil. 1:29)

And of this gospel I was appointed a herald and an apostle and a teacher. That is why I am suffering as I am. Yet I am not ashamed, because I know whom I have believed, and am convinced that he is able to guard what I have entrusted to him for that day. (2 Tim. 1:11–12)

In fact, everyone who wants to live a godly life in Christ Jesus will be persecuted, while evil men and impostors will go from bad to worse. (2 Tim. 3:12–13)

Peter similarly says, "To this you were called, because Christ suffered for you, leaving you an example, that you should follow in his steps" (1 Peter 2:21). In one of the last books of the New Testament to be written, the apostle John calls for a similar mind-set: "Do not be surprised, my brothers, if the world hates you" (1 John 3:13). Paul was beheaded by the emperor Nero, Peter was crucified upside down, and John was exiled during much of his later life by the emperor Domitian. Tradition also strongly suggests that John was executed. These men paid the ultimate price for their faith.

What Is the "Fiery Ordeal" That Christians Are Promised?

Peter's words of warning in 1 Peter 4:12 are translated "fiery ordeal" in the NASB, and "painful trial" in the NIV. What exactly is this? Some expositors believe that Peter was using a form of the word *burn* to intentionally relate his warning to Nero's atrocities (the burning of Rome, Christians being burned at the stake and used as burning torches). Though this may be the case, the term is more probably a metaphorical reference to the refining process to which Peter refers in 1:7: "[All kinds of trials] have come so that your faith—of greater worth than gold, which perishes even though refined by fire—may be proved genuine." To use a modern expression, we sometimes "go through the fire" of difficult times to strengthen and prove the reality of our faith.

The condition—"If you are insulted because of the name of Christ" (1 Peter 4:14)—narrows the scope of trials that qualify in this category. Even more specifically, in verses 15–16 the apostle draws a contrast between suffering for our own sins (murder, theft, meddling) and suffering *as a Christian*. Although it is possible to bring suffering upon ourselves through our own faults, what Peter has in mind here is a particular kind of trial that comes as a result of representing Christ.

I first met Leah, my wife, at a small Bible school in England. During our term there, a group of students began to follow the dubious leadership of an unusual fellow student who declared that he had discovered a deeper spiritual experience than the rest of us. He and his followers would not speak to or associate with anyone outside their group. Many of them wore odd clothing and did not take showers or fix themselves up in any way. After a while, we were actually grateful that they kept to themselves! They called themselves "Fools for Christ," but in the eyes of the other students they were just being fools, and it had nothing to do with Christ. In a similar way, Christians today sometimes identify problems that they have brought on themselves as spiritual warfare or persecution for the cause of Christ. Peter and the other New Testament writers would not agree with that assessment. Yes, personal problems from our own sin or choices may be genuine trials, but they are not the same as suffering persecution for the cause of Christ.

The New Testament records several types of suffering that the early Christians faced. They knew that there would likely be a price to pay for following Jesus, and many of them paid dearly. In the twenty centuries since the church was established, Christians around the world have continued to face such trials. The following are examples of what Peter means by "fiery ordeals":

- *Persecution, being excluded, insulted, disgraced, slandered.*

  Blessed are you when people insult you, persecute you and falsely say all kinds of evil against you because of me. (Matt. 5:11)

  And everyone who has left houses or brothers or sisters or father or mother or children or fields for my sake will receive a hundred times as much and will inherit eternal life. (Matt. 19:29)

  Blessed are you when men hate you, when they exclude you and insult you and reject your name as evil, because of the Son of Man. (Luke 6:22)

  If they persecuted me, they will persecute you also. (John 15:20)

  They will put you out of the synagogue. (John 16:2)

  When we are persecuted, we endure it; when we are slandered, we answer kindly. . . . We have become the scum of the earth, the refuse of the world. (1 Cor. 4:12–13)

  Everyone who wants to live a godly life in Christ Jesus will be persecuted. (2 Tim. 3:12)

You were publicly exposed to insult and persecution; at other times you stood side by side with those who were so treated. (Heb. 10:33)

If you are insulted because of the name of Christ . . . (1 Peter 4:14)

• *Hatred from others.*

All men will hate you because of me. (Matt. 10:22)

Blessed are you when men hate you. (Luke 6:22–23)

That is why the world hates you. (John 15:19)

I have given them your word and the world has hated them. (John 17:14)

Do not be surprised, my brothers, if the world hates you. (1 John 3:13)

• *Loss of property, beating, imprisonment, martyrdom.*

Be on your guard against men; they will hand you over to the local councils and flog you in their synagogues. On my account you will be brought before governors and kings as witnesses to them and to the Gentiles. (Matt. 10:17–18)

Brother will betray brother to death, and a father his child; children will rebel against their parents and have them put to death. All men will hate you because of me, but he who stands firm to the end will be saved. (Matt. 10:21–22)

But when Herod heard this, he said, "John, the man I beheaded, has been raised from the dead!" For Herod himself had given orders to have John arrested, and he had him bound and put in prison. . . . So he immediately sent an executioner with orders to bring John's head. The man went, beheaded John in the prison, and brought back his head on a platter. (Mark 6:16–17, 27–28)

For we who are alive are always being given over to death for Jesus' sake, so that his life may be revealed in our mortal body. (2 Cor. 4:11)

Remember those earlier days after you had received the light, when you stood your ground in a great contest in the face of suffering. . . . You sympathized with those in prison and joyfully accepted the confiscation of your property, because you knew that you yourselves had better and lasting possessions. . . . (Heb. 10:32, 34)

They were stoned; they were sawed in two; they were put to death by the sword. They went about in sheepskins and goatskins, destitute, persecuted and mistreated. . . . They wandered in deserts and mountains, and in caves and holes in the ground. (Heb. 11:37–38)

Further examples in the stories of the apostles are found in the following passages:

Arrest and imprisonment of apostles (Acts 4:3; 5:18, 40; 12:4; 16:23; 23:35)

Martyrdom of Stephen and James (Acts 7:58; 12:2)

Imprisonments of Paul (Eph. 3:1; 4:1; 6:20; Phil. 1:7, 13; Col. 4:3, 18; 2 Tim. 1:8, 16; 2:9)

During my years as a professor, I have met many students who have paid a tremendous price to attend a Christian seminary, and I do not mean just tuition! One such student, who came from a Jewish family background, was removed from the family will and ostracized by other members of his family. When he became a Christian, his father held a funeral for him and spoke of him as if he had died. For this young man, following Christ meant giving up relationships in life that most of us take for granted.

Why a Privilege? Why Rejoice?

Perhaps you can understand and accept the natural consequences of bearing a testimony for Christ. When other people live in darkness and the light of Christ shines on them, they become angry, and we Christians are their only visible target. But why see it as a privilege? If you are asking this question right now, it is a legitimate one. Peter, the other New Testament writers, and Jesus not only promise persecution, but they actually describe it as a blessing, a privilege, and a reason for rejoicing!

Blessed are you when people insult you, persecute you and falsely say all kinds of evil against you because of me. (Matt. 5:11)

Blessed are you when men hate you, when they exclude you and insult you and reject your name as evil, because of the Son of Man. Rejoice in that day and leap for joy, because great is your reward in heaven. For that is how their fathers treated the prophets. (Luke 6:22–23)

The apostles left the Sanhedrin, rejoicing because they had been counted worthy of suffering disgrace for the Name. (Acts 5:41)

I want to know Christ and the power of his resurrection and the fellowship of sharing in his sufferings, becoming like him in his death, and so, somehow, to attain to the resurrection from the dead. (Phil. 3:10–11)

Dear friends, do not be surprised at the painful trial you are suffering, as though something strange were happening to you. But rejoice that you participate in the sufferings of Christ, so that you may be overjoyed when his glory is revealed. If you are insulted because of the name of Christ, you are blessed, for the Spirit of glory and of God rests on you. . . . If you suffer as a Christian, do not be ashamed, but praise God that you bear that name. (1 Peter 4:12–14, 16)

These statements about persecution provide some answers for why we should count it as a privilege. Christians are not masochists who enjoy pain for pain's sake. Peter's exhortation involves an attitude that is set on the truth rather than subject to the winds of our emotions and feelings. These passages give five reasons for considering suffering and persecution a privilege and a reason for rejoicing:

1. When we are persecuted because of Christ we experience deeper fellowship with Jesus by participating in his sufferings. In 1 Peter 4:13, the verb translated "participate" is from the same word as the common biblical word *koinonia,* meaning a shared or close relationship and most often translated "fellowship." Paul likely means the same thing when he says, "I want to know Christ and the power of his resurrection and the fellowship of sharing in his sufferings" (Phil. 3:10; see also 1:29). Our suffering for Christ is not an offering for our sins as Christ's was, but it does become a shared experience with Jesus. Just as he was hated and persecuted for righteousness' sake, we represent him in the continued persecution that has always attended the cause of Christ. Though persecution is not something we would choose, it is perhaps the deepest dimension of our fellowship with Christ.

During a church planting experience in 2004, I served on a new leadership team of elders. We got along very well and seemed to have complementary gifts that enabled us to work well together. At one point, when we had to deal with a very difficult family situation, it became obvious that the challenge drew our team together more effectively than any prior experience. In my years of Christian ministry, I have seen this happen many times. If this "fellowship of suffering" can unite a group of people on a purely human level, how much more will our fellowship with Christ be welded together through the heat of battle and conflict. We come to depend more on his power as we continue the spiritual battle that he began.

2. A faith response to conflict, persecution, and suffering for Christ produces a spiritually prosperous state of God's blessing in our lives. Peter's words about the meaning of persecution, "you are blessed" (1 Peter 3:14; 4:14), are reminiscent of Jesus' teaching in the Sermon on the Mount: "Blessed are you when people insult you, persecute you and falsely say all kinds of evil against you because of me" (Matt. 5:11). "Blessed are you when men hate you . . . exclude you . . . insult you . . . reject your name as evil, because of the Son of Man" (Luke 6:22). Here is a promise exactly opposite to our human expectations or natural emotions. Most of us do not enjoy rejection or persecution. In fact, when conflict exists, we assume that life is not as it should be. But Jesus says just the opposite about our Christian experience. If persecution and rejection come as a result of our commitment to the cause of Christ, it is evidence that we are being blessed by God. Knowing that this is true and that God is with us may be all we need when this kind of suffering occurs.

When Mei Mei became a believer in Jesus Christ, she was one of the first members of her ethnic group to believe.[2] Her people are devout practitioners of a form of Buddhism mingled with a pre-Buddhist animistic faith. In her community, allegiance to the faith is supreme. In the eyes of the government, allegiance to the state and its political ideologies is essential. But Mei Mei found both the faith and the ideologies lacking.

When she was a first-year university student, she began attending a small Bible study in her native language. The following year, she professed faith in Christ and was baptized into the family of God. Few people knew of her decision, only the other girls she worshiped with and a few other Christian friends. To tell her family would risk their anger and potential ostracism; to tell her friends at school would risk becoming a social outcast, something less than a true member of her ethnic community.

The society in which Mei Mei lives has long considered Christianity a threat to its ideologies and agendas. Despite modern reforms moving toward religious freedom, there is a long history of religious oppression, and the pressure to remain "pure" and free from the taint of religious "superstitions" is heavy.

At the time when Mei Mei was beginning her walk with Christ, a growing number of students were beginning to explore Christianity. As the administrators of the school she attended began to hear rumors, they actively sought to stifle the small beginnings of this movement of faith.

Students were summoned to a special "lecture" given by a member of the national security bureau, who denounced the evils of Christianity. He claimed that Christianity was a tool of foreign oppression and that foreign missionaries were sent by their national governments to manipulate young, impressionable students for their own countries' political gain. He said that students contacted by missionaries were being preyed upon, lied to, and brainwashed. Christianity was portrayed as nothing more than a means to get Mei Mei and her classmates to betray their nation and give foreign nations a political foothold in the motherland.

At the same time, the authorities began to apply pressure to individuals to abandon their interest or faith in Christianity. The school administrators knew that one of Mei Mei's friends was a Christian. They tapped her phone, searched her room, and confiscated her Bible and other religious books. Mei Mei and the other three girls who worshiped together were scared. If their friend's phone was tapped, theirs probably were too. If the authorities had been listening to the one girl's phone calls and knew she was a Christian, they surely knew about the others as well. Mei Mei took all of her Christian books and worship tapes and left them in the apartment of a friend who was not a student.

"It is very hard to be a Christian here," Mei Mei said. "It is easy in other countries, but here it is dangerous. I am scared." Less than a year after her baptism, Mei Mei has known real fear because of her faith, but her faith is growing stronger. She knows that the pressure will not be lifted any time soon, and that she faces the possibility of further persecution from both the government and her community in the years to come. Her prospects for marriage are very slim; no men from her ethnic group have yet come to faith. But more than ever, she knows who she is and why. She has grown confident in her identity as a child of God, a follower of Christ.

3. Suffering for Christ demonstrates that God considers us "worthy" to represent Christ. When God allows persecution, it indicates that he has granted us the privilege of representing Christ. Not every Christian grows to the stage of being able to handle such persecution; when we suffer for Christ, we share in that privilege.

In Acts 5, Luke records an early example of persecution in a story about the first Christians. The disciples of Jesus were zealous in publicly proclaiming the message of the risen Christ in Jerusalem where Jesus had ascended into heaven (Acts 1:11). They were witnesses to Christ's resurrection from the dead, and they were now beginning the first phase of a mission that would ultimately spread the message of Christ to the whole world (v. 8). Peter preached the first message in Jerusalem on the Jewish feast day of Pentecost (2:1–41) and continued to speak of Christ around the temple area (3:11–26). Many from the crowd responded and the church began to grow in numbers and in unity (2:42–47).

This new activity presented a particular problem for a Jewish leadership group known as the Sadducees. They were the religious party of Israel's priests, and for more than 150 years they had been in charge of the sacrificial system in the temple. But, like the Pharisees at that time, this leadership group had become corrupt and misused their power. The story of Jesus casting out the moneychangers from the temple (probably twice, as recorded in John 2:13–22 and Matt. 21:12–17) reveals a corrupt sacrificial system in which the poor were contributing to the coffers of the wealthy Sadducees. This group no longer represented the pure religion of Judaism prescribed in the Old Testament. Consequently, the preaching about Jesus threatened them in two ways. First, the early church was meeting and growing in numbers on the Sadducees "turf," the temple area. This would certainly have been a great embarrassment to those who had crucified Jesus. Luke tells us they were "filled with jealousy" at the overwhelming response to the apostles' ministry (Acts 5:12–17). Second, the central truth preached by the apostles was Jesus' bodily resurrection (2:24, 31–33), a doctrine that the Sadducees did not believe or accept.

Thus began the persecution that Jesus had promised to those who would follow him. The Sadducees arrested Peter, John, and other apostles, and placed them in the public jail, only to find that an angel had delivered them to again begin preaching the message of the risen Christ in the temple courts (Acts 5:18–21). After another arrest and warning by the high priest and his council, Peter and the other apostles responded, "We must obey God rather than men," and proceeded to preach the message of the risen Christ before the ruling council (vv. 22–32). Some Sadducees were ready to kill the apostles, but others acted with caution, beat the apostles, and again released them with the command that they should not speak the name of Jesus (vv. 33–40). Luke captures the spirit of the early Christians amidst such opposition: "The apostles left the Sanhedrin, rejoicing because they had been counted worthy of suffering disgrace for the Name" (v. 41).

Polycarp, bishop of Smyrna in Asia Minor, was arrested, tried, and executed in A.D. 155 for being a Christian. He had been a disciple of the apostle John. At his death, Polycarp had the opportunity to recant but insists that the tortures of this life are far to be preferred to the eternal torments for those who deny Christ. An eyewitness account, perhaps the earliest story of martyrdom to be preserved outside of the New Testament, records that Christians were condemned simply for refusing to worship the state gods or to give reverence to the emperor:

> Therefore, when he was brought before him, the [Roman] proconsul asked if he were Polycarp. And when he confessed that he was, the proconsul tried to persuade him to recant, saying, "Have respect for your age. . . . Swear by the Genius of Caesar; repent; say, 'Away with the atheists!'" [the Christians]. So Polycarp solemnly looked at the whole crowd of lawless heathen who were in the stadium, motioned toward them with his hand, and then (groaning as he looked up to heaven) said, "Away with the atheists!"
>
> But when the magistrate persisted and said, "Swear the oath, and I will release you; revile Christ," Polycarp replied, "For eighty-six years I have been his servant, and he has done me no wrong. How can I blaspheme my King who saved me?" But as he continued to insist, saying "Swear by the Genius of Caesar," he answered: "If you vainly suppose that I will swear by the Genius of Caesar, as you request, and pretend not to know who I am, listen carefully; I am a Christian. Now if you want to learn the doctrine of Christianity, name a day and give me a hearing. . . ."
>
> Then he said to him again: "I will have you consumed by fire, since you despise the wild beasts, unless you change your mind." But Polycarp said: "You threaten with a fire that burns only briefly and after just a little while is extinguished, for you are ignorant of the fire of the coming judgment and eternal

punishment, that is reserved for the ungodly. But why do you delay? Come, do what you wish."[3]

As he was burned alive before the crowd, Polycarp's prayer included these words, "I bless you because you have considered me worthy of this day and hour, that I might receive a place among the number of martyrs in the cup of your Christ, to the resurrection of eternal life, both of soul and of body, in the incorruptibility of the Holy Spirit."[4]

4. Perseverance through suffering serves as a testimony to encourage others to follow Christ. Paul speaks of his imprisonment for the gospel: "Now I want you to know, brothers, that what has happened to me has really served to advance the gospel" (Phil. 1:12). This principle, explained more extensively in chapter 3 of this book, has special meaning when the reason for a trial is persecution for Christ. Paul's faith throughout his incarceration in Rome served as an example to bring others to the Lord. Almost all of the apostles, and many other early Christians beginning with Stephen (Acts 7), suffered and died for their faith. Their powerful examples inspired many others to follow, especially in the Roman empire.

Eusebius recounts the effects of such persecution in his *Ecclesiastical History.* A severe persecution took place at Lyons in Gaul (France) in 177. During a holiday to celebrate the greatness of Rome, members of the sect known as Christians were to be publicly tortured. Christianity had come to Gaul about twenty-five years earlier when Polycarp of Smyrna sent Pothinus as a missionary. As the groups of converts grew in size, resistance had mounted. Christians were shut out of houses and businesses, robbed, beaten, and stoned. In 177, some Christians were falsely accused of cannibalism and incest and were awaiting the arrival of the governor. They were confined in the worst prison cells, some of which were smaller than a modern refrigerator. Many of the saints died of suffocation. Some Christians were placed in stocks or were tortured by being forced to sit on a red-hot iron grill. Others were devoured by wild beasts in the amphitheater as the crowd watched in amusement. At the onset of this persecution, many Christians denied Christ in response to the gruesome public tortures.

But when they saw the faithful dying for their faith, most of them changed their minds and were emboldened, as a direct result of seeing others suffer for Christ. The historian Eusebius writes:

> But the intervening time [of public torture] was not idle or fruitless for them [the martyrs] but through their endurance was manifested the immeasurable mercy of Christ, for through the living [the martyrs] the [spiritually] dead were being quickened and martyrs gave grace to those who had denied. . . . For through them [the martyrs] the majority of those who had denied were again brought to birth and again conceived and quickened again, and learned to confess [Christ], and now alive and vigorous, made happy by God who wills not the death of the sinner, but is kind towards repentance, [they] went to the judgment-seat, in order that they might again be interrogated by the governor. For Caesar had written that they should be tortured to death, but that if any should recant they should be let go. . . . He [the governor] accordingly examined them again, beheaded all who appeared to possess Roman citizenship, and sent the rest to the beasts. And Christ was greatly glorified by those who had formerly denied but then confessed contrary to the expectation of the people.[5]

5. *It means we share also in future glory.* Peter, Paul, and Jesus all made an intentional connection between the experience of trials and the glory of eternal life. As discussed in chapter 4, perseverance through trials in this life is rewarded in heaven. Paul expresses it like this, "The Spirit himself testifies with our spirit that we are God's children. Now if we are children, then we are heirs—heirs of God and co-heirs with Christ, if indeed we share in his sufferings in order that we may also share in his glory" (Rom. 8:17–18; see also Luke 6:22–23; 2 Tim. 2:12; 1 Peter 1:7; 4:14; 5:1, 10).

Only a Christian Would Brag About This Résumé

It seems as if I have been in school all my life. While I was completing a degree in electrical engineering in my early twenties, the Lord led me into a Christian ministry that necessitated my starting over in college. Three theology degrees later, my wife says I became a professor because I have always loved school, and she may be right. There are aspects of the academic world, however, that really annoy me. Arrogance about grades, résumés, or other career accomplishments have always been a turnoff for me, because all these things are merely means to an end. That's why I love the apostle Paul's attitude after his conversion. Of all young Jewish leaders in the first century, Paul had every reason to brag about his credentials. He makes this point as he contrasts himself to some Jewish false teachers in Philippi:

> Watch out for those dogs, those men who do evil, those mutilators of the flesh. For it is we who are the circumcision, we who worship by the Spirit of God, who glory in Christ Jesus, and who put no confidence in the flesh—though I myself have reasons for such confidence. If anyone else thinks he has reasons to put confidence in the flesh, I have more: circumcised on the eighth day, of the people of Israel, of the tribe of Benjamin, a Hebrew of Hebrews; in regard to the law, a Pharisee; as for zeal, persecuting the church; as for legalistic righteousness, faultless. (Phil. 3:2–6)

His credentials as a Jew and a Pharisee were impeccable, and though others would use such material as a reason to boast, Paul would not. He goes on to reflect his change of heart from an arrogant Pharisee to a humble servant of the living Christ:

> But whatever was to my profit I now consider loss for the sake of Christ. What is more, I consider everything a loss compared to the surpassing greatness of knowing Christ Jesus my Lord, for whose sake I have lost all things. I consider them rubbish, that I may gain Christ and be found in him, not having a righteousness of my own that comes from the law, but that which is through faith in Christ—the righteousness that comes from God and is by faith. I want to know Christ and the power of his resurrection and the fellowship of sharing in his sufferings, be-

coming like him in his death, and so, somehow, to attain to the resurrection from the dead. (Phil. 3:7–11)

What a transformation of attitude! His initial references to "profit" and "loss" in verse 7 are accounting terms, showing that his value system had now radically changed. The accomplishments and credentials of an educated Pharisee, previously a source of pride, moved from the positive to the negative side of the ledger. Pride in human righteousness and accomplishments is now seen as a handicap ("I now consider loss," "I consider them rubbish") to true spirituality. The term translated "rubbish" in Philippians 3:8 is actually so strong in the Greek that the translators have not used the literal meaning—dung or manure. Paul is disgusted and repulsed by his former attitudes as a Pharisee, and now values the righteousness of Christ over all. The bragging points on his former résumé have been deleted so that he can focus on Christ's accomplishments rather than his own.

In this passage, we find that Paul's new passion includes knowing Christ through "the fellowship of sharing in his sufferings" (Phil. 3:10). Those who hated Christ looked upon his suffering and death as a symbol of weakness and defeat, but early Christians saw them as symbols of victory. How do you view them? Was Jesus weak when he did not fight back? Was he a failure because he accepted and submitted to suffering? Of course not! How about you? Are you willing to be persecuted for Christ? Can you accept that status quo in the Christian experience guarantees you will have suffering and trials? This is a crucial question for all of us because it determines how we view our lives.

The apostle Paul—the transformed Pharisee—boasted in his suffering. In 2 Corinthians 11:30, he says, "If I must boast, I will boast of the things that show my weakness," and later concludes, "For when I am weak, then I am strong" (12:10). The formerly proud Pharisee brags about a new identity that was completely foreign to his previous ways of thinking. As in the Philippian church, some false teachers had evidently infiltrated the Corinthian church and had led the Corinthian Christians astray through a false gospel. They also brought false charges against Paul (10:7–11; 11:12–15). Because these false teachers deceived the Corinthians through boasting about their superior credentials, Paul is tempted to boast of his qualifications as well (11:18, 21–23). He, too, came from the best Hebrew stock and had demonstrated unsurpassed dedication to his spiritual leader, Christ. As Paul recounts his sacrificial service (vv. 23–29), he realizes that all the things he is "boasting" about would be seen in his former life as evidence of failure—in prison frequently, flogged severely (thirty-nine lashes five times), beaten with a rod (three times), stoned, and so forth. That is the reason he exclaims, "If I must boast, I will boast of the things that show my weakness" (v. 30).

By all standards, ancient and modern, Paul's training and position of authority within Judaism were very impressive. But after meeting Christ, he defined success and presented his résumé differently. What he previously considered qualities of weakness were now badges of success. Why? Because he had adopted Jesus' way of looking at life. As he processed life, he regularly asked the question, "What would Jesus think about this?" This is what makes Christians so different from other people.

Are you willing to wear that badge? Historically, living for Jesus has meant imprisonment for some, physical beatings for others, and even the death of a martyr for yet others. Early Christian Jews were excommunicated from the temple and synagogues, stripped of their possessions, and ostracized from family and friends.

For most of us in the contemporary church, there are lesser prices to pay. Living the moral life of a Christian may mean that we are ostracized by friends because we just do not fit into an accepted lifestyle. It may determine who will go out on a date with you, and ultimately who you will marry. I recently talked with a Christian secretary who had been fired from her job because she was unwilling to cover up the unethical practices of her boss and lie to clients over the phone. Living the moral life of a Christian may mean that we encounter ethical conflicts with the world.

The Fragrance of a Wallflower

The Merriam-Webster Dictionary defines *wallflower* as "a person who from shyness or unpopularity remains on the sidelines of a social activity." Wallflowers experience an array of emotions relating to this isolation. In athletics, it's the sadness I can remember feeling as a child when we chose up sides to play softball and I was the last one to be picked. Socially, it's the loneliness felt by someone who is never invited out by a group of friends. Or, perhaps it's the sadness that comes when you visit a church several times and no one talks to you. Almost all of us enjoy being included in a group and would not choose to be a loner or a wall-flower. But, as the Scripture passages we have investigated in this chapter remind us, sometimes being different is good! Though persecution for the cause of Christ can be a brutal trial or at best a difficult pill to swallow, it is only through such experiences that people really see the difference that Jesus makes. It is the unexpected responses, like the football player with spit on his face, that speak the loudest and don't go unnoticed.

While I was going to seminary, I took an evening job as a janitor to pay the tuition bills. Though I got along fine with the other night-shift janitors, it became obvious that I did not enter into their coffee break conversations, which usually centered on dirty jokes and discussions about their latest sexual conquests. My lack of participation was not viewed favorably by most members of the group, and they would have nothing to do with me. I hadn't said a word about Jesus, but one of the young men asked me privately if I was a Christian. My silent lifestyle witness attracted the interest of two men in that group, and I was able to share the good news of Christ with them.

This story illustrates something very significant about trials that result from living for Jesus. What we would seek to avoid may actually be God's preferred way of doing things. As Paul explains in 2 Corinthians 2:15–16, "We are to God the aroma of Christ among those who are being saved and those who are perishing. To the one we are the smell of death; to the other, the fragrance of life." The very reason why some people hate Christians and the lifestyle we live is because they hate Christ and the righteousness he represents. A non-Christian may not understand that, but we who follow Christ *must* understand it. As we saw earlier in the chapter, a sinful world has a built-in antagonism to the righteousness of Christ. Remember, if you are living for the Lord, your life is part of a bigger story. This is not personal rejection but adversity to Jesus. But that same "smell of death" (v. 16) for some is a "fragrant aroma" for others as they see the refreshing difference that Christ makes. Just as hatred is not really directed toward us but to Christ, so a favorable response is not directed to us but to Christ who lives in us. Divine appointments often come during times of trial when people see in us a response that is unexpected but refreshing. Jesus says this when he commands us to love our enemies:

> But I tell you who hear me: Love your enemies, do good to those who hate you, bless those who curse you, pray for those who mistreat you. If someone strikes you on one cheek, turn to him the other also. If someone takes your cloak, do not stop him from taking your tunic. . . .
>
> If you love those who love you, what credit is that to you? Even "sinners" love those who love them. And if you do good to those who are good to you, what credit is that to you? Even "sinners" do that. And if you lend to those from whom you expect repayment, what credit is that to you? Even "sinners" lend to "sinners," expecting to be repaid in full. But love your enemies, do good to them, and lend to them without expecting to get anything back. Then your reward will be great, and you will be sons of the Most High, because he is kind to the ungrateful and wicked. Be merciful, just as your Father is merciful. (Luke 6:27–29, 32–36)

Arthur's Story: Loving Those Who Have Hated You

There is a church in the town of Nyarubuye, Rwanda, that is no longer a place of worship but a tomb for thousands of Rwandans massacred there in the genocide of 1994. They were not killed because they were Christian, but because they were Tutsis, the Rwandan minority that was threatened with extermination at the hands of the Hutu majority. In four short months, more than 800,000 Tutsis were hunted down and brutally murdered by former friends, neighbors, and even family members.

Arthur was a teenager at the time of the genocide, a member of a well-known and prosperous Tutsi family. During the nightmare months of the massacre, he was forced to flee his home and run for his life, pursued by crazed Hutu militia members armed with machetes. He slept in the jungle, hid in toilet pits, and was shot but survived. He returned to his hometown to find rotting bodies lying in the streets and homes. Eventually he escaped Rwanda, and with two brothers and a sister, entered America as a refugee.

The Catholic and Anglican traditions of faith have a strong following in Rwanda, and Arthur was familiar with the gospel when he arrived in America. After beginning at a university on the West Coast, he became a devoted follower of Christ, growing into a strong love of the Lord and a commitment to be fully obedient to his Word.

After graduation, Arthur married a longtime friend and classmate, and as the genocide faded into a vague memory for most of the world, Arthur and Amy began to pray to discern whether God would use them as ambassadors of his love and healing in Rwanda.

Eight years after the genocide, Arthur and his new wife returned to the church in Nyarubuye, to the memorial place of the horror that had threatened to destroy him, his family, and his nation. They had heard the Lord's clear calling on their lives to return to Rwanda, to work alongside the Hutu farmers, to use their lives to give physical expression of the love of the Father to his wounded and broken children.

Arthur's body bears physical scars of a crime that was meant to take his life and that threatened to destroy an entire people. But the physical wounds are only a reflection of the deep spiritual wounds that have scarred the hearts of Hutus and Tutsis alike. Arthur and Amy have returned to Rwanda to share the love of Christ in a very tangible way— through forgiveness, compassion, and mercy. Their love is not just for fellow Tutsis who suffered so horribly but also—equally—for the Hutu oppressors. Arthur and Amy's physical ministry of mercy is an outward expression of the spiritual reconciliation they are seeking, a healing of the relationships between one person and another, and between humankind and God.

DISCUSSION QUESTIONS

1. Have you experienced a trial that came upon you as a result of something you said or did as a Christian? What specifically brought on the response you received? Did the incident result in a positive testimony for Christ? If you had it to do over again, would you say or do the same thing?

2. As you reflect on stories from the New Testament about Christian persecution, why do you think many Christians today do not go through as much persecution as the early Christians did? Comparing the cultural situation in the New Testament to the way things are today, do you think the experience of persecution has a positive effect on Christians and the church?

3. What do you think Peter means in 1 Peter 4:13 when he says we "participate in the sufferings of Christ" when we are persecuted for him? In what way do we share in Christ's sufferings, and what aspects do we not share?

4. Read the story of Arthur at the end of chapter 6. As best you can, describe how you would respond to the genocide of your own family and people? What would it take for you to love your enemies as Arthur did?

5. Imagine yourself as a successful Christian businessperson. Think through the implications of Paul's statement, "When I am weak, then I am strong" (2 Cor. 12:10). If you really want to exemplify an attitude of humility, in what areas of your career and life will you have conflicts?

Part 3

LIFE'S HARDSHIPS AND HEARTACHES

Thinking Right When Things Go Wrong

Chapter 7

Life's Full of Tough Choices, Isn't It?

One of my daughters' favorite movies, which they owned and watched repeatedly growing up, was the full-length animated version of *The Little Mermaid*. Like dads of daughters do, I watched it with them numerous times. The music is catchy and memorable, but my favorite character in the story is the villain Ursula, an unscrupulous octopus sea hag. She skillfully makes a bargain with Ariel to help the little mermaid attract the human prince whom she loves. Ursula offers to make Ariel human for a limited time, *but* if the prince does not respond, Ariel will forever be the slave of the wicked Ursula. As Ariel contemplates how much she might lose in the process, Ursula offers this brutal assessment of life: "Life's full of tough choices, isn't it?"

Yes, life is like that. Some of the toughest choices appear in the most difficult of times, when we are in the "survival mode" of life, just trying to cope with difficult people or circumstances. During these times, it feels as if even God has abandoned us; we wonder if it's time to give up and take matters into our own hands. Like Ursula, Satan's words are brutal and honest: "Life's full of tough choices, isn't it?" Much like the decisions that Eve and Adam had to make in Eden, the choices we must make about God when we suffer are not easy. And it isn't easy to think clearly while under pressure, which is all the more reason to prepare for that moment, so that when it comes we will know how to react and what to choose.

Thus far, we have focused on some important questions about God:

"What is the Lord doing when he permits trials to enter our lives? What are *his* purposes for allowing suffering in our life experiences? God does not leave us without resources, as we will see in the final two chapters. But first I want to focus on you—and me! How do we respond when trials come? Two factors that might cause us to miss God's best are ignorance and lack of obedience. Without knowledge of the truth from Scripture about suffering, we are left to decipher life on our own without the advantage of a larger, divine perspective. But even if we read and digest every word of Scripture on the subject of suffering, we may still fail to see the results that God promises for our lives. How so? Knowledge must always be followed by obedience. We may miss God's best simply because we do not practice what we know to be true. In one of Jesus' greatest recorded messages, the Sermon on the Mount, he concludes with the following warning:

> Therefore everyone who hears these words of mine and puts them into practice is like a wise man who built his house on the rock. The rain came down, the streams rose, and the winds blew and beat against that house; yet it did not fall, because it had its foundation on the rock. But everyone who hears these words of mine and does not put them into practice is like a foolish man who built his house on sand. The rain came down, the streams rose, and the winds blew and beat against that house, and it fell with a great crash. (Matt. 7:24–28)

Jesus knew that truth will be tested by the storms of life, and that it will not have its intended effect until it is acted upon.

I have officiated at many weddings and have learned that the words spoken by the pastor are appreciated most when they are personal and brief. One of the words of wisdom I try to pass along in every wedding (to the couple *and* the audience) is that the covenant of marriage will be tested most during the storms of life, not when life is going well. In life, as in marriage, the ultimate test of how firmly we have embraced the truth is found when we face adversity.

God has a greater perspective than we do about the role of suffering in our world, and for that reason he has given us specific commands, or exhortations. The primary focus in this chapter will be to revisit some of the passages on trials and to define more clearly what we are commanded to think or do in difficult situations. In preparation for this, however, we begin with some wisdom from the Old Testament that provides a very helpful backdrop to wise New Testament living.

How Does God "Make Your Paths Straight"?

I recently bought my wife a Hallmark anniversary card that begins, "I wouldn't change a thing—not one second . . . not one syllable . . . not one smile or sorrow of all we've shared over all the years." Yes, after more than thirty years of marriage, our life together is still a wonderful journey. In the early days, we adopted Proverbs 3:5–6 as our life verses, and we have often found these words to be relevant:

> Trust in the LORD with all your heart
>   and lean not on your own understanding;
> in all your ways acknowledge him,
>   and he will make your paths straight.

Though the last line is sometimes translated "and he will direct your paths," the intent is more than simple guidance. The words literally mean that God will "make your paths straight," promising guidance *and* a smoother or better way of life. Later in the same passage, this idea is supported by the statement that wisdom's "ways are pleasant ways, and all her paths are peace" (Prov. 3:17). The same God who places or allows obstacles in the pathways of life may also remove them and protect us from other problems. These verses in Proverbs are part of the wisdom literature of Israel, the collection of inspired sayings for God's covenant people. Writings such as Job, Proverbs, Ecclesiastes, and the wisdom psalms taught the Israelites how to live life as God intended it to be lived. Put simply, wisdom literature was intended to teach followers of God the skill of living life. Living skillfully does not come naturally because in most cases sin leads to self-centered choices. We need the instruction of God's wisdom to be successful at life, at least the way God designed us to live. Proverbs 3:5–6 are actually part of an excellent summary of wise living:

Let love and faithfulness never leave you;
    bind them around your neck,
    write them on the tablet of your heart.
Then you will win favor and a good name
    in the sight of God and man.

Trust in the LORD with all your heart
    and lean not on your own understanding;
in all your ways acknowledge him,
    and he will make your paths straight.

Do not be wise in your own eyes;
    fear the LORD and shun evil.
This will bring health to your body
    and nourishment to your bones.

Honor the LORD with your wealth,
    with the firstfruits of all your crops;
then your barns will be filled to overflowing,
    and your vats will brim over with new wine.

My son, do not despise the LORD's discipline
    and do not resent his rebuke,
because the LORD disciplines those he loves,
    as a father the son he delights in.

Blessed is the man who finds wisdom,
    the man who gains understanding,
for she is more profitable than silver
    and yields better returns than gold.
She is more precious than rubies;
    nothing you desire can compare with her.
Long life is in her right hand;
    in her left hand are riches and honor.
Her ways are pleasant ways,
    and all her paths are peace.

> She is a tree of life to those who embrace her;
> those who lay hold of her will be blessed.
>   —Prov. 3:3–18

Notice the intentional pattern in this passage. A blessed life doesn't happen by chance but comes through a healthy relationship of obedience to God's commands. The cause-and-effect relationship between our obedience and God's blessing pervades this section of Scripture:

Attitudes of Wise Living	Blessings from Wise Living
Faithful commitment to God: "love and faithfulness" (v. 3).	Favor and good reputation with God and others (v. 4).
Dependence on God in our thinking, rather than on our limited human understanding: "trust," "lean not" (vv. 5–6).	Guidance and favor in life's circumstances: "he will make your paths straight" (v. 6).
Humility and obedience to God's commands: "do not be wise," "fear the Lord," and "shun evil" (v. 7).	Good health (v. 8).
Generosity in worship and giving to God: "Honor the Lord with your wealth" (v. 9).	Material blessings (v. 10).
Submission to God's discipline: "do not despise," "do not resent" (v. 11).	We know God's discipline is that of a loving father (v. 12).
Summary—live wisely (vv. 13–18): "finds wisdom," "gains understanding" (v. 13), "those who lay hold of her [wisdom]" (v. 18).	Blessedness (vv. 13, 18), long life (v. 16), riches (v. 16), honor (v. 16), a pleasant and peaceful life (v. 17).

Good Choices Pay Off and Poor Choices Bring Consequences

When my daughter Kara and my son-in-law Casey were married, two families that have quite a legacy of married life were joined together. Present at the wedding were all four sets of grandparents, all of whom had been married fifty years or more; and parents on both sides who had been married more than twenty-five years. The total of all six original marriages represented a legacy of more than 280 years, which was now being passed along to Kara and Casey. James Dobson's *Focus on the Family* picked up the story, and even Paul Harvey reported it as something extraordinary today. Our marriages are not perfect, but the statement we made to our children was intended to make an impact on their future choices as well.

My wife and I have tried to pass along a spiritual heritage to our children and grandchildren. Both of our daughters now live productive adult lives and have chosen to follow God in their relationships and their pursuits. We know that this is true partly because of the spiritual encouragement from our home, plus a huge measure of God's grace on our family. My wife and I are proud of them and the choices they have made in life.

Of course, children may in some cases choose to go their own way, even in a godly home (Prov. 30:11). But if parents train up a child in the ways of the Lord (22:6) and model authentic faith in the home (Deut. 6:6–7), children are far more likely to follow the Lord in their adult lives. This is a principle that my wife and I have lived by, even though we knew we would not be perfect parents. We passed along a value system and a spiritual example from our parents that our children will likely pass along to their children. Our family legacy is centered in our relationship with God and is built on the premise that obedience to God pays off in life.

The model of life pictured in Proverbs 3:3–18 is one that God gave to his Old Testament covenant people, Israel. It was not a new idea even then, for the conviction that there are good and bad consequences to the choices we make has always been foundational to healthy civilizations, homes, and relationships since the Garden of Eden. God formalized this principle in the covenant he made with Israel, which is summarized in

Exodus 19–24 and the book of Deuteronomy. Though Deuteronomy is sometimes characterized as a book of rules and laws, there is actually more there about the affectionate love of God for his people than in any other Old Testament book. Jesus quoted Deuteronomy more than any other book, because it describes the essential relationship between blessing and obedience, between loving God and obeying him.

Moses recorded God's law in Deuteronomy much like a contract would be established between a great king and his people. One of the most important chapters is Deuteronomy 28. After all the details of God's commands were stipulated in earlier chapters, chapter 28 promises (and accurately predicts) what would happen in response to Israel's choices. Put simply, their obedience would result in abundant blessing, but their disobedience would lead to God's discipline. This chapter, in fact, provides a template to understand the rest of the story of the Old Testament. When Israel or her leaders followed God, they were blessed with victory and prosperity; in contrast, when they disobeyed and followed other gods (which was most of the time), God withheld blessing and disciplined them.

This cause-and-effect pattern is reflected in Israel's wisdom literature as well, and especially in statements like those in Proverbs 3 above. Because we as Christians do not live in a theocracy like Israel (a government with God as the head), there are obviously things

> God responds with blessing when we obey him, but with discipline when we disobey.

that differ in our new covenant relationship. Material prosperity, for example, is not emphasized in the same way in the New Testament as it was in the Old Testament. Though many of us as Christians have received God's material blessings when we give to the Lord first and generously (Prov. 3:9–10), we are not to take this as an absolute promise or blame God when it doesn't happen. Such thinking is a distorted view of God's principles from the Old Testament, for even the Israelites did not think this way. Having recognized these old and new covenant differences, however, please don't miss the principle that is exactly the same in the Old and New Testaments: God responds with blessing when we obey him, but with discipline when we disobey. I have already addressed the subject of disobedience in chapter 1, but what are some examples of God's blessing of obedience?

Let's return to Proverbs 3:5–6: "Trust in the LORD with all your heart . . . in all your ways acknowledge him, *and he will make your paths straight*" (italics added). Later in the same context, verse 17 says of living wisely, "[Wisdom's] ways are pleasant ways, and all her paths are peace." *Shalom.* Peace. Life at its best. This blessing is more than just God's guidance; it also embodies God's actual intervention of blessing into our lives. When God "makes your paths straight" he may be keeping you from harm or tragedy that can easily befall any of us in a sinful world. But, even if trials or suffering come upon us, we live in his *shalom,* the peace of God. Paul says, "Do not be anxious about anything, but in everything, by prayer and petition, with thanksgiving, present your requests to God. And the peace of God, which transcends all understanding, will guard your hearts and your minds in Christ Jesus" (Phil. 4:6–7).

Life is full of tough choices, but knowing the relationship between obedience and God's hand of blessing motivates us. Consider these additional statements about God's *shalom* from the wisdom of Proverbs:

> When calamity overtakes you like a storm,
> when disaster sweeps over you like a whirlwind,
> when distress and trouble overwhelm you.
> Then they [mockers and fools] will call to me
> but I will not answer;
> they will look for me but will not find me. . . .
> But whoever listens to me will live in safety
> and be at ease, without fear of harm.
> —Prov. 1:27–28, 33

> He holds victory in store for the upright,
> he is a shield to those whose walk is blameless,
> for he guards the course of the just
> and protects the way of his faithful ones.
> —Prov. 2:7–8

My son, preserve sound judgment and discernment,
> do not let them out of your sight;
they will be life for you,
> an ornament to grace your neck.
Then you will go on your way in safety,
> and your foot will not stumble;
when you lie down, you will not be afraid;
> when you lie down, your sleep will be sweet.
Have no fear of sudden disaster
> or of the ruin that overtakes the wicked,
for the LORD will be your confidence
> and will keep your foot from being snared.
>
> —Prov. 3:21–26

Thinking Right When Things Go Wrong

With this background, let's return to the major New Testament passages on trials and look specifically at the commands that God gives us. Are you surprised that almost all of them are *attitudes* rather than *actions*? Thinking correctly means we have "the mind of Christ" when trials come upon us. Let's take a closer look at the three most prominent commands that appear in God's wisdom about suffering.

1. Don't be surprised by trials and suffering—expect and prepare for them. Several years ago, a young couple in our church met with me to talk about a serious health issue that had been diagnosed in their newborn baby. I expressed my concern for their situation and prayed with them about it, but the conversation quickly turned to the question of healing. While I assured them that God could heal their child, I told them I did not know 100 percent that he would. I offered to come with our elders and pray for the healing of their baby, but they seemed more interested in pursuing an extended theological discussion about healing. Ultimately, after several subsequent meetings, the couple left our congregation for another church that held views more compatible with their theology. At their new church they were told that if they sought God with enough faith, their baby would be healed. I felt deep sorrow for this young couple. Life had dealt them tragic circumstances, but their tragedy was compounded by a viewpoint that would not let them trust in and submit to God's plan, whatever it might be.

As we've seen in several Scripture passages (i.e., 2 Tim. 3:12; 1 Peter 2:21; 4:12; James 1:2; 1 John 3:13), trials are inevitable for Christians. Job's story in the Old Testament indicates that trials may come for God's glory in order to build in us a deeper faith. Therefore, we must prepare ourselves mentally and spiritually. James, in writing to Christians who were suffering, gives these commands for spiritual preparation:

> Come near to God and he will come near to you. Wash your hands, you sinners, and purify your hearts, you double-minded. Grieve, mourn and wail. Change your laughter to mourning and your joy to gloom. Humble yourselves before the Lord, and he will lift you up. (James 4:8–10)

Hebrews 12:1, which was also written to suffering Christians, shows the importance of a humble and repentant heart: "Let us throw off everything that hinders and the sin that so easily entangles, and let us run with perseverance the race marked out for us." Running this race means we cannot think like the world thinks, for when we do we usually misconstrue suffering. Notice the advice that the apostle Paul gives the church in Rome about the importance of right thinking:

> Don't let the world around you squeeze you into its mold, but let God remold your minds from within, so that you may prove in practice that the plan of God for you is good, meets all his demands and moves toward the goal of true maturity. (Rom. 12:2 PHILLIPS)

The most effective preparation for facing trials happens long before the trials themselves. It involves developing a biblical, spiritual mind-set that humbles itself before God and is willing to serve him wherever that may lead. You may be reading this book right now because you are going through a trial and are seeking answers. As important as your immediate need is, the future is perhaps even more important. I hope the truth found in Scripture will become a part of the way you process and perceive life in days to come. What you learn from God's Word right now may have its greatest payoff years from now. Preparation is the key.

Many of us witnessed the 2004 Summer Olympics in Athens, Greece, where the best athletes in the world competed for gold, silver, and bronze medals. We saw stellar performances by Olympic champions. But the real story of each victory was not the emotional medal ceremony or the exciting finish to a race or competition. The real story was told in the years of disciplined training and practice—four years, eight years, an entire career—that developed the skills and fortitude necessary to win. Victory came because the athletes were already prepared. Likewise, if we want to be victorious when trials come our way, we must be prepared. Paul borrows athletic terminology from ancient Greece in describing the preparation necessary for living the Christian life:

> Everyone who competes in the games goes into strict training. They do it to get a crown that will not last; but we do it to get a crown that will last forever. Therefore . . . I beat my body and make it my slave so that after I have preached to others, I myself will not be disqualified for the prize. (1 Cor. 9:25–27)

2. *Don't resent trials or passively tolerate them; rejoice in them, value them, be content in them, for they provide God's greatest opportunities for growth and witness.* The single most impressive command in the Bible about trials is one we would least expect to find: "Rejoice!" Jesus said it (Matt. 5:12; Luke 6:23), and every major biblical writer who writes about suffering says exactly the same thing.

- Luke, about the apostles (Acts 5:40–41) and about Paul and Silas (Acts 16:25)
- Paul (Rom. 5:3–5; 2 Cor. 6:3, 10; 11:30; 12:10; Phil. 4:11–13)
- The writer of Hebrews (Heb. 12:11)
- James (James 1:2)
- Peter (1 Peter 1:6; 4:12–14, 16)

As explained in more detail in chapter 2, the command to rejoice in times of suffering is one of the more difficult aspects of God's instruction to understand and practice, because it goes against the grain of human logic and emotions. However, the frequency of this command in Scripture indicates that it must be very important. Moreover, because the concept of rejoicing is usually found in the form of a command, we can conclude that joy in such situations *is* possible through the resources that God provides for us. He would not command us to do something that is completely impossible—which isn't to say we can do it in our own strength. Certainly, the powerful ministry of the Holy Spirit within us is capable of producing the fruit of joy, peace, and patience in any situation (Gal. 5:22–23).

Joy, or rejoicing, is not primarily an emotion but an act of the will. Because it is commanded, I choose to do it or not do it. Our feelings about a trial, whether positive or negative, will ultimately proceed from the choices we make. The most important thing to remember about biblical joy is that it begins not with our emotions but with our will. Feelings of joy ultimately proceed from a decision to be joyful. In this regard, rejoicing is like contentment; I can choose both regardless of my circumstances. Paul says, "I have learned to be content whatever the circumstances. I know what it is to be in need, and I know what it is to have plenty. I have learned the secret of being content in any and every situation" (Phil. 4:11–12).

One of the more intriguing book titles on my shelf is *Happiness Is a Choice.*[1] I must admit that when I first saw the title, I hated it. At the time, my brother-in-law was in the grasp of clinical depression, and the title seemed to suggest that a depressed person should just change his mind and "snap out of it." After I read the book, however, I understood what the authors were saying and I came to appreciate the title. Here are some of their conclusions after years of education and research in the field of psychotherapy:

> Both of us can say with a deep inner conviction that a majority of human beings do *not* have the inner peace and joy about which I am thinking. We are also convinced that all human beings are capable of having this inner joy and peace if only they will choose it *and* follow the right path to obtain it. It is difficult for many laymen to comprehend that anyone would choose unhappiness

and depression over peace and happiness, but many people do so for a variety of reasons of which they are unaware. Some choose unhappiness to punish themselves for guilt feelings. Others choose unhappiness to manipulate their mates and friends by enlisting their sympathies. . . . Many people do choose happiness but still do not obtain it. The reason for this is that even though they choose to be happy, they seek for inner peace and joy in the wrong places. They seek for happiness in materialism and do not find it. They seek for joy in sexual prowess but end up with fleeting pleasures and bitter long-term disappointments. They seek inner fulfillment by obtaining positions of power in corporations, in government, or even in their own families (by exercising excessive control), but they remain unfulfilled. . . . They have everything this world has to offer except one thing— inner peace and joy.[2]

Apart from severe conditions, such as clinical depression, we do make choices about our attitudes toward life, and those choices have a significant effect on the way we relate to others and to God. As expressed in an earlier quote from Charles Swindoll, we cannot change or control the adverse circumstances of life, but we do have a choice about our attitude toward them.[3]

Biblical joy (or rejoicing) is not devoid of clear thinking and reason; it is simply based on what we know to be true. It is not a blind leap of faith. Granted, joy amidst tragedy is a different response than people would normally expect, but it comes from the conviction that God is at work. Though the circumstances may *feel* negative, God is able to do something positive, and in this we *choose* to rejoice. What exactly is God capable of doing through our trials? Sometimes we know immediately, but most of the time we do not. We may ultimately see God's purposes, but sometimes (like Job) we'll never know. This is where faith is essential for a Christian. Regardless of whether we can see or understand God's desired ends, we can trust that he will "work all things together for good" (Rom. 8:28). In his Word, God has revealed to us an arsenal of truths to equip us to face trials, including the purposes reflected in the chapters of this book. I believe we can prepare for trials by knowing God's truth ahead of time. But, remember, knowing this information is just the first step. We must go on to practice and live the truth as we mature in the Lord.

3. *Don't lose heart, give up, or be ashamed during trials, but persevere through them.* On October 29, 1941, British Prime Minister Winston Churchill visited Harrow School, which he had attended as a boy, and delivered a speech that contained this famous quote:

> Never give in—never, never, never, never, in nothing great or small, large or petty, never give in except to convictions of honour and good sense. Never yield to force; never yield to the apparently overwhelming might of the enemy.

This statement captures Churchill's "bulldog" spirit that galvanized the British people against Nazi Germany during World War II. As we encounter spiritual warfare, we must also have a bulldog spirit of perseverance. Our inspiration to "run with perseverance the race marked out for us" (Heb. 12:1) happens when we "fix our eyes on Jesus, . . . who . . . endured the cross, scorning its shame, and sat down at the right hand of the throne of God" (v. 2). The writer of Hebrews says that when we "consider him who endured such opposition from sinful men, . . . [we] will not grow weary and lose heart" (v. 3). Though Winston Churchill was a man to be admired, he is not our primary inspiration for spiritual battles. Jesus is. His perseverance through suffering demonstrates a tenacity of human spirit that can only come by the Spirit of God. This concept was defined and described in more detail in chapter 2, and here we see it as an act of obedience to God.

> Therefore we do not lose heart. Though outwardly we are wasting away, yet inwardly we are being renewed day by day. For our light and momentary troubles are achieving for us an eternal glory that far outweighs them all. (2 Cor. 4:16–17)

Why Keep on Keeping On?

School was all but impossible for Sparky. He failed every subject in the eighth grade. He flunked physics, Latin, algebra, and English in high school. He didn't do much better in sports. Although he did manage to make the school golf team, he promptly lost the only important match of the year. There was a consolation match and he lost that, too.

Throughout his youth, Sparky was socially awkward. He was not actually disliked by the other students; he wasn't considered consequential enough for that! He was astonished if a classmate ever said hello to him outside of school hours. He never found out how he would have fared on a date. In high school, he never once asked a girl out. He was too afraid of being rejected.

In the eyes of many, Sparky was a loser. Everyone else knew it, so Sparky simply accepted it. But one thing was important to him—drawing—and it was one thing he did well. He was proud of his artwork. Of course, no one else appreciated it. During his senior year in high school, Sparky submitted some cartoons to the editors of his yearbook. They were turned down. Despite this particularly painful rejection, Sparky had found his passion.

After graduating from high school, he wrote a letter to Walt Disney Studios. He was told to send some samples of his artwork, and the subject matter for a cartoon was suggested. Sparky drew the proposed cartoon. He spent a great deal of time on it and on the other drawings. Finally, the reply from the Disney Studios came. He had been rejected once again.

Sparky wrote his own autobiography in cartoons. He described his childhood self, a little-boy loser and chronic underachiever. He was the little cartoon boy whose kite would never fly, who never succeeded in kicking the football, and who became the most famous cartoon character of all: Charlie Brown.

Sparky, the boy who failed every subject in eighth grade and whose work was rejected again and again, was Charles Schulz.

Charles Schulz persevered. He succeeded beyond his wildest imagination. He earned and deserved that success. He had failed at everything else he had tried. He endured rejection. It took a lot of trial and error to finally find out what it was that he was supposed to do. But he never quit. Because Charles Schulz persevered, the world is richer.[4]

Why persevere? I am learning more about this as I watch my grand-daughter develop mobility in her little world. As I write, she is six months old and absolutely determined to get from here to there. First it was rolling over. Now she is beginning to crawl. Determination is written all over her face as she spots a toy across the room and expends tremendous energy to reach her goal. Next she will be learning to walk, then run, skate, ride a bike, and drive a car. Who among us would have succeeded as an adult without a willingness to stick with the learning process until they had mastered these simple skills? And now they come as second nature to us. Perhaps that's why God uses the picture of walking to picture our growing relationship with him. Put simply, we persevere because it is the only way to succeed. When we persevere, we cannot fail.

Present, Past, and Future

There are two extremes that cause us to miss much of life. One is living in the past. Regrets, unfulfilled dreams, guilt about failures, and sins that will not go away all lead to a terrible obsession with what might have been. Living with these thoughts can paralyze our lives and steal the joys and opportunities of the present moment.

The other extreme, living in the future, can be just as devastating. Exaggerated fears of future danger, the humiliation of what people might say if we fail, the obsession of living only for our own selfish goals—these can restrict us as well. If we try to live life in the future, it will never allow us to break the limits of our greatest fears and obsessions.

How much of your life do you live in the past, or in the future. How often do you fail to see the importance of the present moment? The Bible talks about all three time frames, and in so doing it provides us with a healthy balance to guide our thinking. God's proper name in Scripture is *Yahweh*, a Hebrew word meaning "I am who I am," the eternally existent one, the eternally present one. Yet our finite knowledge of God is intricately related to things he has done in the past and things he promises to do in the future. This "past and future" perspective is a great model for our relationship with God and how we process the trials and the blessings of life in the present.

When making choices during times of trial or suffering, thinking about the past can remind us of God's power and his faithfulness. What has God done in your life to bring you to this point? If he has always been faithful, does it make sense that he would fail you now? What things have you learned about God when you faced tough times before? In the words of Psalm 143:4–5, "So my spirit grows faint within me; my heart within me is dismayed. I remember the days of long ago; I meditate on all your works and consider what your hands have done."

How about the future? The charge has sometimes been brought against Christians that we are "so heavenly minded that we're of no earthly good." Taken to the extreme, a future-orientation can distract us from necessary concerns in the present. But the future can also motivate us to live for God. If our difficult moments in the present are part of God's bigger story, then our choices do matter, for the results may have eternal significance. The Bible presents a worldview that includes a view of heaven and God's eternal kingdom that should motivate us to live for him in the present. Perseverance during trials on earth will result in eternal rewards (James 1:12).

Don't let the past or the future dominate your present thoughts and actions, but allow the Lord to use both as you live for him right now. Life is full of tough choices, isn't it? Trials or suffering may make us feel as if God has abandoned us, but he hasn't. He is ever present and available to do his greatest work. Seize the moment!

DISCUSSION QUESTIONS

1. What are some of the tough choices you have had to make in life? Why were they difficult, and how did you go about making a decision? If you had it to do over again, would you choose differently?
2. Read Proverbs 3:5–6 and name one or two examples of times in your Christian life when you have seen this principle at work. What specifically did it mean that God "[made] your paths straight"?
3. What are some of the practical areas of your spiritual life that must be included in the expression "trust in the LORD with all your heart"? Realizing that all of us sin and have areas of immaturity, what things do you consider essential for you to know you are trusting God?

4. Consider the following quote from Charles Swindoll:

> The longer I live, the more I realize the impact of attitude on life. . . . The remarkable thing is we have a choice every day regarding the attitude we will embrace for that day. We cannot change our past. . . . We cannot change the fact that people will act in a certain way. We cannot change the inevitable. The only thing we can do is play on the one string we have, and that is our attitude. . . . I am convinced that life is 10 percent what happens to me and 90 percent how I react to it.[5]

   Do you believe that happiness is a choice? Is happiness the same as contentment? Are there other factors beyond our control that also determine our happiness?

5. How have the past or the future controlled your attitude about life? Have you dealt with guilt or regret that paralyzed your ability to live in the present? If so, what was the cause and why did you allow it to control you? Are there some unfulfilled goals or dreams for the future that keep you from enjoying your life now?

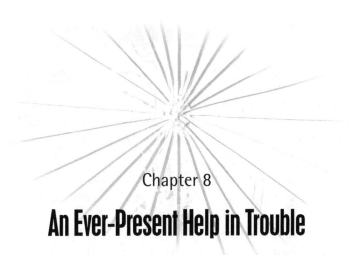

Chapter 8

An Ever-Present Help in Trouble

Ruth's memorial service was exactly the way she wanted it. Everyone present—her two teenage sons, her husband, and her closest friends—saw how personal her relationship with God had been, especially during the difficult battle with liver cancer. Psalm 34 was her favorite passage of Scripture, and Ruth had given me clear instructions to include excerpts from it in her funeral service:

> I sought the LORD, and he answered me;
> he delivered me from all my fears. . . .
>
> Taste and see that the LORD is good;
> blessed is the man who takes refuge in him.
> Fear the LORD, you his saints,
> for those who fear him lack nothing.
> The lions may grow weak and hungry,
> but those who seek the LORD lack no good thing. . . .
>
> The eyes of the LORD are on the righteous
> and his ears are attentive to their cry. . . .
>
> The LORD is close to the brokenhearted
> and saves those who are crushed in spirit.
>
> —Ps. 34:4, 8–10, 15, 18

"Especially those last two verses," instructed Ruth. "I want you to tell people how responsive God has been to me when I was 'brokenhearted and crushed in spirit.'" I had read verses 15 and 18 to her after she learned the news about the cancer. She would not know her grandchildren . . . oh, there were so many experiences that this disease seemed to steal away! Yet God enabled her to understand that she really lacked no good thing. He had used the Psalms, and especially this psalm written by David, to speak to Ruth's soul in a time of great need.

Have you had similar experiences with the Psalms? Have you noticed that often they seem to have been written for just the situation you are in? One of my favorite plans for personal devotions with the Lord is to read five psalms a day, along with the chapter of Proverbs that corresponds with the day of the month. By following this plan, one can read through the entire books of Psalms and Proverbs each month and twelve times in a year. I don't think I have ever done this perfectly, without missing a day, but I am continually amazed at how God uses a particular psalm on a particular day to relate to something in my life. I have often prayed after reading a verse, "Lord, how did you know exactly what I would be going through today?"

The enduring popularity of the Psalms for the past three thousand years demonstrates their unusual connectedness with real life. They describe daily situations as they really happen, yet their brutal honesty is not pessimistic or discouraging. In fact, it's just the opposite. Even in the darkest times of life, the Psalms provide hope, which has united and encouraged generations of believers in a common faith experience.

> The dynamism of history and personal encounter with God exudes from these songs [the Psalms]. They have not only arisen out of history and personal encounter, but have also stood the test of the same. To read and pray the Psalms is to join the voices of numberless people who too have read and prayed them, have felt their joy, anguish, and indignation.[1]

Why do the Psalms minister so effectively? How are they distinctive when compared with other parts of Scripture? How can they be used during times of trial or suffering? These are some of the questions we will address as we seek to understand the unique role of the Psalms in ministry to us during trials.

The Psalms: Divinely Inspired Prayers of Many

How are the Psalms unique when compared to other parts of Scripture? The first and most obvious distinction is that they are in the form of prayers to God. Typically, we think of the Bible as a message *from* God, revelation from God to man. Some of it is even presented as coming directly from the mouth of God. The Old Testament prophet Amos, for example, repeats the phrase "thus says the LORD" forty-one times as he "footnotes" his prophetic message. The same is true of much of the material that Moses received from God on Mount Sinai.[2] In fact, the vast majority of material in both Old and New Testaments was also presented as revelation from God and is recognized as such. The narrative stories of the Old Testament, the wisdom writings (such as Job and Proverbs), the written and spoken messages of the prophets, the Gospel accounts about Jesus, the story of the early church in Acts, and the epistles of Paul, James, Peter, John, and Jude were all addressed to human readers and eventually recognized as God's Word spoken through them (2 Tim. 3:16–17). But the Psalms are different! With the exception of Habakkuk's prophecy, which is also in the form of prayers to God, Psalms represents a unique type of literature in the Bible—prayers, but not just any prayers. These prayers were later incorporated into the Jewish and Christian Scriptures as the Word of God. Revelation from God, but in the form of human expression.

A second unique feature of the Psalms is that they represent a *collection* of writings from many authors[3] over a period of at least nine hundred years.[4] The only other similar biblical collection of writings is Proverbs. The vast majority of biblical books represents a unified message by one author (historical narratives, wisdom writings, prophetic messages, gospels, epistles) who was guided by the Holy Spirit as he wrote (2 Peter 1:20–21).[5] But Psalms represents a collection of the prayers of several writers, and we are encouraged to see what we share in common with them.

What bearing do these historical features have on the ministry of the psalms? As human prayers to God by a variety of believers, they represent common, shared experiences of life. Because they seem to reflect similar situations that are not confined to a particular time or culture, they are believable and true to life. The very purpose for the Psalms requires an honesty on the part of the psalmists. This refreshing authenticity invites us to read on and share in their experiences. We resonate with many of the descriptions and read them as if they were our own. We are encouraged that so many before us have gone through the same struggles, questions, and joys. Both the function of the Psalms, and some of their literary features, make this "up close and personal" experience come alive. In the following sections, we will explore some of the reasons why the Psalms are able to communicate so effectively.

Lament in the Psalms:
An Example of Honesty with God and Others

Deanne recently gave her testimony during our church service. I can remember hearing only one other testimony like it in my life, and both were unique and refreshing in a church setting. Deanne became a Christian as a young adult after growing up with no religion in her family. She was raised by her mom and never personally knew her father. Her mother always said that she had become pregnant as a teenager but had never married. After reaching early adulthood, Deanne decided to try meeting her dad, with no ulterior motives in mind. Her mother gave reluctant approval for her to contact the man she believed was the father. Though making contact was difficult, Deanne finally did and was shocked to find out that the man had no idea he had a child. In fact, he was so surprised that he asked for a paternity test to determine whether it was true. Deanne agreed. When the test results came back negative, Deanne became angry with her mother for the lie she had lived, and demanded the truth. Out came the story that her mother had been unwilling to face: She had been raped and had never told anyone about it. After discovering her pregnancy, she went on believing (perhaps hoping) that the young man she was dating was the father.

Not only would Deanne never know who her father was, but she was now extremely angry with her mother as well. As she shared her story with tears in her eyes, she came to the only reasonable conclusion she could reach in such circumstances: Life stinks! But she went on to share the story of how she came into a relationship with Jesus Christ, and how he transformed her life and gave it meaning. Her story is a powerful, honest reminder of the transformation that God can make in all of us. Through the love of Christ that other Christians have shown her, Deanne is now a beautiful, warm Christian woman. I am so glad she told her story, as difficult as it must have been. Sometimes life really is tough and not fair, and we in the church need to have a place to share our questions, our fears, our struggles, and our growth with others.

Israel did this type of thing through a group of psalms called the lament psalms.[6] These were songs used in worship that honestly expressed the psalmists' concerns, fears, and frustrations about trials and difficult times in life, followed by a statement of trust in God. Put simply, in a lament psalm the psalmist is crying out to God:

> I'm hurting.
> The enemy is winning.
> God, you don't seem to care.

We all know that life on earth isn't always fair, and we don't need to pretend that it is. When I heard Deanne's testimony, I thought immediately of the lament psalms. These songs provided an opportunity for the psalmist to tell his story to the community, and in so doing his honesty served as an encouragement to others who might experience the same thing. But the psalm was not just a gripe session. It also remembered God's deliverance in the past, expressed present trust or confidence in him, and vowed to praise God again in the future. This dynamic is precisely what Paul means in his description of the church as the body of Christ, "If one part suffers, every part suffers with it; if one part is honored, every part rejoices with it" (1 Cor. 12:26). Christians are to share one another's joys, but also one another's sorrows.

When the church fails to be a place where Christians can be honest with one another about the struggles and suffering of life, we become "posers," posturing ourselves to look like something we are not. Our church gatherings can be lonely times with superficial smiles and greetings but little honesty about life. I remember another courageous personal testimony like Deanne's, shared in a large fellowship group of young adults. Tom, who had been a member of the group, had asked the class leader if he could share something very personal with the class. With his wife at his side before a relatively large group, he shared how he had become enamored with another woman who worked in his office, had an affair with her, and seriously considered leaving his wife and children. You could have heard a pin drop in that room, for this was not the usual Sunday morning testimony. Tom then told the story of how the Holy Spirit had convicted him of his sin, and how he had completely broken off the relationship and was trying to restore his marriage. He asked for prayer and support from the group in the days to come. How difficult that must have been! Yet, how refreshing to witness someone who was honest before God and transparent with his Christian friends.

Because the lament psalms can be so encouraging during times of trial, I have included an illustration of one later in this chapter. In short, they model for us the appropriateness of crying out to God when we are hurting. Like Job's lament (Job 3), Jonah's prayer in the belly of the fish (Jonah 2), and Elijah's despair because of the wicked Jezebel (1 Kings 19:1–5), we all hit rock bottom at times. It is not sinful to feel the despair that comes from difficult times. Through the examples of these stories and the lament psalms, we are invited to pour out our hearts to God. We can be honest without being irreverent. In these psalms, lament turns to reflection, and reflection to praise and trust in God. This is exactly where God wants to take us in our spiritual pilgrimage through trials. In addition, some of the lament psalms were intended to be expressed in the congregation, showing the importance of looking to other Christians for support and strength. Don't be a poser! Your honest testimony about the struggles of life can be a great encouragement to others around you.

The Praise of the Psalms: Boasting About God

Even if you have never taken a class on the Hebrew language, you already know one of the most important Hebrew words in the Old Testament: *hallelujah!* It is a two-part word that expresses the central theme of all the Psalms:

Hallelu = give praise to
yah = a short form of Yahweh, the proper name of God

Hallelujah is usually translated "praise the LORD," but this simple expression, which has almost become a cliché in the church, does not fully express the impact of the word. It is a word of excitement, exuberance, and enthusiasm. When one surveys the various examples of praise in the Psalms, they often include the element of boasting. This is not the kind of empty bragging that comes from our own inflated egos. The psalms brag about God, specifically who he is and what he has done. For example, Psalm 113:4–9 describes God as follows:

Who God Is (Descriptive Praise)	What God Has Done (Declarative Praise)
The LORD is exalted over all the nations, his glory above the heavens. (v. 4)	He raises the poor from the dust and lifts the needy from the ash heap; (v. 7)
Who is like . . . the One who sits enthroned on high, (v. 5)	he seats them with princes, with the princes of their people. (v. 8)
who stoops down to look on the heavens and the earth? (v. 6)	He settles the barren woman in her home as a happy mother of children. (v. 9)

Psalms of praise are enthusiastic testimonies about God. When shared with other people, they become tremendously encouraging. To brag about yourself is to be an egotist, and others will ultimately not pay any attention to you. But when you brag about God, you offer people something more substantial, for they can experience a relationship with the same God. And if what you say is true, the same God can meet their needs, just as he has met yours. Listen to the words of David after God's deliverance from a trial:

> I waited patiently for the LORD;
>   he turned to me and heard my cry.
> He lifted me out of the slimy pit,
>   out of the mud and mire;
> he set my feet on a rock
>   and gave me a firm place to stand,
> He put a new song in my mouth,
>   a hymn of praise to our God.
> Many will see and fear
>   and put their trust in the LORD.
>   —Ps. 40:1–3

David's words of praise have a threefold effect: Godward, outward, and inward. God receives praise and honor for what he has done. Others are invited to trust in God and experience the same kind of deliverance. And by praising God we draw our attention away from the hopelessness of our situation to the hope we can find in the Lord. This change in attitude is part of a growth process that enables us to look at future trials with greater faith. This kind of growth is an integral part of what James means when he writes, "Consider it pure joy . . . whenever you face trials" (James 1:2).

Poetry of the Psalms: Words That Visualize Experiences

One of the distinguishing characteristics of the Psalms is that they are all written as poetry. Hebrew poetry provided natural lyrics for worship songs in ancient Israel as it does for the church today. On the surface, the choice of the poetic form seems to affect only the way in which words are arranged on the page. But Hebrew poetry possesses distinct characteristics that add to its effectiveness in communication. Some of these poetic features enhance the Psalms' ability to minister to us in different life situations, especially when we are going through times of suffering or trial.

First, poetry effectively communicates feelings and passion as well as content. It conveys information, but also involves the reader in an experience. When evaluating the message of a psalm, we should ask more than "What does it say?" We must also consider *how* it says what it says. The use of various figures of speech is more common in poetic expression than in prose. One poetic device is the use of metaphor—words that describe through analogies or comparisons. Consider, for example, the introductory words from Psalm 40:1–2:

> I waited patiently for the LORD;
>   he turned to me and heard my cry.
> He lifted me out of the slimy pit,
>   out of the mud and mire;
> he set my feet on a rock
>   and gave me a firm place to stand.

The psalmist, David, has experienced a trial—one that would not go away. Evidently he prayed for God's deliverance, but initially it did not come. So he waited patiently. Have you ever been in that kind of situation? Of course; we all have. Waiting patiently for God to answer prayer is not easy. We become anxious, and the circumstances of life sometimes seem to have a stranglehold on us. In David's situation, he pictures God as a friend or rescuer who hears a cry for help, offers him a strong arm, and lifts him out of "the slimy pit, out of the mud and mire."

Why does David describe his situation like this? Why not just say that he had a problem but God answered his prayer and delivered him? Because by using poetic expression, the powerful word pictures take us into an analogous experience that is much like going through a trial ourselves. We may not have experienced David's exact situation, but it is not difficult to imagine.

As a young boy, I would often visit my cousin, who lived near a river. Because he was older, he was usually the leader for some exciting adventures. One morning very early we walked down to the mudflats, which glistened with a layer of ice from the cold night before. I began to explore, not paying attention to the fact that the warm sun was beginning to melt the ice. Down I went, up to my chest in the slimy pit, the mud and the mire! I was grateful that it was not quicksand and that there was a bottom, but I was truly stuck. If I tried to move forward or climb out, it was as if there were suction cups holding me down. I was scared. My cousin responded to my cries for help, but he could not get near me without sinking himself. So instead he went for help, and I can still remember how fearful I was that I would never get out. He finally came back, this time with a rope, and was able to pull me out while standing on the shore. I will never forget the victorious feeling of standing with my cousin on the rocks at the side of the river, but I will also never forget the relentless hold of that mud.

The details of David's specific problem and deliverance are never mentioned, but we can suggest several possible situations based on information about his life recorded in the historical portions of the Old Testament (1 Sam. 16–2 Sam. 24; 1 Chron. 11–29). For example, is David remembering his experiences as a fugitive after he had been anointed king by Samuel but was hunted by King Saul? Is he making a veiled reference to his adulterous affair with Bathsheba? We simply don't know, and in the nature of the Psalms, David does not tell us specifically. In my opinion, it was God's intent that the psalmist omit specific information about his circumstances because it allows us to relate more readily to the trial. If we knew the specific situation that David is describing, we might dismiss his words with the attitude, "I've never gone through anything like that, so it doesn't apply to me." By using a general metaphor, with no specifics, it allows us to relate our own "slimy pit" experience to David's. His words of testimony encourage us to wait on the Lord, whatever our trial. Even though we feel trapped, God can deliver us to firmer ground.

In this brief metaphor, we also see God pictured as one who initially doesn't know about or respond to David's problem. Depicted in human terms, David says, "He turned to me and heard my cry." This poetic expression, technically called *anthropomorphism* (God described in human terms), is not saying that God all of a sudden discovers that something is wrong. As God, he is all-knowing and aware of every situation you and I encounter. This expression more aptly describes God's response *as we experience it.* Remember, the purpose for poetic expression is to help us enter into an experience. When God answers prayer after we've been waiting on him, it *seems* as if he is just now giving attention and hearing us. There are many examples in Psalms of God being described in human terms. One of my favorites is Psalm 8:3, "When I consider your heavens, the work of your fingers, the moon and the stars, that you have set in place." Our universe, which itself is still beyond the grasp of the most intelligent scientific minds, was simple fingerwork for our Creator God.

Finally, as already mentioned, the experience of helplessness I felt when caught in a pit of mud so aptly describes our feelings during trials. Have you felt trapped by financial needs? Have you felt helpless when someone close to you was diagnosed with cancer? Have you felt sucked in and dragged down by a persistent temptation to sin? The slimy pit, the mud and mire, warn us about the deceptiveness of sin—how what initially seems so innocent can ultimately grasp us like mud in the bottom of a pit.

In contrast, the sensation of having our feet planted firmly on a rock brings feelings of security and hope. Before man-made building materials such as concrete were developed, bedrock was the most stable and secure place for standing or building. Jesus describes one who obeys him as "like a wise man who built his house on the rock" (Matt. 7:24), picturing a life of stability and security.

Many of the psalms that reassure us during times of suffering do so with word pictures. These metaphors are much like abbreviated parables, using familiar images and experiences to encourage believers through unfamiliar times. Think of the encouragement brought through these examples:

1. One who believes in, meditates on, and obeys God's Word is described as "a tree planted by streams of water, which yields its fruit in season and whose leaf does not wither" (Ps. 1:3). This metaphor is especially meaningful in a dry and barren land like Israel, where nothing grows without a source of water nearby.
2. "The LORD is my rock, my fortress and my deliverer; my God is my rock, in whom I take refuge. He is my shield and the horn of my salvation, my stronghold" (Ps. 18:2). This series of metaphors communicates the strength and security to be found in God during times of trial.
3. "The LORD is my shepherd" (Ps. 23:1; see also 80:1) is perhaps the best-known psalm about God's care and guidance of his own, especially when we're walking through the valley of the shadow of death. Anyone who understands the intimate, personal relationship between

a dutiful shepherd and each of his sheep is instantly reassured through this metaphor.[7]

4. "You [God] are my hiding place; you will protect me from trouble" (Ps. 32:7). Psalm 32 was written after David's great moral failure with Bathsheba and his experience of repentance and forgiveness. These words describe the safety and security he found (and that we can find) by seeking God.

5. "As the deer pants for streams of water, so my soul pants for you, O God" (Ps. 42:1). These words, written in a time of trial, describe the desperation of a helpless deer to find life-sustaining water (Ps. 42:3, 5–6). They communicate the kind of intense spiritual dependence and thirst we are to have for God.

6. "God is our refuge and strength, an ever-present help in trouble" (Ps. 46:1). This psalm of confidence pictures God's personal presence among his people, especially during times of natural disaster (vv. 2-3) or times of insecurity, such as war (vv. 6, 9). In the repeated theme of the psalm, God is referred to with the metaphors "our refuge," "our strength," and "our fortress," and he is described in the phrase "an ever-present help in trouble" (vv. 1, 7, 11). These pictures of God appear together often in the Psalms and communicate the security we find by trusting in him during trials.[8] God, as our strength, is there for us in the times when we feel very weak. As our refuge, he is the source of our safety, rest, and security. The fortress was an elevated, protected place during war from which soldiers could withstand the attacks of the enemy. The New Testament makes it clear that we are regularly engaged in spiritual warfare (Eph. 6:10–18), and that this conflict is related to our trials and suffering. How comforting to know that God is our fortress in such times!

7. "Save me, O God, for the waters have come up to my neck. I sink in the miry depths, where there is no foothold. I have come into the deep waters; the floods engulf me. I am worn out calling for help" (Ps. 69:1–3; see also vv. 14–15). Here, the slimy pit metaphor is expanded to picture David being engulfed by rising floodwaters. There is an urgency about his prayer, and God is dramatically pictured as rescuing him from the waters of a flood.

8. Psalm 80:8–16 develops the metaphor of Israel as a precious vine

and God as the vinedresser who protects it and nurtures it to produce fruit. It is not an accident that Jesus' "I am" statements in the gospel of John intentionally use these word pictures to describe himself in the messianic role.

9. "The LORD has established his throne in heaven, and his kingdom rules over all" (Ps. 103:19). This is a powerful psalm that praises God with a litany of his qualities and works of redemption—forgiveness of sins (vv. 3, 12), healing of disease (v. 3), redemption (v. 4), love (vv. 4, 8, 11, 17), compassion (vv. 4, 8, 13), renewal (v. 5), righteousness (vv. 6, 17), justice for the oppressed (v. 6), graciousness (v. 8), and longsuffering (v. 8). God's rule from his throne is a picture in the Old Testament of his omnipotence and sovereignty over all others.

Poetry of the Psalms:
The Value of Restatement and Repetition

My favorite Latin expression is *repetitio est mater estudiorum,* "repetition is the mother of learning." It is my favorite, in part because it is the only phrase I can remember from two years of high school Latin, but more importantly, because it is true. The Psalms utilize repetition and restatement effectively and artistically to help us understand and learn. Hebrew poetry provides a natural way to do this, called *parallelism.* One of the common features of Western poetry is the repeating and rhyming of sounds, especially those at the ends of lines. Consider Robert Louis Stevenson's poem "The Swing," in which we can observe repetitive rhyme:

> Wouldn't you like to go up in a swing
>   Up in the sky so blue?
> Oh I think it's the pleasantest thing
>   Ever a child can do.

Part of the artistry of the poem is the common ending sound of every other line. Rather than paralleling sounds of words, however, Hebrew poetry "rhymes" ideas, placing them alongside one another. Two (sometimes three) lines are written together (as a unit), and the relationship of their meaning is intended by the poet to add artistry and meaning to the poem. There are many types of parallelism, but by far the three most common are comparisons, completions, and contrasts.

Type of parallelism	Meaning	Example
Comparisons	Line B essentially restates line A in different words.	**A** The heavens declare the glory of God; **B** the skies proclaim the work of his hands. (Ps. 19:1)
Completions	Line B elaborates on the meaning of line A.	**A** But his delight is in the law of the LORD, **B** and on his law he meditates day and night. (Ps. 1:2)
Contrasts	Line B presents the opposite of line A.	**A** For the LORD watches over the way of the righteous, **B** but the way of the wicked will perish. (Ps. 1:6)

The Hebrew poets, including David, were masters in the artistry of parallelism. Some psalms contain even more sophisticated types, but I have introduced these few examples simply to help you appreciate some of the depth of the Psalms, including their ability to teach us truth that is vital in helping us face life's challenges. Comparisons, for example, are often used to restate and repeat an idea in different words, which helps us to understand the idea more clearly. Contrasts, which usually include the word *but* in the translation, clarify ideas by providing a contrasting side of the truth. Completions, as the word suggests, finish an idea by providing further explanation or information. Perhaps the best way to appreciate parallelism, as well as the other distinctives of the Psalms, is by exploring how these unique features of poetry contribute to the ministry of a psalm.

Psalm 32: The Joy of Experiencing Forgiveness

The paralysis of extreme guilt is one of the more difficult trials we can face. We may fear that our lives will never be right again. My daughter Kara has participated in a prison-visitation ministry at the state penitentiary and discovered during her visits that the most serious barrier to the female inmates' salvation was their inability to believe that God could forgive them for what they had done. Psychologists tell us that the most common factor leading to serious emotional problems or depression—for all of us, not just prisoners—is the inability to experience complete forgiveness.

In Psalm 51, King David writes about the most serious moral failure of his life: his adultery with Bathsheba, the subsequent murder of her husband, and the deception that accompanied it. Although these events are not directly mentioned in the psalm, a notation at the beginning gives us the background information: "For the director of music. A psalm of David. When the prophet Nathan came to him after David had committed adultery with Bathsheba."[9] In the psalm, David confesses his guilt and cries out to the Lord for mercy:

> For I know my transgressions
> and my sin is always before me.
> Against you, you only, have I sinned
> and done what is evil in your sight,
> so that you are proved right when you speak
> and justified when you judge. . . .
>
> Cleanse me with hyssop, and I will be clean;
> wash me, and I will be whiter than snow.
> Let me hear joy and gladness;
> let the bones you have crushed rejoice.
> Hide your face from my sins
> and blot out all my iniquity.
>
> Create in me a pure heart, O God,
> and renew a steadfast spirit within me.
> —Ps. 51:3–4, 7–10

Although the notation to Psalm 32 does not give any background information beyond David's authorship, scholars generally agree that this psalm makes reference to the same situation as Psalm 51.

Psalm 32 is especially helpful to any Christian who lives with the guilt of serious sin. It is an uplifting psalm of praise that grows out of the glorious transformation and happiness that David finds as a result of knowing and experiencing true forgiveness. Placed in the prominent (beginning) position of the psalm, this is the heart of David's praise:

> Blessed is he
>   whose transgressions are forgiven,
>   whose sins are covered.
> Blessed is the man
>   whose sin the LORD does not count against him
>   and in whose spirit is no deceit.
> —Ps. 32:1–2

In order to help us fully appreciate the height of joy that he expresses in the opening verses, David then takes us back to the depths of his time of guilt. In verses 3–5, he recounts the misery of his life in the aftermath of his sin, the process of coming to his senses, and finally his confession:

> When I kept silent,
>   my bones wasted away
>   through my groaning all day long.
> For day and night,
>   your hand was heavy upon me;
> my strength was sapped
>   as in the heat of summer. Selah.
>
> Then I acknowledged my sin to you
>   and did not cover up my iniquity.
> I said, "I will confess
>   my transgressions to the LORD"—
> and you forgave
>   the guilt of my sin. Selah.

Psalms of praise often contain a section that looks back at a past time of need in order to understand the present reason for praising God.

David's silence before God was for the same reason we sometimes refuse to acknowledge sin. "After all, no one knows about it," we reason to ourselves. "Nobody will ever know." How naive! God knows, and if you are a child of God, God's Holy Spirit lives within you. It's just a matter of time until your conscience, prompted by the Holy Spirit, will begin speaking to you. Remember, as a loving Father, God disciplines those whom he loves (Heb. 12:7–11). He does this through the process of conviction in our hearts, but he also might discipline us using circumstances or other people.

We know from 2 Samuel 12:1–11 that God sent a prophet named Nathan to confront David about his sin. What courage it must have taken for Nathan to do this! David, who was one of the most powerful kings in the world at that time, would have been "above the law" in any other situation. But no one is above God's law, and a confrontation with a true prophet of God was exactly what David needed. Psalm 32 reveals that David was experiencing physical or psychosomatic problems as a result of his refusal to confess his sin. "My bones wasted away" and "my strength was sapped as in the heat of summer" may be poetic ways of describing psychological phenomena, but I am more inclined to take them literally. As a result of his guilt, God had brought upon David physical sickness, and he was miserable—physically, emotionally, and spiritually. This "looking back" section is intended to show the sharp contrast between his situation before and after his confession, thus establishing the reason for praise.

In verse 5, David summarizes his confession:

> Then I acknowledged my sin to you
>   and did not cover up my iniquity.
> I said, "I will confess
>   my transgressions to the LORD"—
> and you forgave
>   the guilt of my sin. Selah.

In Psalm 51, we find an extended expression of the content of David's actual confession, which is only summarized in Psalm 32. Both psalms use the same terminology for sin, and the same words for David's confession, which is the reason that most scholars associate these psalms with the same event.

In Psalm 32, David artistically uses parallelism at its best. He makes three essentially synonymous statements about his sin:

> Blessed is he
>> whose transgressions are forgiven,
>> whose sins are covered.
> Blessed is the man
>> whose sin the LORD does not count against him
>> and in whose spirit is no deceit.
>> —Ps. 32:1–2

The reason we find different terms in our English translations is that David chose three different Hebrew words to describe the various facets of sin. He also chose three distinct words to characterize God's complete forgiveness of sin, which can be summarized as follows:

Sin	What God Has Done with It
transgressions—act of rebellion against God's law and disloyalty to him (v. 1)	*are forgiven*—taken away, showing God's removal of sin, guilt, and remembrance of them
sins—behavior that misses (often intentionally) God's revealed will (v. 1)	*are covered*—God's act of atoning for sin, covering it from his presence and reconciling the sinner to God
sin—iniquity, often an intentional act to do wrong (v. 2)	*does not count against him*—focusing upon God's attitude toward the sinner, who is justified (i.e., declared right with God)

The intentional choice of different words by David in the span of just two sentences is more than stylistic. He uses parallelism to show the complexity of sin and the complete forgiveness of God. The various definitions of these terms, accessible in any good Bible commentary and some study Bibles, show that David had reflected on the far-reaching effects of his sin. I am reminded of the old saying that also applies here: "Oh what a tangled web we weave when first we practice to deceive." When David stood on his rooftop that night and his attention was drawn to a beautiful woman bathing, he could never have known how the simple decision to dwell on her beauty could lead to such ugly complications.

Who would have believed that such a simple choice could lead to the multiplicity of sins that followed—lust, adultery, lying, betrayal, murder, deception. Through the use of various descriptive words, David brings attention to the fact that sin is complicated. Not only had he transgressed the standards of God's law and "fallen short of the mark" of what God expected of him as the king and as a believer (cf. Ps. 51:1–3), he also sinned against other people. He abused his power as Israel's king and ordered the premature death of Uriah, a devoted, effective leader. His lustful actions led to the shame and anguish of a young woman, who was guilty of adultery and lost her husband. In addition, because of David's prominence as king, the scandal became known throughout Israel, and his reputation and influence as a spiritually minded king were permanently diminished.

As David tells his story through poetry, he invites us to enter into his experience. He had been caught in the tangled web of sin, which at the time had seemed so innocent but ultimately was so deceptive. Knowing this, how amazing and thorough was God's forgiveness and restoration? Psalm 32:1–2 is an introductory summary of David's reason for praise and his restored happiness after he received forgiveness. Again, he uses three different terms for God's cleansing because forgiveness is multifaceted and thorough. God covers sin, takes it away, and justifies the sinner. David's cry of freedom, "O the happiness of the one whose transgressions are forgiven!" says it all.

Are you experiencing this kind of forgiveness? Or does the tangled web of sin have its grasp on you? Guilt can be one of the most miserable trials you will ever experience, and the Psalms help map out a road to freedom.

After recounting his great sin and the joy of forgiveness, in a verse of descriptive praise David invites all of us to enter into the joy and peace he has found (Ps. 32:7). God is David's "hiding place," his protection from trouble, one who brings "songs of deliverance." These songs were songs of praise that would have been sung after God delivered Israel from an enemy. David has been delivered from the enemy of guilt and sin.

The psalm goes on to explain why David's story—both his sin and his forgiveness—is being told to others. As indicated in the superscription, it is a *maskil* psalm. Though this Hebrew term at times gives direction to the musicians who accompanied it, the actual root of the word *maskil* probably means "instruction" or "teaching." In other words, David's experiences have been recorded in order to be applied to our lives with the purpose of teaching us. Elaborating on this, David speaks as if his words were directly from God himself. We could legitimately add the words, "Thus says the LORD" before Psalm 32:8–9:

> I will instruct you and teach you in the way you should go;
>> I will counsel you and watch over you.
> Do not be like the horse or the mule,
>> which have no understanding
> but must be controlled by bit and bridle
>> or they will not come to you.

Here we have a powerful illustration that relates to God's discipline. The bit and bridle used when directing a horse are the only ways a human rider can communicate with the animal. The bridle moves the bit in the horse's mouth to produce pressure, perhaps discomfort at first, and the animal learns to respond correctly. God says to us, "You are intelligent human beings, created in the image of God to have an intimate relationship with me. You know my will and desire for your life. Don't be like an animal, requiring me to use the bit and bridle of discipline for sin, to redirect your life in the right direction. Make that decision yourself."

Has God had to use "the bit and bridle" of discipline to lead you away from sin? It's never too late to simply walk with God and experience the joy that David writes about:

Rejoice in the LORD and be glad, you righteous;
sing, all you who are upright in heart!

—Ps. 32:11

Psalm 13: How Long, Lord?

Loneliness hurts. It often comes as the result of a trial. The relenting loneliness of life after your wife of fifty years dies. The loneliness of daily life when your husband's job takes him away from home six days a week; of a young woman who doesn't have a boyfriend when others do; of a middle-aged woman whose husband has just divorced her; of a teenage boy who just doesn't fit in socially. When we feel lonely, it seems as if everyone around has forgotten us— maybe even God has forgotten!

> Though we know that God does not forget anything, nor does he hide his face from us, during a prolonged time of suffering it *seems* as if he does.

The prominence of someone like David causes us to forget that he was human just like we are. He, too, experienced times of intense loneliness in his life. One of the great values of the poetry of the Psalms is its capacity to express this kind of experience. As we read, we are invited to enter into the experience of the writer, to identify with the moods of the psalmist. Such is the case with Psalm 13, a psalm of lament. Bible scholar Claus Westermann identified the typical elements that characterize this type of psalm.[10] In a sense they form a template that helps us to understand the order of Psalm 13 (see page 204).

If God is an eternal God, and he forgets about you, will he forget you forever? Though we know that David did not necessarily believe this literally, this psalm is written when it seems as if God has forgotten about him, maybe even forever! Here the figures of speech, which are common ones in the Psalms, help us to understand the psalmist's desperation. Though we know that God does not forget anything, nor does he hide his face from us, during a prolonged time of suffering it *seems* as if he does. In his cry for help and lament to God, David repeats the question,

Typical Features of a Lament Psalm		Psalm 13
Introductory cry for help		How long, O LORD? Will you forget me forever? (v. 1)
Lament	The enemy	How long will my enemy triumph over me? (v. 2)
	I	How long must I wrestle with my thoughts and every day have sorrow in my heart? (v. 2)
	You (God)	Will you forget me forever? How long will you hide your face from me? (v. 1)
Confession of trust		But I trust in your unfailing love; my heart rejoices in your salvation. (v. 5)
Petition	Hear!	Look on me and answer, O LORD my God. (v. 3)
	Save!	Give light to my eyes, (v. 3)
	Punish!	
Reasons for this petition		or I will sleep in death; (v. 3) my enemy will say, "I have overcome him," (v. 4) and my foes will rejoice when I fall. (v. 4)
Vow of praise		I will sing to the LORD, (v. 6)
Declarative praise		for he has been good to me. (v. 6)

"How long?" four times in just two verses. This is a deeply moving cry for help, and the repetition here shows the intensity of David's raw emotions. It draws our attention to one of the most difficult aspects of David's trial—its longevity. He has prayed and prayed, but God has given no indication that he plans to answer this prayer.

As with most of the psalms, we do not know exactly what David's trial was or who the "enemy" is in verse 4. We do know that the trial had gone on a long time (vv. 1–2) and that David feared death as a result (v. 3). Again, the historical account in 1 and 2 Samuel provides helpful background; we can at least postulate what his circumstances might have been. I think the most likely possibility are the events recorded in 1 Samuel 13–31, *after* David had been named king by God's prophet, Samuel, and *before* the present king, Saul, died. Saul had become insanely jealous of David and continually tried to kill him. During these years, Saul tried to kill David with a spear at least three times, he sent servants to kill him, and he forced David to live in exile (including a stint with the despised Philistines). To add insult to injury, Saul gave David's wife, Michal, to another man. David knew that he had been anointed king, but he was a man of principle and would not kill Saul, even when he had the chance. During these years, David watched Saul's kingdom, *his* kingdom, deteriorate before his eyes because of Saul's obsession to kill David. One year . . . five years . . . ten years . . . for fourteen years this went on! No wonder David pondered the possibility that God had forgotten him.

This is the most difficult part of some situations—it isn't just the trial but also the timing! Through the psalms of lament, God gives us permission to cry out to him. In his prayer, David was honest with God about his anxiety, his sorrow, his doubts—all of his experiences. This is not an unspiritual, selfish prayer but a very spiritual prayer of honesty and trust. David boldly asks God to answer his prayer and deliver him. Because the psalm intentionally does not give the identity of the enemy, we can read it with our own situations in mind. Notice the boldness of David's requests, even giving God reasons why he should deliver him.

The ending of the psalm is perhaps the most important part. Lament psalms are not just "gripe sessions"; they regularly include words of praise and declarations of the psalmist's faith in God. The Hebrew word translated "unfailing love" (Ps. 13:5) is one of my favorites. Sometimes translated "lovingkindness" in the Psalms, this word speaks of the kind, affectionate love that God has for his people, but also the loyalty he promises through his covenant. The loyalty of his love is great encouragement when the circumstances of life make it seem as if God has forgotten us.

This vow of trust in God's loyal love expresses itself in various ways in Psalm 13:5–6:

- *Present*—"My heart rejoices in your salvation"
- *Future*—"I will sing to the LORD"
- *Past*—"For he has been good to me"

The ability to rejoice in God even amid trials gives us the confidence to look forward to days when we will sing praise to God because we know the history of his past deliverance. Past, present, and future are all connected because we can experience God in all of them.

Meditation: The Experience of a Masterpiece

The Psalms have been viewed by many as masterpieces of literature that have perhaps affected more people in human history than any other single collection of writings. Several years ago, I learned something about masterpieces when my wife and I visited the Italian cities of Florence and Rome. We were with a good friend who knew much more about art than we did. When we stood before several masterpieces, our schedule often allowed enough time to take it all in. There is a reason why a work of art is called a "masterpiece." One simply cannot experience and appreciate everything about it in a short time. As we sat near *David*, Michelangelo's famous sculpture, and later viewed some of his paintings and sketches, we were overwhelmed by the artist's detailed knowledge of the physiology of the human body combined with his talent to express it so artistically. We simply could not appreciate everything unless we took sufficient time.

So it is with the Psalms. Not only are they human masterpieces of literature, but they carry with them the voice of the Holy Spirit speaking to our souls. Meditating on the Psalms is not just a spiritual discipline to be admired but an investment of time with huge spiritual payoffs. When we meditate on the Psalms, we allow time for our minds to absorb the truths that are expressed so uniquely there. Like a beautiful sculpture or painting, these masterpieces stimulate mind, emotions, and will. As we think deeply about the meaning of the poetic expressions, we learn a great deal about ourselves and about life. Because many of the psalms were written during or after times of trial, we also learn much about God's presence during tough times. They offer hope and peace and forgiveness, no matter what we are facing. They teach the value of being honest with God as we lament life's struggles; they teach us to praise God, no matter what the test.

DISCUSSION QUESTIONS

1. Reflecting upon the definition and nature of poetry as presented in this chapter, why is so much of the Bible written in this form? What advantages does it have over prose or nonpoetic language?

2. Why were lament psalms an important part of Israel's worship? What do we learn from them that encourages us during times of trials?

3. What is the difference between the words of a lament psalm and a "gripe session" about God? Though a lament psalm expresses dissatisfaction about life's circumstances, in what way does it carry a positive and encouraging message?

4. What is "praise" in the Psalms? Though it's similar to thanksgiving, how is praise slightly different?

5. In what settings in your Christian experience do you praise God? Do you feel you have enough opportunities to do that? What are some of the results when a Christian praises God?

Chapter 9

Standing on the Promises

O ur journey through life—as we know it and as God designed it—will include bumps and potholes, and even some deep valleys. Each of these may become an obstacle or an opportunity, a stumbling block or a stepping-stone, depending on how we respond. Because we all react poorly to trials at times, one of the purposes of this book is to encourage us that there is great hope for growth and maturity in this area. Two significant ingredients bolster our growth process during trials: *an experienced faith* that has already trusted God for smaller things and found victory in the midst of them; and *a focused faith* that finds hope in the greatness of God and his resources, rather than dwelling on the hopelessness of our situation. Just as muscles develop through exercise, so too our "faith muscles" grow when they are tested, and the result is greater strength to face future challenges.

David, the Giant Slayer

One of the all-time favorite children's Bible stories is that of David and Goliath. It is unfortunate that this biblical event has remained a children's story to most Christians, because it possesses a tremendous message for our adult experiences of faith. The setting of David's showdown with the giant Goliath is a military battle in the Valley of Elah. Israel's king and military leader, Saul, had already shown himself to be a man of weak faith (1 Sam. 13:1–14; 15:1–35), unable to deliver Israel from the humiliating domination of their enemies. The battle was not only political but spiritual as well, for Philistine warriors like Goliath used every opportunity to blaspheme the name of God. David at the time was just a teenage shepherd boy, not even old enough to serve in the army. While bringing supplies to his brothers on the battlefield, he overheard the challenges of Goliath. David's response was one of faith: "Who is this uncircumcised Philistine that he should defy the armies of the living God?" (17:26). His words to Saul, who was warning him not to go to battle, illustrate the first ingredient of faith:

> Your servant [David] has been keeping his father's sheep. When a lion or a bear came and carried off a sheep from the flock, I went after it, struck it and rescued the sheep from its mouth. When it turned on me, I seized it by its hair, struck it and killed it. Your servant has killed both the lion and the bear; this uncircumcised Philistine will be like one of them, because he has defied the armies of the living God. The LORD who delivered me from the paw of the lion and the paw of the bear will deliver me from the hand of this Philistine. (1 Sam. 17:34–37)

David had developed his spiritual muscles in the everyday, mundane tasks of life. He valued courage and knew the importance of trust in God, so he capitalized on his experiences as a shepherd to build those qualities early in life. David had not done this to impress anyone, because he was probably all alone at the time, but he developed his faith because he wanted to serve God effectively. As a result, Goliath, though a daunting enemy, represented the same challenge and opportunity as the earlier challenges. Are you facing situations that seem small and insignificant, where it seems unnecessary to trust God? Perhaps these are the "lions" and "bears" that God wants to use in your life to strengthen and prepare you to face giants in the future.

David's faith was not only an experienced faith but also a focused one. As he went into battle, he confronted Goliath with the following words:

> You come against me with sword and spear and javelin, but I come against you in the name of the LORD Almighty, the God of

the armies of Israel, whom you have defied. This day the LORD
will hand you over to me. . . . All those gathered here will know
that it is not by sword or spear that the LORD saves; for the battle
is the LORD's, and he will give all of you into our hands. (1 Sam.
17:45–47)

David's words reflect the faith of a young man who viewed his life as
part of a bigger story. He considered the battle as God's battle rather
than his own. His faith is contrasted in this story with Saul's lack of
faith. Saul was self-absorbed and looked at the impossibility of his human circumstances, but David was God-centered and focused upon the
resources provided by God. His courageous faith and victory over Goliath
inspired Israel's armies to future victories over the Philistines, and David's
kingdom experienced more freedom than Saul's.

Jesus had the same focus when he was tested in the wilderness by
Satan. In each of the three temptations (Matt. 4; Luke 4), Satan tries to
lure Jesus to a self-serving perspective—to satisfy his hunger, concern
for his safety, to enjoy his glory. When Jesus answered each temptation
with a quotation from God's Word, he was countering Satan's strategy
with one of his own—keeping the focus upon God and the available
resources that he provides.

In my own experience, I find this aspect of facing trials one of the
most challenging—to focus on God and his resources rather than on
my own impossible circumstances. Do you struggle with this as well?
That is why I find the Psalms so helpful as prayers during trials. In the
previous chapter, we saw how they strike a healthy balance by expressing
honesty with God about our insecurities, but at the same time praise
him for his attributes that bring us security.

Five years ago, my father began to show signs that he might have
Alzheimer's disease. His behavior and mental deterioration since that
time has confirmed the diagnosis. My eighty-year-old mother has been
his primary caregiver during these years, and as his condition has dete-
riorated it has become the most difficult thing she has ever faced. But
she is a woman with amazing faith in God, and the Lord has sustained
her each step of the way. My siblings and I are involved in supporting
roles in whatever ways we can, and recently I have been in contact with

my mom almost daily. She simply needs someone to talk to, to encourage her, and to let her know that she is not alone in facing this situation. Based on the typical scenario of this disease, caring for my dad will get much more difficult than it is now, and the day will come when my mother will not be able to do it all alone. But until that day comes, she daily faces "impossible" tasks and continually looks to God for her strength.

Most of us do not face extreme daily challenges like this one, but we regularly face the same question my mom does: Am I going to focus on the frustration and impossibility of life's circumstances, or am I going to focus on God and the resources he can provide?

The Most Important Thing About You

A. W. Tozer, in his classic book about the attributes of God, writes, "What comes into our minds when we think about God is the most important thing about us."[1] Tozer says that no religion has ever been greater than its idea of God. "We tend by a secret law of the soul to move toward our mental image of God."[2] In my estimation, Tozer has given to us great insight into a particular needy area of our lives—our thinking process when we face suffering. Even the most nonreligious person thinks about God when a crisis happens. Large natural disasters are sometimes blamed on God: "Why does God let these things happen to innocent people?" The helplessness everyone feels when nature manifests itself through earthquakes, tornados, hurricanes, or floods leads even agnostics or atheists to mention God. Sadly, his name is rarely uttered when lives are miraculously spared or good things happen. Most people have a weak and inadequate understanding of God.

> What comes to your mind when you think about God during a time of trial or suffering?

What comes to your mind when you think about God? If it is indeed the most important thing about you, then this question deserves your attention. But let's restate it as the Big Idea for this chapter: What comes to your mind when you think about God during a time of trial or suffering? Like natural disasters, personal disasters reduce us to our greatest sense of helplessness, and instinctively we turn to the only God we know. Do you picture him as an angry God, who is punishing you for your sins? Is he a helpless and weak God, unable to protect or deliver you when you really need it? Perhaps when things go wrong, God seems distant and out of touch. Maybe he forgot about you, or perhaps he is not interested in unimportant details like your feelings. All of these responses are common, yet inadequate, views of the God of the Bible.

Knowing God and his promises has a tremendous bearing on the way we face trials. Who is he and what resources does he provide that equip us to face the most difficult times of life? What do we see of God's plan, purposes, and character in the scriptural passages about trials? How does this knowledge help us to think right when things go wrong?

Reassurance About My Relationship with God

It is ironic but true that we spend more time cultivating a rich and authentic relationship with God during trials than we do when life is rosy. I wish that were not true (and so does God), but it seems to be human nature that peace and prosperity lead to illusions of self-sufficiency. If adverse circumstances draw us closer to God and make us more sensitive to his voice, what are we to learn from him?

1. God's discipline proves that I am a child of God and have been chosen for a mission. When our daughters were two and three years old, we put them down for a nap one afternoon and decided to take a quick walk around the block. Returning about ten minutes later, we saw their sad faces in the window with tears streaming down their cheeks. They had heard us close the front door when we departed. And when they peeked out the window and saw us walking down the street, they were sure that Mom and Dad were abandoning them. This is often the way we feel about God during our experiences of suffering. Though difficult times may give us the emotional sense of abandonment by God, disciplinary trials are actually evidence that he loves us and accepts us as children:

And you have forgotten that word of encouragement that addresses you as sons:

> "My son, do not make light of the Lord's discipline,
>   and do not lose heart when he rebukes you,
> because the Lord disciplines those he loves,
>   and he punishes everyone he accepts as a son."
> —Heb. 12:5–6 (which includes a
> quote from Prov. 3:11–12)

God disciplines us so that "we may share in his holiness" (Heb. 12:10) and our lives will produce "a harvest of righteousness and peace"(Heb. 12:11). It is clear that when God is proactive in allowing trials into our lives, his purposes are grounded in character qualities like love, holiness, righteousness, and peace. Trials in general are designed to make our lives more Christlike for the mission of representing him in a hostile world (John 15:20; 17:14).

2. Persevering through trials, especially persecution for Christ, indicates blessing from God (Matt. 5:11–12; Luke 6:22–23; James 1:12). The preponderance of statements in the Bible connecting words like "Blessed are . . ." with references to suffering is impressive. These statements certainly challenge our value system about life experiences. A good friend who was reflecting on a trial she has undergone for several years said she had learned that it is important to share her story with others: "What a privilege to share it; if we don't, it was all for nothing!" Rather than responding with resentment and bitterness, she has learned to value the experiences that God has taken her through.

3. We are reassured, renewed, and do not lose heart during trials, knowing that perseverance will be rewarded by God in heaven (Matt. 5:11–12; 19:29; Rom. 8:18; 2 Cor. 4:16–5:7; 1 Thess. 2:19; 2 Tim. 4:6–8; James 1:12; 1 Peter 5:4). This future reward is described as the "crown of righteousness" (2 Tim. 4:8), "the crown of glory" (1 Peter 5:4), and "the glory that will be revealed in us" (Rom. 8:18). The terms translated "glory" throughout the Bible sometimes speak of a physical manifestation of God's majesty, but most often represent the composite essence of all Godlike qualities. The crown of eternal life we will receive is a final transformation to become like Christ, culminating the process described by Paul in 2 Corinthians 3:18: "And we, who with unveiled faces all reflect the Lord's glory, are being transformed into his likeness with ever-increasing glory." Remember this advice from Paul when you go through difficult days:

> Therefore we do not lose heart. Though outwardly we are wasting away, yet inwardly we are being renewed day by day. For our light and momentary troubles are achieving for us an eternal glory that far outweighs them all. So we fix our eyes not on what is seen, but on what is unseen. For what is seen is temporary, but what is unseen is eternal. (2 Cor. 4:16–18)

In these verses, Paul uses a play on words, because the root meaning of the Greek word translated "glory" comes from a common Old Testament Hebrew word meaning "weightiness" or "heaviness." To be "weighty" describes the glory of one who is prosperous, mighty, or honored for accomplishments. Here the apostle says that our eternal glory "far outweighs" any glory we could have on earth. Our hope through difficult days comes by keeping our focus on God and what he has promised, rather than on any temporary glory we may have here. When Jesus invited Peter to join him in walking on the Sea of Galilee (Matt. 14:22–33), Peter was successful until he took his eyes off Jesus and looked at the uncertainty of his circumstances. So it is with us. If we claim a relationship with God, Scripture makes it clear that our motivation to follow him and persevere through suffering is only possible when we see the bigger perspective of eternity. Through reading and studying the Bible, we see more of God's true character and the resources we already possess to take us through difficult times.

Promises About Personal Spiritual Growth

1. God is a nurturing God. When we persevere through trials, he offers us a growth process that produces maturity, proven character, and hope (Rom. 5:3–5; Heb. 12:10–11; James 1:3). This promise, which we discussed thoroughly in chapter 2, is a major reason why we can rejoice during difficult times. Through our suffering, God develops in us qualities that cannot be produced in any other way. Here is a vivid illustration of this principle in the life of a dear friend, shared in her own words:

> Within a short time after the birth of our second child, I had hepatitis three times. Having barely regained my strength from this ordeal, I was diagnosed with a premalignant colon. I had surgery to have my colon removed, went through chemotherapy, all of this requiring me to be in the hospital months at a time. Even though after two and a half years the doctors finally gave me a clear diagnosis, my body had suffered irreversible damage. Scar tissue had formed in my intestinal tract, requiring another very painful surgery and long recovery time. The removal of my colon requires me to live daily with a small plastic pouch into which my small intestine empties. All of this came in my life when my two children were under four years of age.
>
> I would love to tell you that I was at peace the entire time and the extensive time it took to get well, but that would not be true. I was frantic over what this was doing to my daughters emotionally. During my long stays in the hospital, they were terrified that Mommy would never come home. We also had an overwhelming financial burden with little income, and I regularly had serious doubts that I would ever get well. Once, while in the hospital, I considered taking my own life by hoarding sleeping pills and planning to take them all at once. Thoughts of how much worse a suicide would be for my children held me back, and I threw away the pills.
>
> I do not believe I would have had the enormous faith-building experience if I had not lived through it in just the way I did. I made it through these years by putting one foot in front of the other one, often reluctantly. After it was all over and we were looking back, I realized I could now say I wouldn't change the past in any way. I was truly "standing on the promises" because even though I was so very sick, and frightened out of my wits, I continued to cling to all I had learned as a Christian growing up. I did not always feel it, but I knew it was true. I tried

to remember the advice, "Do not doubt in the dark what God has taught you in the light."

God encouraged me by giving me experiences of his presence in moments of crisis. Once, when I was all alone going into surgery, God sent me a Christian nurse who held my hand, talked to me, and seemed to understand exactly what I needed. Afterward, I could see how she was the "angel" I needed at that moment. Often I was too ill to read the Bible, but God encouraged me with just a few Scripture passages that really spoke to my heart:

> The LORD your God is with you,
> he is mighty to save.
> He will take great delight in you,
> he will quiet you with his love,
> he will rejoice over you with singing.
>
> —Zeph. 3:17

> Can a mother forget the baby at her breast
> and have no compassion on the child she has borne?
> Though she may forget,
> I will not forget you!
>
> —Isa. 49:15

Looking in the "rear view mirror," we saw how there were so many, many needs that had been answered and dealt with before we even knew what they were. Child care was completely provided by people who really loved my girls, not strangers; shortly before I became ill we had just taken out a new insurance policy; we had just become a part of a new church home, etc. I could go on and on. Living through that time showed me how reliable God's promises were and that even when you do not feel his presence or even feel peaceful, it does not change who God is, what He does, or how much He loves you. You learn to just believe without any "decoration." I believe that who I, my husband, and our daughters are today is due in large part to living through that nightmare. Believing is often painful, but never without reward.[3]

2. God is faithful, loving, and gracious. He provides strength during our times of weakness and enough grace to bear up under every test and temptation. One of the most encouraging passages about handling temptation gives this assurance:

> No temptation has seized you except what is common to man. And God is faithful; he will not let you be tempted beyond what you can bear. But when you are tempted, he will also provide a way out so that you can stand up under it. (1 Cor. 10:13)

This promise of God, rooted in his *faithfulness,* reassures every Christian who faces temptation that several things are true. First, your temptation is not different from or more difficult than temptations that others face. One of the seductive elements of many temptations is the sense that our situation is somehow unique. I remember a heartbreaking conversation with a friend who had committed adultery and was now preparing to leave his wife and two children to marry his mistress. In response to the pleas of several friends he said, "You just don't understand my situation." He explained that he had married the wrong woman, and God had now led him to the right one. My friend rationalized divorce and the breaking up of two families because he believed his circumstances were somehow different than the temptations of other married men. In this case, his pride led him to believe this deception.

Sometimes, loneliness or lack of friendships can lead to "isolationism" in the area of temptation. Honest friendships that provide accountability and encouragement are essential to good spiritual health. A good friend can help us correct our thinking before we begin to rationalize sin and give in to it. During the past year, my wife and I have been part of a group that is planting a new church. We have served in large churches most of our adult Christian years and welcomed the different dynamic offered by a smaller group. Within our congregation, most people also participate in small group Bible studies that meet during the week. After one year, we are still making new friends and getting to know others in the group, and we are discovering that regardless of the size of the church, one has to work at building relationships.

After comparing church experiences, however, I am convinced that large churches provide a much greater opportunity for Christians to hide from the friendships and accountability that are absolutely essential for healthy spiritual growth. Of course, this can happen in a small church, too, but large congregations provide a perfect climate for isolationism. But when people in a congregation are anonymous to one another, they miss out on much of the dynamic of what the church was designed to be. As Christians, we need to be talking about the common challenges, temptations, and sins that undermine our faith, and encouraging one another that "no temptation has seized you except what is common to man." Remember, you're not all alone in facing temptations or trials.

A second promise resonating from 1 Corinthians 10:13 is that God will provide a way out of temptation before it becomes sin, and he will never allow us to experience greater temptation than we are capable of handling. This is tremendous encouragement for all of us who are honest about the way temptation works. In order to understand this idea more clearly, consider James's description of temptation:

> When tempted, no one should say, "God is tempting me." For God cannot be tempted by evil, nor does he tempt anyone; but each one is tempted when, by his own evil desire, he is dragged away and enticed. Then, after desire has conceived, it gives birth to sin; and sin, when it is full-grown, gives birth to death. (James 1:13–15)

James makes it clear that God does not tempt us to sin, because his nature does not allow that. Our own desire to act independently of God has a powerful influence upon us, however, and tempts us toward sin. The desire itself is not yet sin, but when we entertain what it offers and give it opportunity, sin is born. Martin Luther, one of the leaders of the Protestant Reformation, said of temptation and sin, "You can't stop the birds from flying over your head, but you can keep them from building a nest in your hair!" In 1 Corinthians 10:13, Paul describes the opportunity we have after we are tempted but before sin is born. He says that

God will never allow the pressure of that moment to be too great for us, and he will provide some way for us to say no and escape.

Because James and Paul use a word that can be translated either "temptation" or "trial," I believe this principle applies to every trial of our faith. In the broadest sense, every trial is a temptation to act independently of God. God intends it for our good, but Satan intends it for our downfall—and our inner desires play into his hands. But here is the glorious promise of 1 Corinthians 10:13, the truth on which we depend: God understands our frailty and will only allow trials or temptations that we are capable of handling. Though at that moment we may *feel* there is no way out, God promises to provide a way out. How and why does he do this?

The third insight from 1 Corinthians 10:13 is that God's faithfulness motivates him to do this. Though faithfulness might be isolated as just one of God's attributes among many (e.g., immutability, omniscience, wisdom, omnipotence, mercy, grace, justice), it may also be applied to any quality that defines his relationship with us. Whatever God does in his relationship with us, he will always be faithful to it. In this verse, Paul tells us that God will be faithful to extend mercy and grace during times of temptation. The prophet Jeremiah strikes a similar chord in the following description of God's attributes:

> Because of the LORD's great love we are not consumed,
>   for his compassions never fail.
> They are new every morning;
>   great is your faithfulness. . . .
> Though he brings grief, he will show compassion,
>   so great is his unfailing love.
>
>   —Lam. 3:22–23, 32

It is God's *grace* that sustains us during the greatest times of testing. When Paul prayed fervently at least three times that God would remove the trial of his thorn in the flesh, God answered no—which is a very difficult answer to hear and accept. Recently we enjoyed a visit from our daughter, son-in-law, and our granddaughter, Elliana. She has recently gained mobility through crawling and loves to pursue *verboten* objects like electrical cords and our dog's tail. She quickly learned the warning "no," though at this stage her interpretation of that word is "pause, think about it for a moment, then grab!" Like Elliana, we rarely appreciate being told no to something we really want, and that is true in our prayer life as well. God actually answered the apostle's request to remove his infirmity. "No," he said, but then he added the following encouragement: "My grace is sufficient for you, for my power is made perfect in weakness" (2 Cor. 12:9). It is God's grace that enables us to "keep on keeping on" even in the most difficult circumstances.

3. God is all-wise and all-knowing. Though he does not promise we will always understand the meaning of every trial, he does invite us to pray for wisdom as we go through them. In chapter 2, we looked closely at James's invitation to pray in times of testing and to pray specifically for wisdom amidst trials.

> If any of you lacks wisdom, he should ask God, who gives generously to all without finding fault, and it will be given to him. But when he asks, he must believe and not doubt, because he who doubts is like a wave of the sea, blown and tossed by the wind. (James 1:5–6)

Tim and Samantha have gone through a trial for several years. They both love children, and it was clear from the beginning of their relationship that a large family was a part of their shared dreams of life together. For several years, infertility prevented that dream. After pursuing the expertise of excellent and expensive medical advice, Samantha became pregnant. She and Tim both thought their trial was over, only to have their hopes dashed by a miscarriage. But they were unwilling to give up. They again pursued the further expense of more medical advice, and again Samantha became pregnant, only to have a second miscarriage. Their experience has taught them many things about the miracle of conception and birth, which are reflected in David's words in Psalm 139:13–14:

> You created my inmost being;
>> you knit me together in my mother's womb.
> I praise you because I am fearfully and wonderfully made;
>> your works are wonderful,
>> I know that full well.

David is offering praise to God for one of the greatest miracles of all, and it is one that so many couples take for granted.

This couple's experiences of waiting, praying, and reflecting have also produced in them greater spiritual maturity, broadening their perspective and teaching them how to minister to others who are going through similar trials. I asked them to write down some of the things they have learned or are still in the process of learning. Here are some examples:

- We need to love God for who he is, not just for what he gives us (or doesn't give us). Suffering helps to purify our motives.
- God has graced us by showing himself in special ways in some of the toughest times. This has given us strength to keep going.
- God's people, when they are present and expressing his love, greatly ease suffering. When they are absent, suffering is greatly increased.
- Sometimes people feel they need to offer some reason or logical explanation in order for their words to be a comfort to us. Encouragement really comes just by knowing that someone is there and cares; words are not always necessary.
- Waiting "stinks," but much of life happens while we wait.
- Suffering times are not wasted times. Other things (like our marriage, our compassion for and understanding of others' struggles) have been strengthened in the process.
- We become deeper people as we suffer.

Samantha said, "Somebody told me that at the end of my infertility journey I would look back and say, 'I wouldn't change a thing.' I thought they were crazy, but they were right. I truly wouldn't change a thing for the sake of the character that has been built, the depth of my marriage, the depth of my ministry, my knowledge of 'infertility land,' and the truest appreciation for God's creation of life. Pain is the gift no one wants."

As I write these words, Samantha and Tim are parents of a healthy baby girl, Abigail. They are thankful for this little life God has entrusted to them, as well as the lessons learned in their journey.

4. God is both compassionate and omnipotent. He gives us comfort and strength to go through even the most difficult times. In chapter 3, we saw that our ministry of comfort to others comes because God is the source of all comfort:

> Praise be to the God and Father of our Lord Jesus Christ, the Father of compassion and the God of all comfort, who comforts us in all our troubles. (2 Cor. 1:3–4)

We are comforted through the confidence that God is in charge, all-powerful, and that his strength is made perfect in our weakness. This confidence leads Paul to conclude, "When I am weak, then I am strong" (2 Cor. 12:10); and, "I can do everything through him who gives me strength" (Phil. 4:13). The inner strength of a Christian is a dynamic quality that people in the world usually cannot understand. In fact, the apostle Paul describes it this way: "God chose the foolish things of the world to shame the wise; God chose the weak things of the world to shame the strong" (1 Cor. 1:27). This is what enables us to "keep on keeping on," even in the most difficult circumstances.

Dixie and Steve, good friends of ours, are in the midst of the greatest trial they have ever faced. Their youngest son, Gabe, is ten years old and has Landau-Kleffner Syndrome (LKS), a rare form of childhood epilepsy. As parents, they began to notice developmental factors when Gabe was very young, and they sought out the best pediatric neurologists when he was less than two years old. Tests were run, but all were inconclusive. Nobody who examined Gabe diagnosed LKS until he was nine years old. This has been especially frustrating to Dixie and Steve, in part because they are both doctors themselves and have great confidence in the techniques of medical testing. At the time I am writing, Gabe continues to have seizures, and his parents have not found a way to address his condition or find any relief.

Meanwhile, I have watched Steve and Dixie continue to raise their three children, serve others successfully in their medical practices, and go about life with great courage. They are, however, in the midst of a trial that makes life extremely difficult. I asked Dixie—a mother who daily watches her son struggle with seizures—how she can "keep on keeping on" when she and Steve have not yet found promising news. She says that the impossibility of the trial has led her back into a more intimate walk with God. Some days are harder than others, but she shared with me some promises from Scripture that have especially encouraged her through the tough times:

> Surely goodness and mercy shall follow me
>   all the days of my life.
>
> —Ps. 23:6 KJV

> Because you are my help,
>   I sing in the shadow of your wings.
>
> —Ps. 63:7

> For you created my inmost being;
>   you knit me together in my mother's womb. . . .
> Search me, O God, and know my heart;
>   test me and know my anxious thoughts.
>
> —Ps. 139:13, 23

> Trust in the LORD with all your heart
>   and lean not on your own understanding;
> in all your ways acknowledge him,
>   and he will make your paths straight.
>
> —Prov. 3:5–6

> Do you not know?
>   Have you not heard?
> The LORD is the everlasting God,
>   the Creator of the ends of the earth.
> He will not grow tired or weary,
>   and his understanding no one can fathom.
> He gives strength to the weary
>   and increases the power of the weak.
> Even youths grow tired and weary,
>   and young men stumble and fall;
> but those who hope in the LORD
>   will renew their strength.

> They will soar on wings like eagles;
>> they will run and not grow weary,
>> they will walk and not be faint.
>>> —Isa. 40:28–31

Come to me, all you who are weary and burdened, and I will give you rest. Take my yoke upon you and learn from me, for I am gentle and humble in heart, and you will find rest for your souls. For my yoke is easy and my burden is light. (Matt. 11:28–30)

Now to him who is able to do immeasurably more than all we ask or imagine, according to his power that is at work within us, to him be glory in the church and in Christ Jesus throughout all generations, for ever and ever! Amen. (Eph. 3:20–21)

Please notice the focus of these words of encouragement from the Bible. They promise comfort by drawing our attention to God—who he is and what he can do during impossible circumstances.

5. God is omnipotent and a God of peace. He comforts our fears, renews our strength, and provides protection and security during trials. We live in an era of history when a new kind of warfare is being fought—terrorism. The fear tactics of terrorists are a relatively new addition to the international political scene, but the father of terror, Satan, has always been successful using them. Terrorists accomplish their goals through the paralysis of fear in society; Satan does so through fear in our hearts. When suffering comes, it is often accompanied by two companions—worry and fear. This stressful combination can reduce us to discouragement, despair, and even depression. Psychiatrists and psychologists tell us that the majority of patients under their care have problems stemming from uncontrolled worry and fear. Someone once documented the things that people regularly worry about, and more than 95 percent of them rarely or never happen! But worries about potential crises can paralyze us just as easily as actual trials.

Jesus provides some rich advice in the Sermon on the Mount that helps us to focus on the right things so that we will not worry unnecessarily:

Therefore I tell you, do not worry about your life, what you will eat or drink; or about your body, what you will wear. Is not life more important than food, and the body more important than clothes? Look at the birds of the air; they do not sow or reap or store away in barns, and yet your heavenly Father feeds them. Are you not much more valuable than they? Who of you by worrying can add a single hour to his life?

And why do you worry about clothes? See how the lilies of the field grow. They do not labor or spin. Yet I tell you that not even Solomon in all his splendor was dressed like one of these. If that is how God clothes the grass of the field, which is here today and tomorrow is thrown into the fire, will he not much more clothe you, O you of little faith? So do not worry, saying, "What shall we eat?" or "What shall we drink?" or "What shall we wear?" For the pagans run after all these things, and your heavenly Father knows that you need them. But seek first his kingdom and his righteousness, and all these things will be given to you as well. Therefore do not worry about tomorrow, for tomorrow will worry about itself. Each day has enough trouble of its own. (Matt. 6:25–34)

Jesus' directive to "seek first his kingdom" is wonderful advice during trials as well. Though we are tempted to worry about our difficult circumstances, God invites us to intentionally refocus on him. It is here we find peace and security in order to face our fears head on.

Meditate on the following Old and New Testament passages. As you read, begin a "Meditation Journal" that answers the following questions:

1. What qualities (attributes) of God does this passage draw attention to?
2. What promises do I receive that address my fears and worries?
3. What trial(s) am I facing right now that might be addressed in this advice?

Set up your Meditation Journal as follows, and add to it as you reread the following passages:

	Attributes of God	Promises Received	Trial I Am Facing
Psalm 18:2			
Psalm 23:1-4, etc.			

The LORD is my rock, my fortress and my deliverer;
  my God is my rock, in whom I take refuge.
He is my shield and the horn of my salvation, my stronghold.
  —Ps. 18:2

The LORD is my shepherd, I shall not be in want.
He makes me lie down in green pastures,
  he leads me beside quiet waters,
  he restores my soul.
He guides me in paths of righteousness
  for his name's sake.
Even though I walk
  through the valley of the shadow of death,
I will fear no evil,
  for you are with me;
your rod and your staff,
  they comfort me.
  —Ps. 23:1–4

You [God] are my hiding place;
  you will protect me from trouble.
  —Ps. 32:7

I sought the LORD, and he answered me;
  he delivered me from all my fears. . . .

Taste and see that the LORD is good;
   blessed is the man who takes refuge in him.
Fear the LORD, you his saints,
   for those who fear him lack nothing.
The lions may grow weak and hungry,
   but those who seek the LORD lack no good thing. . . .

The eyes of the LORD are on the righteous
   and his ears are attentive to their cry; . . .

The LORD is close to the brokenhearted
   and saves those who are crushed in spirit.
                              —Ps. 34:4, 8–10, 15, 18

I waited patiently for the LORD;
   he turned to me and heard my cry.
He lifted me out of the slimy pit,
   out of the mud and mire;
he set my feet on a rock
   and gave me a firm place to stand.
He put a new song in my mouth,
   a hymn of praise to our God.
Many will see and fear
   and put their trust in the LORD.
                              —Ps. 40:1–3

He who dwells in the shelter of the Most High
   will rest in the shadow of the Almighty.
I will say of the LORD, "He is my refuge and my fortress,
   my God, in whom I trust." . . .

If you make the Most High your dwelling—
   even the LORD, who is my refuge—
then no harm will befall you,
   no disaster will come near your tent.

For he will command his angels concerning you
    to guard you in all your ways;
they will lift you up in their hands,
    so that you will not strike your foot against a stone.

                                   —Ps. 91:1–2, 9–12

When calamity overtakes you like a storm,
    when disaster sweeps over you like a whirlwind,
when distress and trouble overwhelm you.

Then they [mockers and fools] will call to me but I will not answer;
    they will look for me but will not find me. . . .
But whoever listens to me will live in safety
    and be at ease, without fear of harm.

                                   —Prov. 1:27–28, 33

So do not fear, for I am with you;
    do not be dismayed, for I am your God.
I will strengthen you and help you;
    I will uphold you with my righteous right hand.

                                   —Isa. 41:10

If God is for us, who can be against us? . . . Who shall separate us from the love of Christ? Shall trouble or hardship or persecution or famine or nakedness or danger or sword? . . . No, in all these things we are more than conquerors through him who loved us. (Rom. 8:31, 35, 37)

Do not be anxious about anything, but in everything, by prayer and petition, with thanksgiving, present your requests to God. And the peace of God, which transcends all understanding, will guard your hearts and your minds in Christ Jesus. (Phil. 4:6–7)

And of this gospel I was appointed a herald and an apostle and a teacher. That is why I am suffering as I am. Yet I am not ashamed, because I know whom I have believed, and am convinced that he is able to guard what I have entrusted to him for that day. (2 Tim. 1:11–12)

6. God is our deliverer and gives us victory. He gives us the power, resources, and ministry of the Holy Spirit to face the spiritual battle of trials. When young David confidently declared, "The battle is the LORD's!" (1 Sam. 17:47), Goliath was already defeated. Sure, David would strategize, gather stones, use the sling, and eventually bring the enemy down, but when he believed by faith that this was God's battle, it was already won. One of the great hymns of the faith says, "Faith is the victory! Faith is the victory! O glorious victory, that overcomes the world."[4]

The reason that faith is the victory is found in God. He has all the resources to defeat the giants in our lives. God's victory may not always come through the removal of adverse circumstances, yet even so he will sustain us through them. "It is not by miraculous deliverance that our faith grows, but by discovering God's faithfulness in the midst of our pain."[5] The Old Testament includes many illustrations—similar to the story of David and Goliath—of victories that came by faith and defeats that happened because of a lack of faith. Another popular children's Bible story, the conquest of Jericho in Joshua 6, is a similar example of a victory that came by faith. God had directed Joshua to conquer this strategic city en route to the Israelite conquest of Canaan. The faith required, however, was not just in God's ability to give the victory but also in the highly unusual tactics of warfare he devised. Armies normally did not conquer cities by marching around them and shouting until the walls came tumbling down; instead, they used battering rams, spears, and arrows. Yet God taught Joshua and the people of Israel that if they would trust in him, even in the details, victory would follow. Stories like Goliath and Jericho illustrate challenges we regularly face, for God often plans to bring victory in completely unexpected and unconventional ways. Isaiah prophesies these words to Israel, anticipating that they would face impossible odds:

> But now, this is what the LORD says—
> he who created you, O Jacob,
> he who formed you, O Israel:

"Fear not, for I have redeemed you;
   I have summoned you by name; you are mine.
When you pass through the waters,
I will be with you;
   and when you pass through the rivers,
   they will not sweep over you.
When you walk through the fire,
   you will not be burned;
   the flames will not set you ablaze.
For I am the LORD, your God,
   the Holy One of Israel, your Savior."

—Isa. 43:1–3

Just as Israel was reassured of God's future victory, including protection physically and spiritually, so are we. Peter says, "The Lord knows how to rescue godly men from trials and to hold the unrighteous for the day of judgment" (2 Peter 2:9).

This battle is accomplished through the Holy Spirit's work in the lives of Christians. The Old Testament account of the history of Israel depicts faith and victory using the physical circumstances of warfare, with unseen spiritual conflict in the background. The stories of Goliath and Jericho are two good examples. Goliath and the Canaanites were participants in ungodly and immoral religions. They saw the God of Israel as their enemy, who therefore needed to be defeated. In contrast, the life of a Christian pictured in the New Testament is framed in a way that depicts only the spiritual battle. Christians are described as living in this world but not being of this world. Though we serve as ambassadors for God, we also engage in a continuous spiritual battle against Satan and all of his demonic resources. Paul gives the best descriptions of this warfare in passages like the following:

For though we live in the world, we do not wage war as the world does. The weapons we fight with are not the weapons of the world. On the contrary, they have divine power to demolish strongholds. We demolish arguments and every pretension that sets itself up against the knowledge of God, and we take captive every thought to make it obedient to Christ. (2 Cor. 10:3–5)

Finally, be strong in the Lord and in his mighty power. Put on the full armor of God so that you can take your stand against the devil's schemes. For our struggle is not against flesh and blood, but against the rulers, against the authorities, against the powers of this dark world and against the spiritual forces of evil in the heavenly realms. Therefore put on the full armor of God, so that when the day of evil comes, you may be able to stand your ground, and after you have done everything, to stand. Stand firm then, with the belt of truth buckled around your waist, with the breastplate of righteousness in place, and with your feet fitted with the readiness that comes from the gospel of peace. In addition to all this, take up the shield of faith, with which you can extinguish all the flaming arrows of the evil one. Take the helmet of salvation and the sword of the Spirit, which is the word of God. And pray in the Spirit on all occasions with all kinds of prayers and requests. With this in mind, be alert and always keep on praying for all the saints. (Eph. 6:10–18)

Notice several things revealed in these descriptions that are important to remember every day. First, our battle is a spiritual one, and thus does not follow the usual rules of engagement. Our struggle is not against things we can see, but against a kingdom of darkness that is well-organized and orchestrated by Satan himself. In order to address such a daunting foe, Paul declares we must "be strong in the Lord and in his mighty power" (Eph. 6:10). Many of the original readers of Paul's letters came from backgrounds in magic, astrology, witchcraft, goddess worship, and various kinds of mystery cults that encouraged dependence upon their gods and goddesses.[6] In our contemporary setting, we rely on other gods or forms of religion to face life—our own strength, humanistic philosophies, or perhaps empty religious rituals. Paul warns us not to underestimate the power of the foe or the battle but to face it daily with the only power that will be successful. As David said, "The battle is the LORD's" (1 Sam. 17:47).

Second, the spiritual battle especially focuses on the mind, thought processes that make war against the knowledge that comes from God. Thus, a crucial part of the battle is to "take captive every thought to make it obedient to Christ" (2 Cor. 10:5). This correlates with Paul's advice in Romans 12:2: "Do not conform any longer to the pattern of this world, but be transformed by the renewing of your mind. Then you will be able to test and approve what God's will is—his good, pleasing and perfect will." The battle is a battle for the mind. J. P. Moreland says of Romans 12:1–2:

> Now these words of Paul's are familiar to many, but the critical point of verse 2 is that we cannot "prove," that is, "make known to ourselves and to others," what God's will is, *without the renewing or transformation of our minds.* This brings the mind to the spiritual stage, front and center! We all want to know God's will, but his text is telling us we can't unless we present our bodies, including our soul and minds, to the Lord for transformation and renewal.[7]

Moreland shows that loving God with all your mind is an essential ingredient of discipleship and spiritual formation. Often, we limit our application of expressions like "conform to the pattern of this world" to moral value issues, such as our views of sexuality or abortion. Yet it is quite possible to be a very moral and upright Christian in areas of popular morality, but when it comes to facing trials we may be no different than anyone else around us. Christ wants ambassadors who think victoriously and face life's trials with all the resources available.

This brings us to the final point: the equipment needed to win the battle is already provided for us. Ephesians 6:13–18 describes metaphorically the defensive and offensive resources that every Christian possesses because we have the Holy Spirit. Paul uses a common illustration of his day to picture these resources, the soldier's armor and sword. Though the most common association made by interpreters has been the armor worn by a Roman soldier, Clinton Arnold suggests that Paul's primary inspiration may have been allusions to the pieces of armor mentioned in the prophecies of Isaiah.[8] Though the equipment of a Roman centurion is quite similar, Paul is simply referring to a soldier's armor and weapons in general. What are some of the specific parts pictured?

- Belt of truth buckled around the waist
- Breastplate of righteousness in place
- Gospel of peace providing swiftness and stability to our feet
- Shield of faith, extinguishing the flaming arrows of Satan
- Helmet of salvation
- Sword of the Spirit, that is, the Word of God
- Prayer in the spirit

All these resources are grounded in the character and qualities of God—truth, righteousness, peace, salvation—and are available to us through the work of God's Holy Spirit.

I must admit that during my early Christian experience I had little understanding of the work of the Holy Spirit. I grew up referring to the third person of the Godhead as the Holy *Ghost,* and my relationship to him was as mysterious as that term implies. As I grew in my faith, through God's Word I began to relate to the Holy Spirit as a person and to understand the resources he provides. In addition to those mentioned above, "the fruit of the Spirit" (Gal. 5:22–23) reassures me that when I trust in God through times of trial, God through the Holy Spirit produces qualities in me that I cannot muster on my own. Love, joy, peace, patience, kindness, goodness, faithfulness, gentleness, self-control—it sounds like a well-designed "response kit" for any difficult time. How does this work? When I face suffering, I know that my natural response will be fear, anxiety, worry, doubt, impatience, frustration, and confusion. When I make a conscious choice to trust God, look to Jesus, and rely on the Holy Spirit, I am enabled to experience joy, peace, patience, and to persevere through the difficult time. God may choose to deliver me from the problem, but even if he doesn't, I will be enabled to experience

- courage instead of doubt or fear
- confidence instead of discouragement or defeat
- peace instead of anxiety
- wisdom instead of confusion

Larry, a friend of mine, has recently gone through the insecurity of a potential job change. He pursued a job opportunity that he was led to believe would be offered to him. Then he received the news that everything was "up in the air" and he would not have an answer for some time. Larry's heart sank, and he realized how emotional this decision had become for him. He reflected back on the fact that when he had started the process, he had entrusted it to the Lord, believing that God was quite capable of guiding every step. Almost instantaneously he experienced absolute peace and renewed courage to face whatever the results would be. What exactly happened to produce this? Larry realized that his thinking processes had been hijacked by terror, which easily could have led to an extended attitude of anxiety, discouragement, and defeat. But when by faith he returned his focus to God, the Holy Spirit supernaturally produced peace, joy, and patience in his heart, even without any resolution of the job situation. By persevering with this attitude, Larry's ability to trust God will progressively become more natural because he knows it works.

Have your thought processes been hijacked by terror, defeat, or anxiety? Have you learned to surrender these challenges in your life to the Lord of all? As you think about these questions, reflect on the things we have learned about trials and suffering. Yes, the problems are very real, but so are the promises of God. Whether you like it or not, your life as a Christian is lived in the midst of a spiritual battle. At the center of that conflict is the battle for your mind. Satan, his demons, and a world alienated to God would like to "take you out" spiritually using whatever means they have. Sometimes it is even your own choices and sins which make this possible. Guilt ... discouragement ... defeat ... anxiety ... spiritual apathy—all of these attitudes play right into the hands of an enemy who wants to destroy you.

But the truth of God has the potential to set you free. Here are some of the things we know about God's plan for our lives when it includes times of trial:

- Trials and times of suffering happen to everyone; they are simply part of living in a fallen world.
- God allows them into the lives of those he loves to get our attention about choices we make; they may point out the need to repent of sin or to reevaluate our priorities. Because God is all-knowing, he may even use a trial to keep us from a potential sin.

- When we persevere through a trial with faith in God's wisdom, it has the potential, more than any other type of experience, to produce tremendous personal growth. We become more mature through trials.
- Experiencing God's comfort through suffering prepares us to help others in the future.
- God may allow trials to show the authenticity of our faith, and in so doing God receives his greatest glory. Satan's purpose in suffering is to prove that our religiosity is a façade in order to destroy us and discourage the faith of others.
- Suffering for our faith in Christ is a privilege, through which others are drawn to Christ and we will receive rewards in heaven. We will never fully understand the purpose of suffering in this life without viewing it from an eternal perspective.
- Good choices in life, especially about our attitudes, enable us to cope with the most difficult human experiences. It is the power of God's Holy Spirit which enables us to think right when things go wrong.
- God is an ever-present help in trouble. During suffering we often feel like God has abandoned us, but he is, in fact, closer than ever. Focusing upon him—his love, compassion, wisdom, faithfulness, and power—enables us to face overwhelming circumstances with confidence. He provides deliverance, victory, and peace amidst the most difficult human circumstances.

Dear Lord, you know the anxiety and fear that dominate my thoughts. Thank you for the promise that you are my rock, my fortress, my deliverer, my shepherd—a very present help in trouble. I confess to you the sin of unbelief, that I have allowed anxiety and fear to replace your presence in my life. Thank you for making me into a new person in Christ, and all the resources available to me through your Holy Spirit. May your will be done in the trial I face, but while it goes on, I am trusting in your power to provide peace and to restore joy. In Jesus' name I pray. Amen.

DISCUSSION QUESTIONS

1. A. W. Tozer once wrote, "What comes into our minds when we think about God is the most important thing about us."[9] What was your mental image of God as you were growing up? Where did this mental image come from? Who in your life helped to shape it? How has this helped or hindered you in your present relationship with God?

2. If you were writing a psalm, what attributes or qualities of God would you want to emphasize? Why are these in particular the most important to you? What experiences in your life support your choice of emphasis?

3. Imagine that you are encouraging and mentoring a young Christian. How would you explain Romans 12:1–2? Why do you think Paul chose the command to "offer your bodies as living sacrifices" to God? What does it mean to "be transformed by the renewing of your mind"?

4. Based on your reading of the chapter, what role does the Holy Spirit have in your Christian growth? Do you understand the role of the third person of the Trinity? Have you ever experienced spiritual warfare? If so, describe what you believe it is and illustrate.

5. Review the six promises about your personal spiritual growth that are explained and illustrated in this chapter. In which of these sections could you write your own story of the way God has proven himself during your trials? What attributes of God have you experienced firsthand in these times of growth?

Appendix

Suggestions for Small Groups

A book about how to face trials can certainly be of great value on a personal level. As you read it, study the Scripture passages, and reflect on and apply the truth to your own life, God can and will use all of these steps to stimulate your personal spiritual growth. However, a book like this will have its greatest impact when you study it with other Christians. With a partner or in a group, you will discover that you are not alone in facing the challenges of life, because trials are a common experience for everyone. In fact, others have had the very same fears, doubts, and questions that you have. Like you, they do not have all the answers, but together you can share the support and wisdom found in Christian community. The Bible says, "Carry each other's burdens, and in this way you will fulfill the law of Christ" (Gal. 6:2). The apostle Paul describes a dynamic process that is all too often absent in our churches: "If one part suffers, every part suffers with it; if one part is honored, every part rejoices with it. Now you are the body of Christ, and each one of you is a part of it" (1 Cor. 12:26–27).

Here are two ways of approaching this study with others. Certainly, other formats can be used as well, so be creative as you talk to others about establishing a study group:

- Study Partners: a friend, an accountability partner, your husband, wife, boyfriend, girlfriend, etc.

- Small Groups: a Bible study group in a home, at church, or at your workplace.

Suggestions and Ideas

- Determine a regular time when you can meet, how long each session will be, and how many weeks your study will span. I suggest a weekly session (or every other week) of sixty to ninety minutes, meeting a minimum of ten times.
- Survey the book before you begin, and agree that, based on the meeting time available, you will prepare for each session by reading a chapter and thinking about the discussion questions.
- Use your meeting times to discuss what you have read, selected biblical passages, and personal experiences that illustrate the things you are learning from Scripture.
- Pray for one another at the end of each session, especially focusing on immediate trials or unresolved conflicts from the past.
- Remember, flexibility is the key! Some partners or groups may choose to go more deeply into Scripture passages, and others may focus more on the application of each chapter. Whatever your goals, make sure you include the following elements in each session: (1) discussion of key Scripture passages, (2) authentic sharing of personal experiences, and (3) prayer for one another.
- Though the focus of this book is the *Christian's* journey through trials and suffering, don't be afraid to invite an interested non-Christian to visit or join your group. Handling trials in life is a subject everyone has questions about, whether Christian or not. You may want to consider inviting a friend to "listen in" as Christians look into the Bible and wrestle with these issues. (See my comments in the Introduction.)

Endnotes

Introduction

1. Used by permission. © ShaRita Wesley, 2005. Recorded on *Swept Away,* a CD by Susan Summers.
2. Frank Minirth and Paul Meier, *Happiness Is a Choice* (Grand Rapids: Baker Book House, 1978), 12. Original source unknown.
3. John Eldredge, *Waking the Dead* (Nashville: Thomas Nelson Publishers, 2003), 9.
4. Ibid., 13.
5. Henry David Thoreau, *Walden; or, Life in the Woods* (Mineola, N.Y.: Dover Publications, Inc., 1995), 4. Republication of the work first published by Ticknor and Fields, Boston, 1854.
6. Margaret Clarkson, *Destined for Glory: The Meaning of Suffering* (Grand Rapids: Eerdmans, 1983), 84.

Chapter 1: May I Have Your Attention, Please?

1. In 1 Kings 19:1–18, the prophet Elijah experiences one of the most devastating trials of his life when his life is threatened by the powerful queen Jezebel. In Elijah's great fear and despair in the wilderness, God speaks to him with encouragement and direction. Elijah sees awesome revelations of God's force through a powerful wind,

an earthquake, and a fire, but God is not in any of them. His message to Elijah comes through a "gentle whisper," as it often does for us.

2. C. S. Lewis, *The Problem of Pain* (London: Collins, 1940), 81.

3. Ibid., 16.

4. Ibid., 36.

5. D. A. Carson, *From Triumphalism to Maturity: An Exposition of 2 Corinthians 10–13* (Grand Rapids: Baker, 1984), 144.

6. Quote taken from e-mail sent to author. The writer's last name and the date of the e-mail have been omitted for privacy.

7. Some Bible expositors view James 1:9–11 as a contrast between wealthy unbelievers (vv. 10–11) and poorer Christians (v. 9). The context in verses 1–2, however, emphasizes the role of trials in the life of a Christian. It seems most natural, therefore, to extend the address to a "brother" (fellow Christian) in verse 9 into the advice of verses 10–11 as well. The advice is therefore to Christians from both rich and poor classes of society. See more on this passage in chapter 4.

8. F. Michael Ferrante, M.D., is professor of clinical anesthesiology and medicine at UCLA. He serves as director of the UCLA Pain Management Center and codirector of the UCLA Spine Center.

9. Ferrante's working definition of pain was proposed by a group of scientists and clinicians called the International Association for the Study of Pain. The widely used definition was originally put forth in the 1970s and was reconfirmed in a meeting of the group in the 1990s.

10. F. Michael Ferrante, M.D., quoted from an interview with the author on July 14, 2003.

11. Paul Brand and Philip Yancey, *In His Image* (Grand Rapids: Zondervan, 1984), 230.

12. Paul Brand and Philip Yancey, *The Gift of Pain* (Grand Rapids: Zondervan, 1997), 192–96.

13. This statement applies primarily to acute pain and not to chronic pain. Acute pain is accompanied by common and identifiable physiological factors and behaviors—increased blood pressure or heart rate, facial expressions of discomfort, clear identification of the area of

pain, etc. With chronic pain, these are not present, even though a person describes his experience as pain. Though both are clinically considered pain, for the purposes of this discussion *acute* pain will be described because it is the most commonly understood type of pain.

14. Quote taken from e-mail sent to author. The writer's last name and the date of the e-mail have been omitted for privacy.

15. C. S. Lewis, *A Grief Observed* (New York: HarperCollins, 2001), 5–6.

Chapter 2: No Pain, No Gain

1. Excerpted from an article I wrote titled "In the Presence of Terminal Illness: The Church's Ministry to Families Facing Death," *Decision* (January 1994), 10–12.

2. Philip Yancey, *Where Is God When It Hurts?* (Grand Rapids: Zondervan, 1990), 19.

3. Margaret Clarkson, *Destined for Glory: The Meaning of Suffering* (Grand Rapids: Eerdmans, 1983), 84.

4. The lament represents a particular genre (category) of psalm. A further explanation of the use of the lament psalms in our Christian experience will come in chapter 9.

5. See Romans 5:3; James 1:2; and 1 Peter 4:13.

6. Donald Burdick, *The Expositor's Bible Commentary* (Grand Rapids: Zondervan, 1981), 12:168.

7. Also note Paul's use of the athletic metaphor in 2 Timothy 2:5 and 2 Timothy 4:7.

8. Charles Swindoll, *Strengthening Your Grip* (Waco, Tex.: Word, 1982), 206.

9. Author unknown.

10. One of the best illustrations of the honest expression of human sorrow alongside rejoicing in God is found in the psalms of lament. Examples are Psalms 6, 13, 22, 102, and 142. Each expresses a prayer that cries out to God in a difficult time (sometimes in doubt), but ends with a statement of confidence in God because of who he is and what he has done in the past.

11. James W. Sire, *Discipleship of the Mind* (Downers Grove, Ill.: InterVarsity, 1990), 15.

12. Burdick, *The Expositor's Bible Commentary*, 12:169.
13. See Matthew 5:1–12.
14. For example, Psalms 1:1; 32:1; 34:8; 84:12.
15. Clarkson, *Destined for Glory*, 84.

Chapter 3: Stretching the Soul

1. Quote taken from e-mail sent to author. The writer's last name and the date of the e-mail have been omitted for privacy.
2. The story of Job records a similar response after Job's extensive losses of all his material possessions: "At this, Job got up and tore his robe and shaved his head. Then he fell to the ground in worship" (Job 1:20–21). Job's worship focuses on the sovereignty of God, whereas Paul's doxology remembers the mercy and compassion of God amidst trials.

Chapter 4: "Well Done, Good and Faithful Servant"

1. R. C. H. Lenski, *The Interpretation of the Epistles to the Hebrews and the Epistle of James* (Minneapolis: Augsburg, 1966), 534–35.
2. Peter Kreeft, *Making Sense Out of Suffering* (Ann Arbor, Mich.: Servant, 1986), 167–84.
3. Kreeft identifies the Renaissance as the time when Western thinking began to formulate new ideas that were not held in the era before that; this was the rise of modernism.
4. Though definitions vary, the most widely held view of the rise of postmodernism is circa 1970. Therefore, those born after that date would have grown up in a cultural shift with postmodern thinking becoming more dominant. Because we are still experiencing this cultural shift, the postmodern generation continues to be influenced by modernist role models (parents, professors, etc.), and thus shares some of the core values of modernism. This is why I believe that Kreeft's observations about modernism can be helpful to all ages.
5. For more specifics about this crucial period in Western thinking, see two articles I have written on the relationship between reli-

gion and the history of modern science: "Darwin's Evolutionary Theory and Nineteenth-Century Natural Theology," *Bibliotheca Sacra* 152 (July–September 1995): 334–54; and "The 'Design' Argument in Scientific Discourse: Historical Theological Perspective from the Seventeenth Century," *Journal of the Evangelical Theological Society* 41 (March 1998): 85–105.

6. In the following summary of postmodernism, I am appreciative of my pastor, Tim Morey, for his insights about the cultural shifts it represents, and for his passion to reach the postmodern generations with the gospel of Jesus Christ. For further reading on the subject of Christian ministry in a postmodern context, I have found the following books to be helpful resources: Eddie Gibbs, *ChurchNext: Quantum Changes in How We Do Ministry* (Downers Grove, Ill.: InterVarsity, 2000); Brian McLaren, *The Church on the Other Side* (Grand Rapids: Zondervan, 2000); and Chuck Smith Jr., *The End of the World . . . As We Know It* (Colorado Springs: Waterbrook, 2001).

Chapter 5: It's All About You, Lord

1. Most scholars believe that Job lived during the patriarchal period of the Old Testament (the era of Abraham, Isaac, and Jacob), for the following reasons:
   - The expression of his wealth is measured in livestock (Job 1:3), just as Abraham's is in Genesis 12:16 and 13:2.
   - Job was a common name in that period.
   - Job served as the priest for his own family, regularly praying and offering sacrifices for his ten children (Job 1:5).
   - Literature similar to the book of Job appears during that time from surrounding cultures.
   - If Job lived to be approximately two hundred years old, his life span would be similar to others of the patriarchal period.
2. Helpful books on spiritual warfare include three by Clinton E. Arnold: *Three Crucial Questions About Spiritual Warfare* (Grand Rapids: Baker, 1997); *Powers of Darkness: Principalities and Powers in Paul's Letters* (Downers Grove, Ill.: InterVarsity, 1992); and *Power*

and Magic: The Concept of Power in Ephesians (Grand Rapids: Baker, 1997); and five by Neil T. Anderson: *The Bondage Breaker* (Eugene, Ore.: Harvest House, 2000); *The Beginner's Guide to Spiritual Warfare,* coauthored with Timothy M. Warner (Ann Arbor, Mich.: Vine, 2000); *Victory over the Darkness* (Ventura, Calif.: Regal, 2000); *Stomping Out the Darkness* (Ventura, Calif.: Regal, 1995); and *Winning Spiritual Warfare* (Eugene, Ore.: Harvest House, 1991).

3. Frank Peretti, *This Present Darkness* (Wheaton, Ill.: Crossway, 2000); and *Piercing the Darkness* (Wheaton, Ill.: Crossway, 2000).

4. The most commonly recognized stages of grief are (1) denial; (2) anger toward others, self, or God; (3) bargaining; (4) depression; (5) acceptance.

5. This meaning is established from passages like Psalm 14:1, "The fool says in his heart, 'There is no God.'"

6. Don Baker and Emery Nester, *Depression: Finding Hope and Meaning in Life's Darkest Shadow* (Portland, Ore.: Multnomah, 1983), 11.

7. Life Stress Test by Tim Lowenstein, 1997, Conscious Living Foundation, http://www.cliving.org/lifstrstst.htm.

8. Margaret Clarkson, *Destined for Glory: The Meaning of Suffering* (Grand Rapids: Eerdmans, 1983), 84.

9. God's reprimand and counsel to Job's friends comes later, in Job 42:7–9.

10. Clarkson, *Destined for Glory,* 84.

11. Rick Warren, *The Purpose Driven Life: What on Earth Am I Here For?* (Grand Rapids: Zondervan, 2002), 17.

Chapter 6: What a Privilege!

1. See also the warnings of inevitable persecution found in Jesus' words in Matthew 5:10–12; 10:17–22; Luke 6:22–23; and John 16:2.

2. This true story was provided by a missionary. Mei Mei is a pseudonym for the name of the Christian, but the name is in no way indicative of the person's nationality, ethnicity, or identity, and thus no inferences should be drawn.

3. Bart D. Ehrman, *After the New Testament: A Reader in Early Christianity* (Oxford: Oxford University Press, 1999), 33.

4. Ibid., 34.

5. Eusebius *Ecclesiastical History* 5.1.45ff.

Chapter 7: Life's Full of Tough Choices, Isn't It?

1. Frank Minirth and Paul Meier, *Happiness Is a Choice: A Manual on the Symptoms, Causes, and Cures of Depression* (Grand Rapids: Baker, 1978).

2. Ibid., 12–13.

3. Charles Swindoll, *Strengthening Your Grip* (Waco, Tex.: Word, 1982), 206.

4. Original source unknown.

5. Swindoll, *Strengthening Your Grip,* 206.

Chapter 8: An Ever-Present Help in Trouble

1. C. Hassell Bullock, *An Introduction to the Old Testament Poetic Books* (Chicago: Moody, 1979), 111.

2. Exodus 19–40, Leviticus, and portions of Numbers are delivered by Moses as direct quotes from Yahweh's instruction on Mount Sinai and subsequent communication. Deuteronomy is also God's Law but is delivered by Moses in a sermonic form at a later time on the Plains of Moab as Israel prepared to enter Canaan. All these books represent information received as direct revelation from God.

3. Though David wrote about half of the Psalms, according to historically reliable superscriptions that appear before the first verse of the Psalms, other authors identified are Asaph (12 psalms), the Sons of Korah (9), Solomon (2), Heman the Ezrahite (1), Ethan the Ezrahite (1), and Moses (1). Fifty-one psalms do not identify their authors.

4. Over half of the Psalms (85) were written in David's time (ca. 1020–970 B.C.), but others range from Moses' Psalm 90 (ca. 1406 B.C.) to Psalms 126 and 136 (postexilic, ca. 500 B.C.).

5. Some modern scholars have doubted this and claimed that many of the biblical writings were not produced by individual writers but by later editors who collated materials. But the evidence of

internal features and external historical evidence supports the more traditional view that each was written by a single author.

6. For more serious Bible students, one of the most helpful ways to categorize and study a particular psalm is to determine whether it naturally fits into a particular genre, or category. Claus Westermann has provided perhaps the simplest approach to genre analysis, recognizing the two major categories as psalms of lament and psalms of praise, with examples of each of these written for the individual and for the community. In the category of "laments of the individual," Westermann includes Psalms 6; 13; 22; 51; 77; 102; 130. Examples of "community" or "national" laments are Psalms 44; 74; 79; 80; 83; and 89. See Claus Westermann, *Praise and Lament in the Psalms,* trans. Keith R. Crim (Richmond, Va.: Knox, 1981), 53–92.

7. Excellent background to understand the shepherd/sheep metaphor in the Bible is available in two books by Phillip Keller, *A Shepherd Looks at Psalm 23* (Grand Rapids: Zondervan, 1970), and *A Shepherd Looks at the Good Shepherd and His Sheep* (Grand Rapids: Zondervan, 1979).

8. A rich and encouraging Bible study is found in the multitude of psalms that speak of God as our "strength" or "stronghold" (see Psalms 27:1; 28:8; 29:11; 37:39; 43:2; 68:35; 71:7; 73:26; 81:1; 84:5; 96:6), our "refuge" (see Psalms 9:9; 14:6; 57:1; 59:16; 61:3; 62:7–8; 71:1, 3, 7; 73:28; 91:2, 9; 94:22; 142:5), and our "fortress" (see Psalms 9:9; 18:2; 31:3; 48:3; 59:9, 16–17; 71:3; 91:2; 144:2). Both the coincidence of these metaphors and the numerous passages in which they appear indicate the importance of these themes in our understanding of God.

9. The background information before verse 1, often called the superscription, supplies the author's name and various musical directions. Fourteen of the Psalms also include historical information (Psalms 3; 7; 18; 30; 34; 51; 52; 54; 56; 57; 59; 60; 63; 142). The exact origin of these notes is unknown. Most scholars believe they were added to the psalms by later editors or arrangers of the psalms for worship, and were in place by 200–100 B.C. Though they should not be treated as divinely inspired text, there is good reason historically to view the information as trustworthy.

10. Westermann, *Praise and Lament in the Psalms*.

Chapter 9: Standing on the Promises

1. A. W. Tozer, *The Knowledge of the Holy: The Attributes of God— Their Meaning in the Christian Life* (New York: Harper and Row, 1961), 9.
2. Ibid.
3. Quote taken from e-mail sent to author. The writer's last name and the date of the e-mail have been omitted for privacy.
4. Public domain. "Faith Is the Victory" first appeared in the *Christian Endeavor Hymnal* and was written in 1891 by John H. Yates. Music by Ira Sankey.
5. Margaret Clarkson, *Destined for Glory: The Meaning of Suffering* (Grand Rapids: Eerdmans, 1983), 84.
6. Clinton E. Arnold, "Ephesians," in *Zondervan Illustrated Bible Backgrounds Commentary*, ed. Clinton E. Arnold (Grand Rapids: Zondervan, 2002), 3:336. On the subject of spiritual warfare, see also Clinton E. Arnold, *Three Crucial Questions About Spiritual Warfare* (Grand Rapids: Baker, 1997); *Powers of Darkness: Principalities and Powers in Paul's Letters* (Downers Grove, Ill.: InterVarsity, 1992); and *Power and Magic: The Concept of Power in Ephesians* (Grand Rapids: Baker, 1997).
7. J. P. Moreland, *Love Your God with All Your Mind: The Role of Reason in the Life of the Soul* (Colorado Springs: NavPress, 1997), 49.
8. Arnold, "Ephesians," 3:337. Isaiah refers to a belt (11:5), breastplate (59:17), feet of those who bring good news (52:7), shield (21:5; also Psalm 35:2), helmet (59:17), and sword (49:2).
9. Tozer, *Knowledge of the Holy*, 9.

Scripture Index